D0347968

# MAUS

I

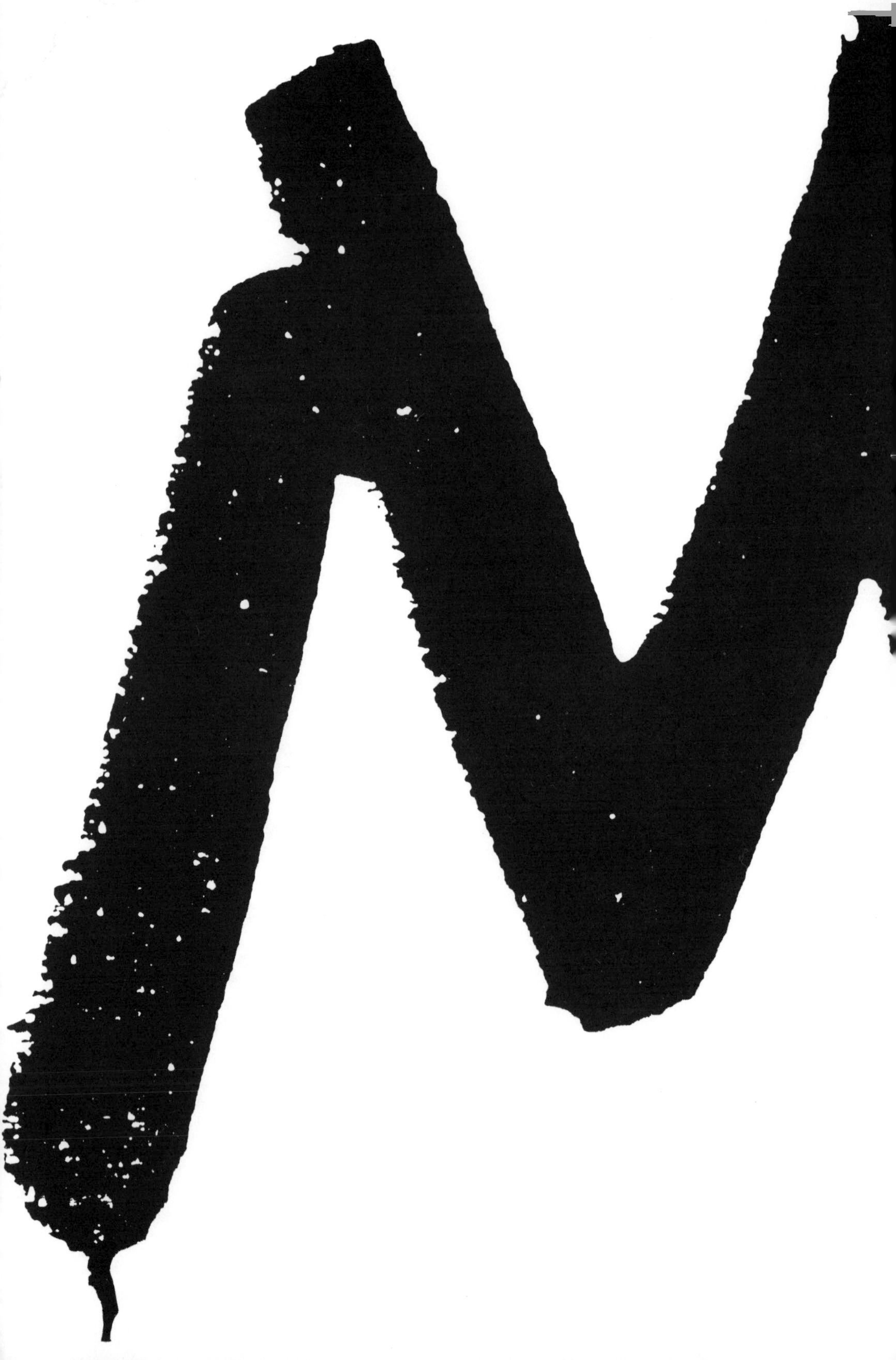

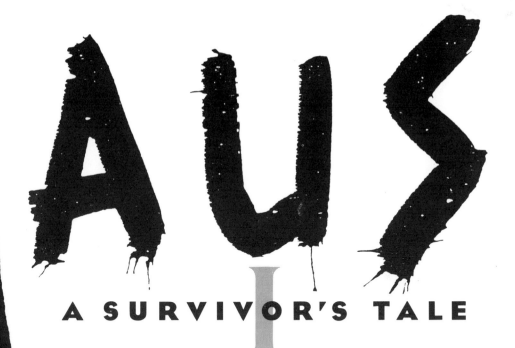

AUS
I

# A SURVIVOR'S TALE

## MY FATHER BLEEDS HISTORY

## art spiegelman

PENGUIN BOOKS

"The Jews are undoubtedly a race,

but they are not human."

Adolf Hitler

Thanks to Ken and Flo Jacobs, Ernie Gehr, Paul Pavel, Louise Fili, and Steven Heller, whose appreciation and moral support have helped this book find its shape.

Thanks to Mala Spiegelman for her help in translating Polish books and documents, and for wanting *Maus* to happen.

And thanks to Françoise Mouly for her intelligence and integrity, for her editorial skills, and for her love.

PENGUIN BOOKS

Published by the Penguin Group
Penguin Books Ltd, 27 Wrights Lane, London W8 5TZ, England
Penguin Books USA Inc., 375 Hudson Street, New York, New York 10014, USA
Penguin Books Australia Ltd, Ringwood, Victoria, Australia
Penguin Books Canada Ltd. 10 Alcorn Avenue, Toronto, Ontario, Canada M4V 3B2
Penguin Books (NZ) Ltd, 182–190 Wairau Road, Auckland 10, New Zealand

Penguin Books Ltd, Registered Offices: Harmondsworth, Middlesex, England

First published in the USA by Pantheon Books, a division of Random House, Inc., 1986
Published in Penguin Books 1987
9 10 8

Copyright © Art Spiegelman, 1973, 1980, 1981, 1982, 1983, 1984, 1985, 1986
All rights reserved

Chapters 1-6 first appeared, in a different form, in
*Raw* magazine between 1980 and 1985
'Prisoner on the Hell Planet' first appeared in *Short Order Comix* #1 1973

Made and printed in Singapore by
Kyodo Printing Co. (s) Pte Ltd.

Except in the United States of America,
this book is sold subject to the condition
that it shall not, by way of trade or otherwise,
be lent, re-sold, hired out, or otherwise circulated
without the publisher's prior consent in any form of
binding or cover other than that in which it is
published and without a similar condition
including this condition being imposed
on the subsequent purchaser

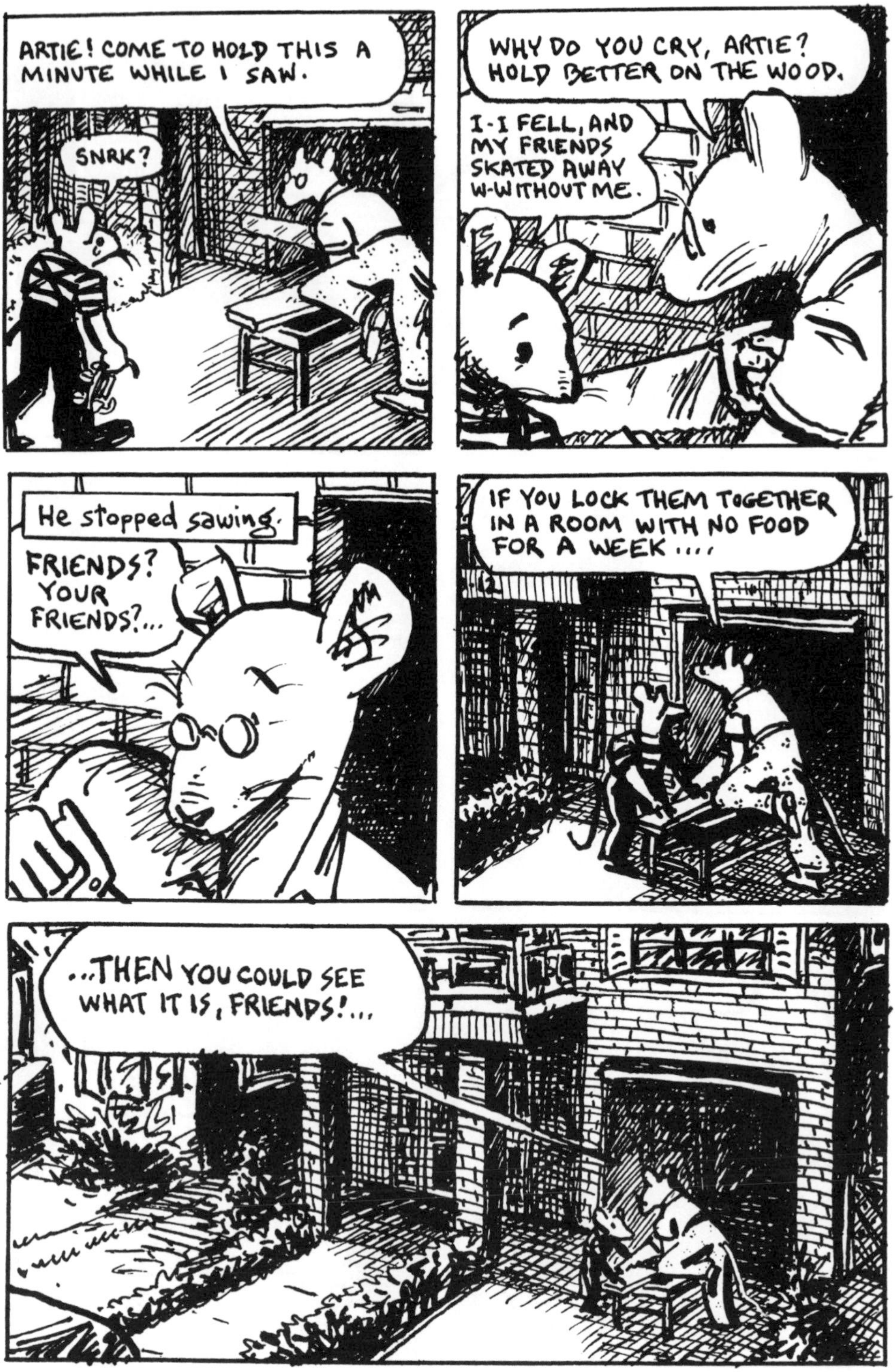
ARTIE! COME TO HOLD THIS A MINUTE WHILE I SAW.
SNRK?
WHY DO YOU CRY, ARTIE? HOLD BETTER ON THE WOOD.
I-I FELL, AND MY FRIENDS SKATED AWAY W-WITHOUT ME.
He stopped sawing.
FRIENDS? YOUR FRIENDS?...
IF YOU LOCK THEM TOGETHER IN A ROOM WITH NO FOOD FOR A WEEK....
...THEN YOU COULD SEE WHAT IT IS, FRIENDS!...

# MY FATHER BLEEDS HISTORY

(MID-1930s TO WINTER 1944)

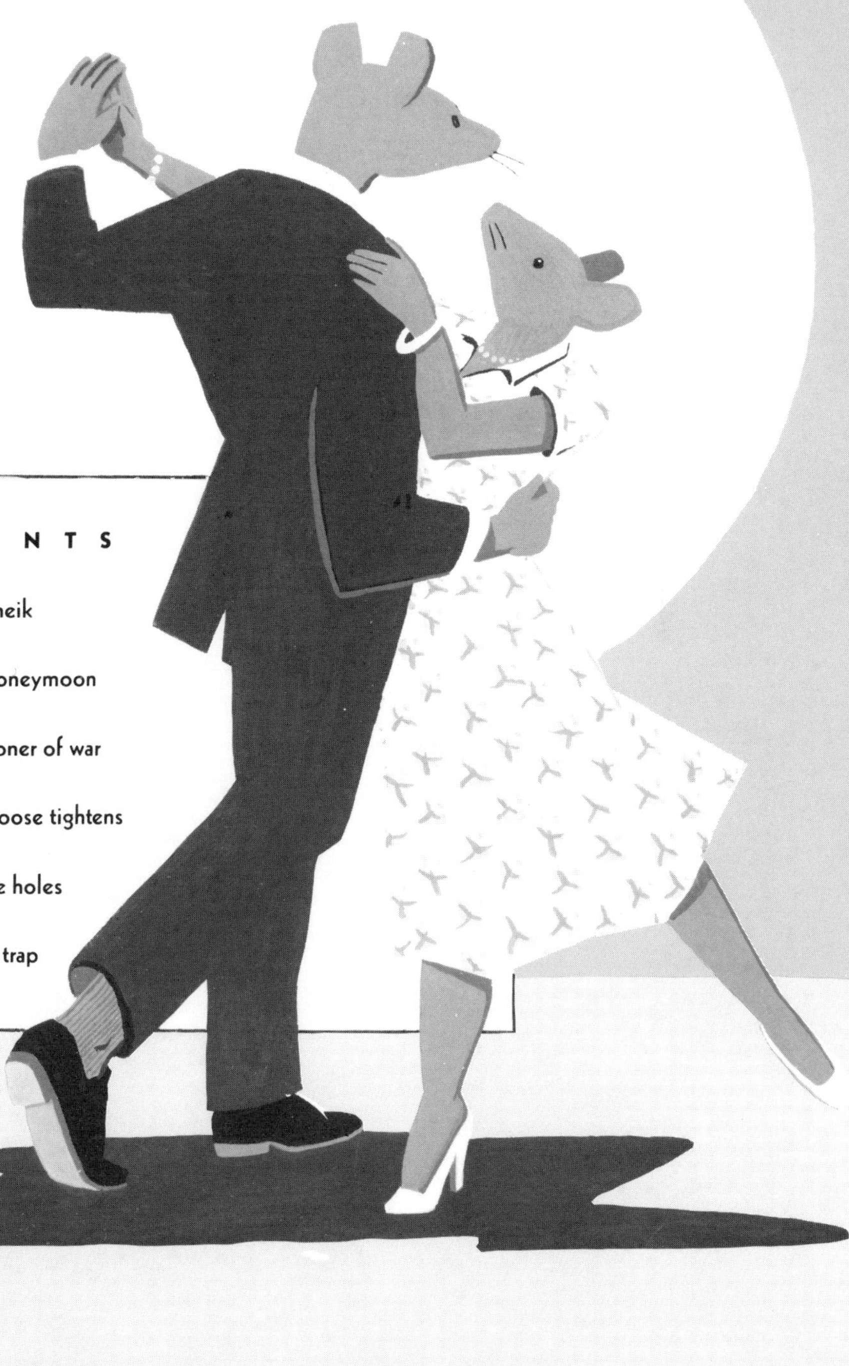

CONTENTS

FOR ANJA

# CHAPTER ONE

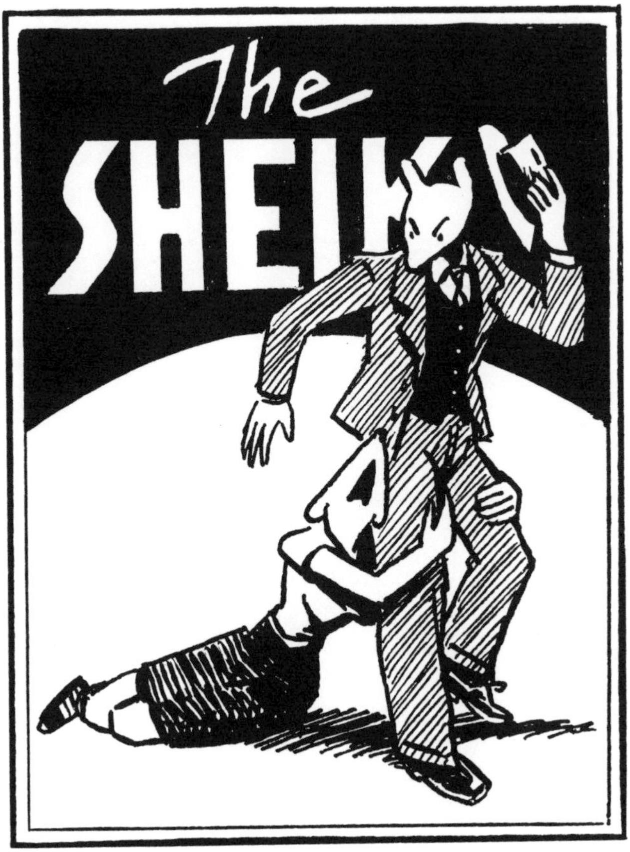
The
SHEIK

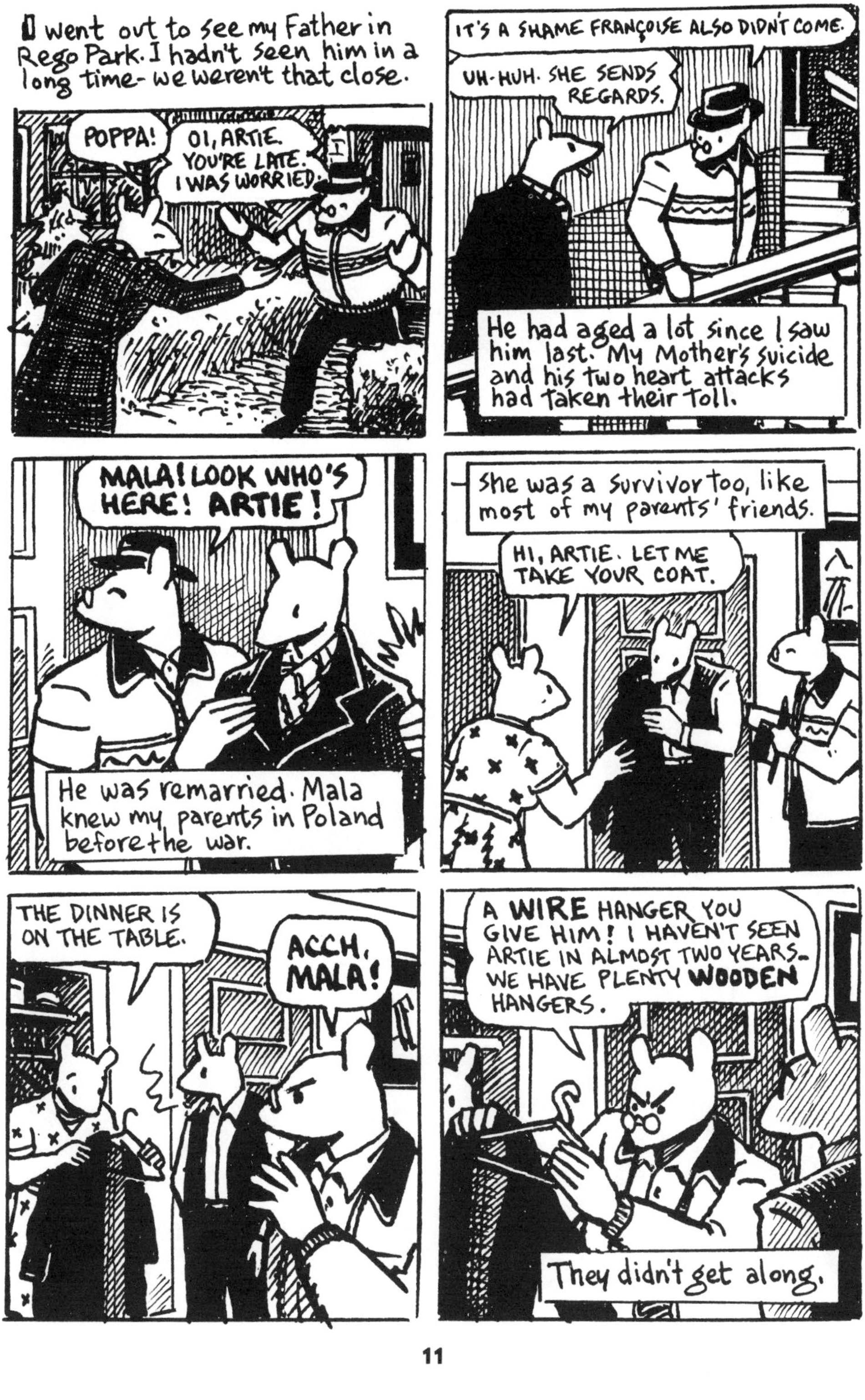
I went out to see my Father in Rego Park. I hadn't seen him in a long time- we weren't that close.
POPPA!
OI, ARTIE. YOU'RE LATE. I WAS WORRIED.
IT'S A SHAME FRANÇOISE ALSO DIDN'T COME.
UH-HUH. SHE SENDS REGARDS.
He had aged a lot since I saw him last. My Mother's suicide and his two heart attacks had taken their toll.
MALA! LOOK WHO'S HERE! ARTIE!
He was remarried. Mala knew my parents in Poland before the war.
She was a survivor too, like most of my parents' friends.
HI, ARTIE. LET ME TAKE YOUR COAT.
THE DINNER IS ON THE TABLE.
ACCH, MALA!
A WIRE HANGER YOU GIVE HIM! I HAVEN'T SEEN ARTIE IN ALMOST TWO YEARS- WE HAVE PLENTY WOODEN HANGERS.
They didn't get along.

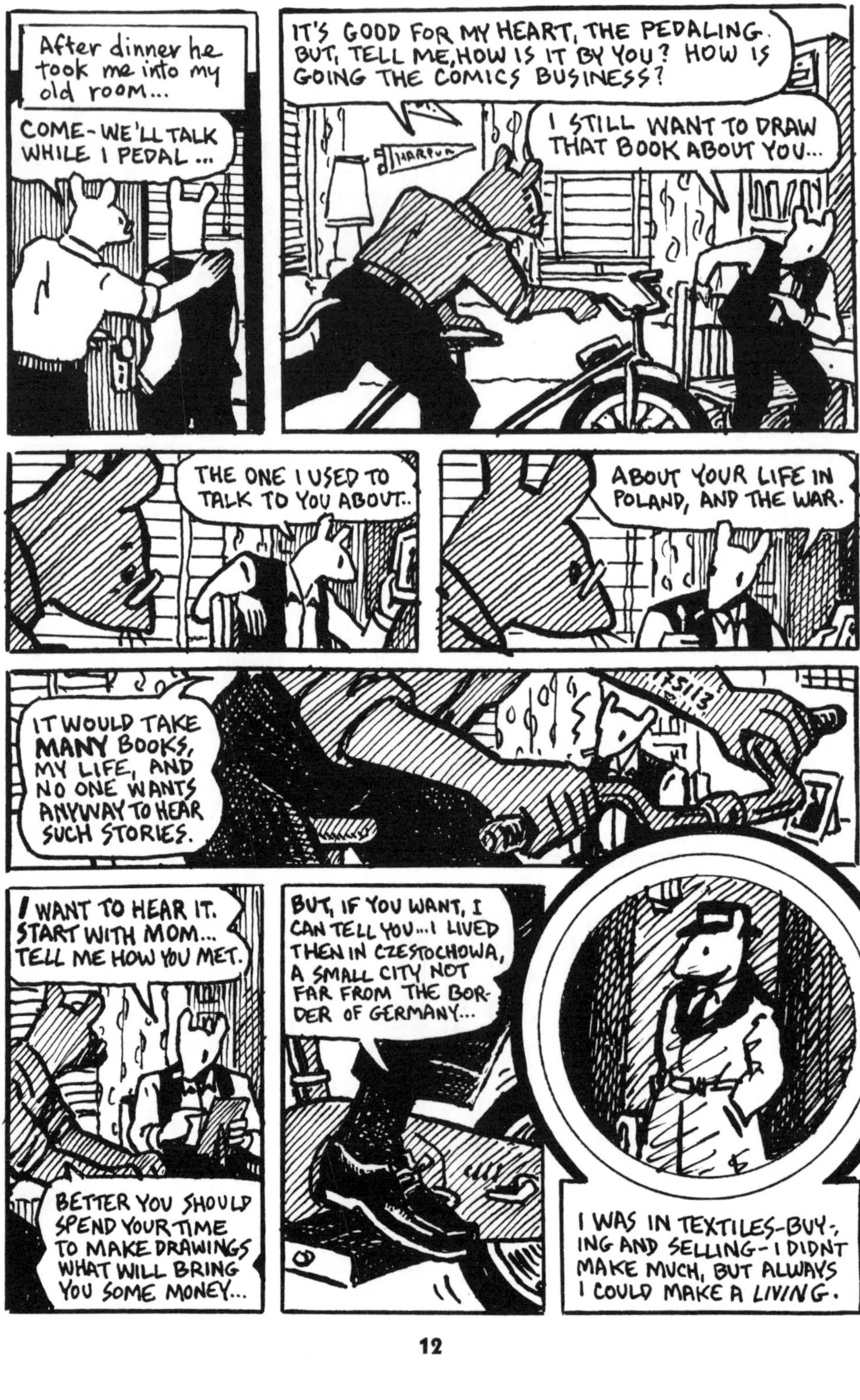
After dinner he took me into my old room...
COME- WE'LL TALK WHILE I PEDAL...
IT'S GOOD FOR MY HEART, THE PEDALING. BUT, TELL ME, HOW IS IT BY YOU? HOW IS GOING THE COMICS BUSINESS?
I STILL WANT TO DRAW THAT BOOK ABOUT YOU...
THE ONE I USED TO TALK TO YOU ABOUT..
ABOUT YOUR LIFE IN POLAND, AND THE WAR.
IT WOULD TAKE MANY BOOKS, MY LIFE, AND NO ONE WANTS ANYWAY TO HEAR SUCH STORIES.
I WANT TO HEAR IT. START WITH MOM... TELL ME HOW YOU MET.
BETTER YOU SHOULD SPEND YOUR TIME TO MAKE DRAWINGS WHAT WILL BRING YOU SOME MONEY...
BUT, IF YOU WANT, I CAN TELL YOU... I LIVED THEN IN CZESTOCHOWA, A SMALL CITY NOT FAR FROM THE BORDER OF GERMANY...
I WAS IN TEXTILES-BUYING AND SELLING- I DIDNT MAKE MUCH, BUT ALWAYS I COULD MAKE A LIVING.

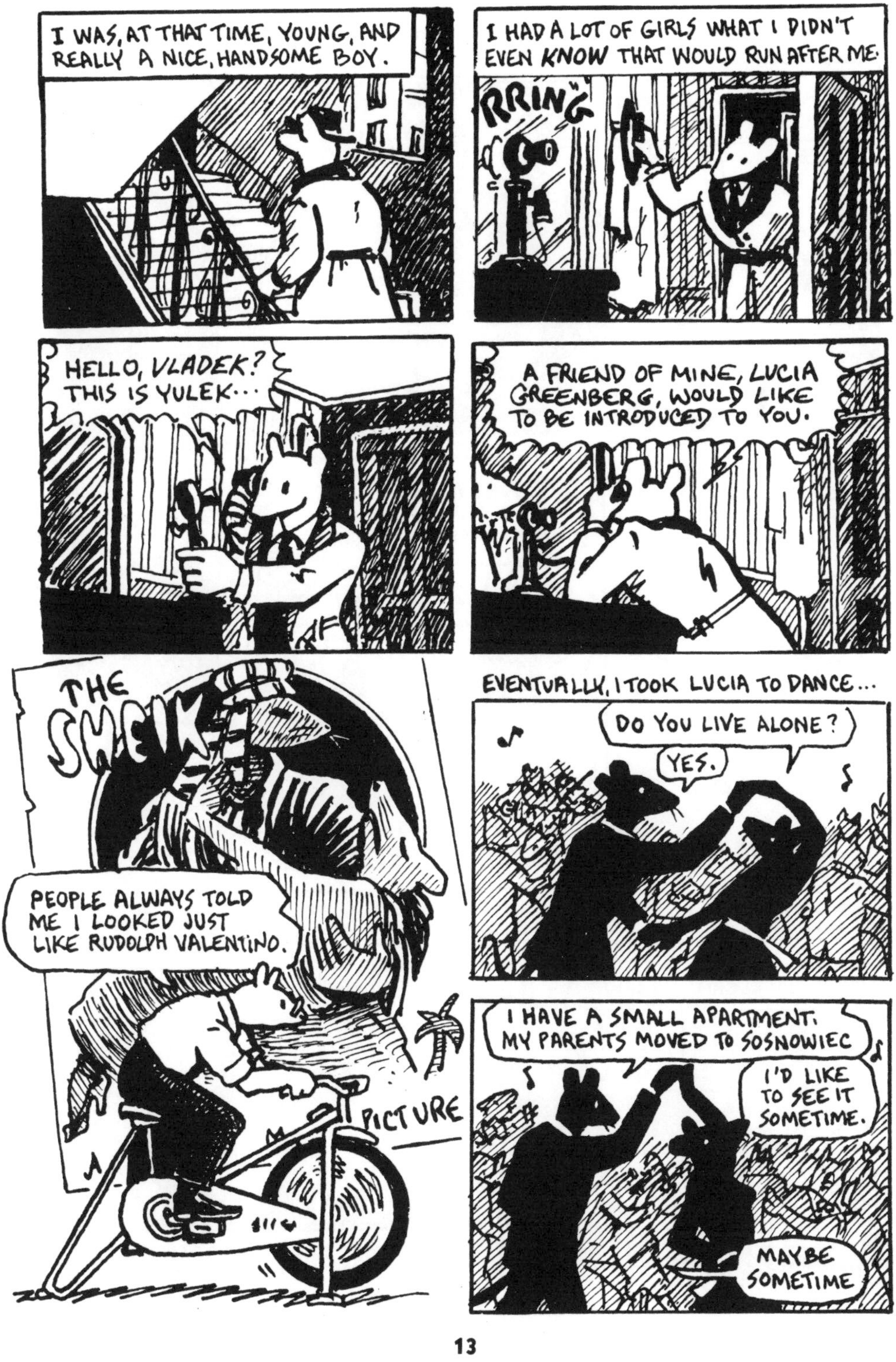
I WAS, AT THAT TIME, YOUNG, AND REALLY A NICE, HANDSOME BOY.
I HAD A LOT OF GIRLS WHAT I DIDN'T EVEN KNOW THAT WOULD RUN AFTER ME.
RRING
HELLO, VLADEK? THIS IS YULEK...
A FRIEND OF MINE, LUCIA GREENBERG, WOULD LIKE TO BE INTRODUCED TO YOU.
THE SHEIK
PEOPLE ALWAYS TOLD ME I LOOKED JUST LIKE RUDOLPH VALENTINO.
PICTURE
EVENTUALLY, I TOOK LUCIA TO DANCE...
DO YOU LIVE ALONE?
YES.
I HAVE A SMALL APARTMENT. MY PARENTS MOVED TO SOSNOWIEC
I'D LIKE TO SEE IT SOMETIME.
MAYBE SOMETIME

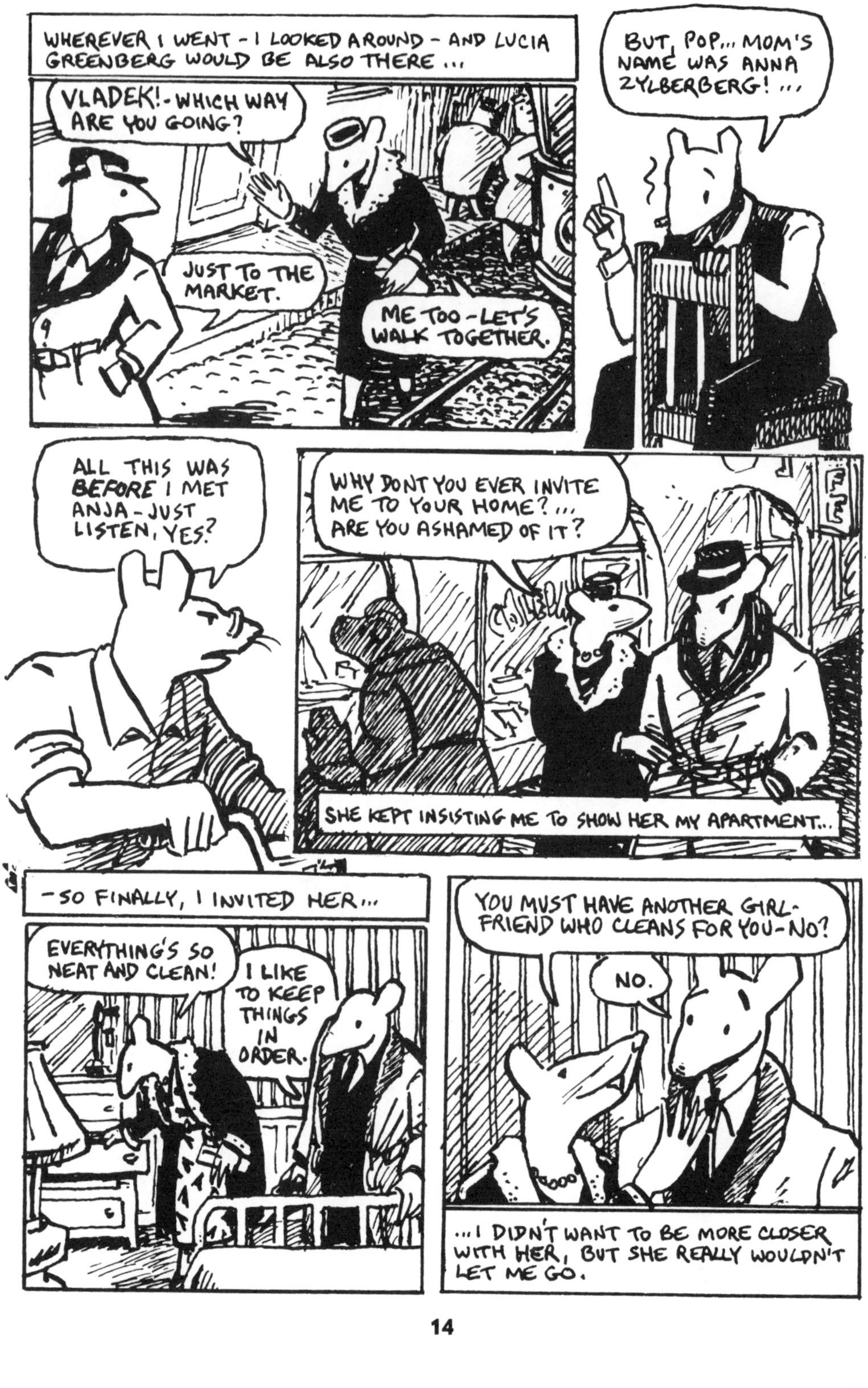
WHEREVER I WENT - I LOOKED AROUND - AND LUCIA GREENBERG WOULD BE ALSO THERE...
VLADEK! - WHICH WAY ARE YOU GOING?
JUST TO THE MARKET.
ME TOO - LET'S WALK TOGETHER.
BUT, POP... MOM'S NAME WAS ANNA ZYLBERBERG!...
ALL THIS WAS BEFORE I MET ANJA - JUST LISTEN, YES?
WHY DONT YOU EVER INVITE ME TO YOUR HOME?... ARE YOU ASHAMED OF IT?
SHE KEPT INSISTING ME TO SHOW HER MY APARTMENT...
-SO FINALLY, I INVITED HER...
EVERYTHING'S SO NEAT AND CLEAN!
I LIKE TO KEEP THINGS IN ORDER.
YOU MUST HAVE ANOTHER GIRL-FRIEND WHO CLEANS FOR YOU-NO?
NO.
...I DIDN'T WANT TO BE MORE CLOSER WITH HER, BUT SHE REALLY WOULDN'T LET ME GO.

WAS SHE THE FIRST GIRL YOU –UH–

YES...WE WERE MORE INVOLVED, SO LIKE THE YOUTHS HERE TODAY.

WE SAW EACH OTHER TOGETHER FOR MAYBE THREE OR FOUR YEARS.

LETS GET ENGAGED, VLADEK.

IT'S LATE. I'LL TAKE YOU HOME.

NOT YET, PLEASE

COME ON – YOUR PARENTS WOULD WORRY.

HER FAMILY WAS NICE, BUT HAD NO MONEY, EVEN FOR A DOWRY.

WELL, EVERY HOLIDAY I WENT TO VISIT MY FAMILY... IT WAS MAYBE A JOURNEY OF 35 OR 40 MILES.

DECEMBER 30 '35

CZESTOCHOWA/SOSNOWIEC

COUSIN VLADEK!

IT'S GOOD TO SEE YOU AGAIN. LISTEN ...

THERE'S A GIRL IN MY CLASS – I WANT YOU TO MEET US TOMORROW – HER NAME IS ANJA.

SHE'S INCREDIBLY CLEVER, FROM A RICH FAMILY... A VERY GOOD GIRL ...

15

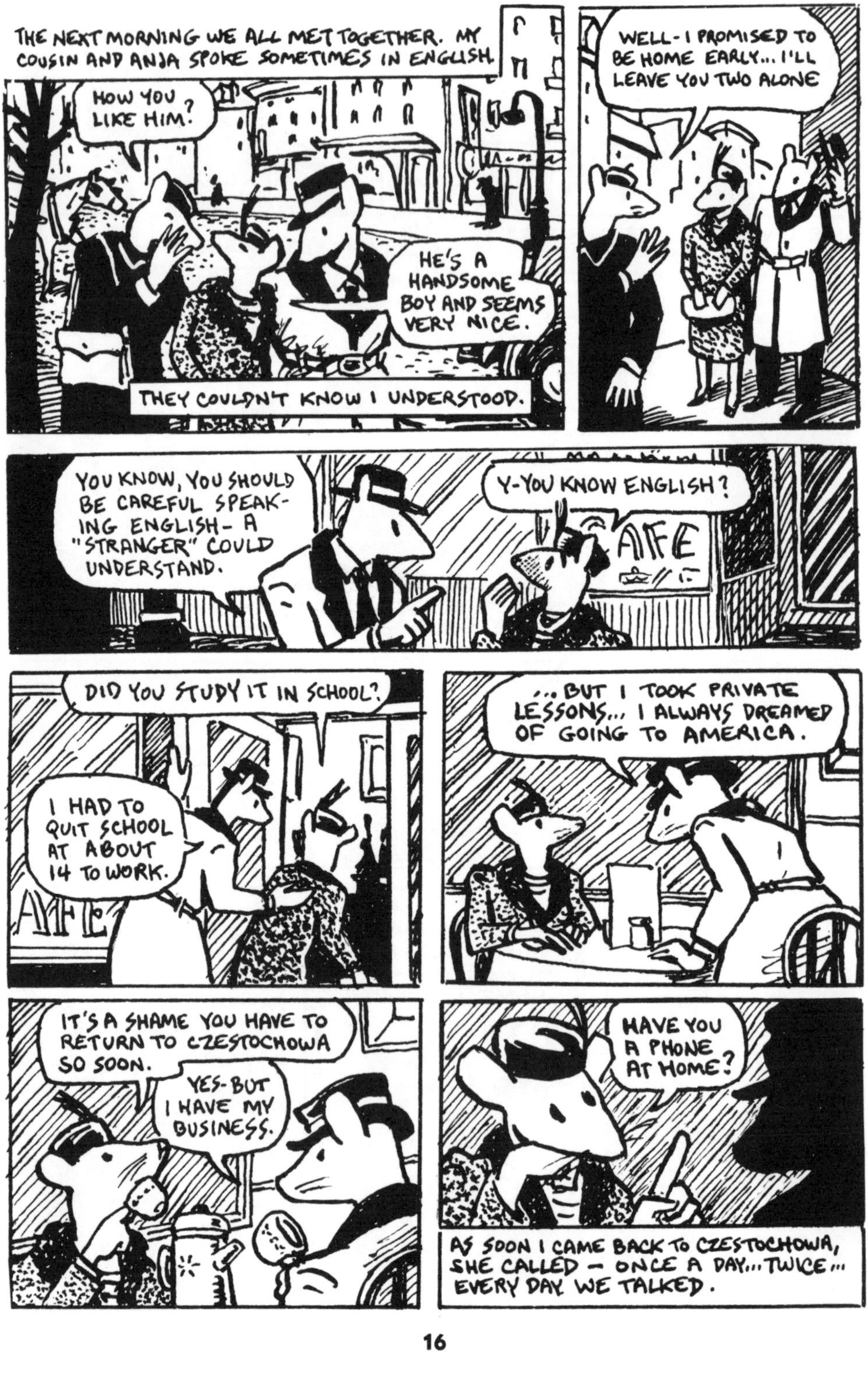
THE NEXT MORNING WE ALL MET TOGETHER. MY COUSIN AND ANJA SPOKE SOMETIMES IN ENGLISH.
HOW YOU LIKE HIM?
HE'S A HANDSOME BOY AND SEEMS VERY NICE.
THEY COULDN'T KNOW I UNDERSTOOD.
WELL- I PROMISED TO BE HOME EARLY... I'LL LEAVE YOU TWO ALONE
YOU KNOW, YOU SHOULD BE CAREFUL SPEAKING ENGLISH- A "STRANGER" COULD UNDERSTAND.
Y-YOU KNOW ENGLISH?
DID YOU STUDY IT IN SCHOOL?
I HAD TO QUIT SCHOOL AT ABOUT 14 TO WORK.
...BUT I TOOK PRIVATE LESSONS... I ALWAYS DREAMED OF GOING TO AMERICA.
IT'S A SHAME YOU HAVE TO RETURN TO CZESTOCHOWA SO SOON.
YES- BUT I HAVE MY BUSINESS.
HAVE YOU A PHONE AT HOME?
AS SOON I CAME BACK TO CZESTOCHOWA, SHE CALLED - ONCE A DAY... TWICE... EVERY DAY WE TALKED.

IT WAS NOT SO EASY TO GET FREE FROM LUCIA.

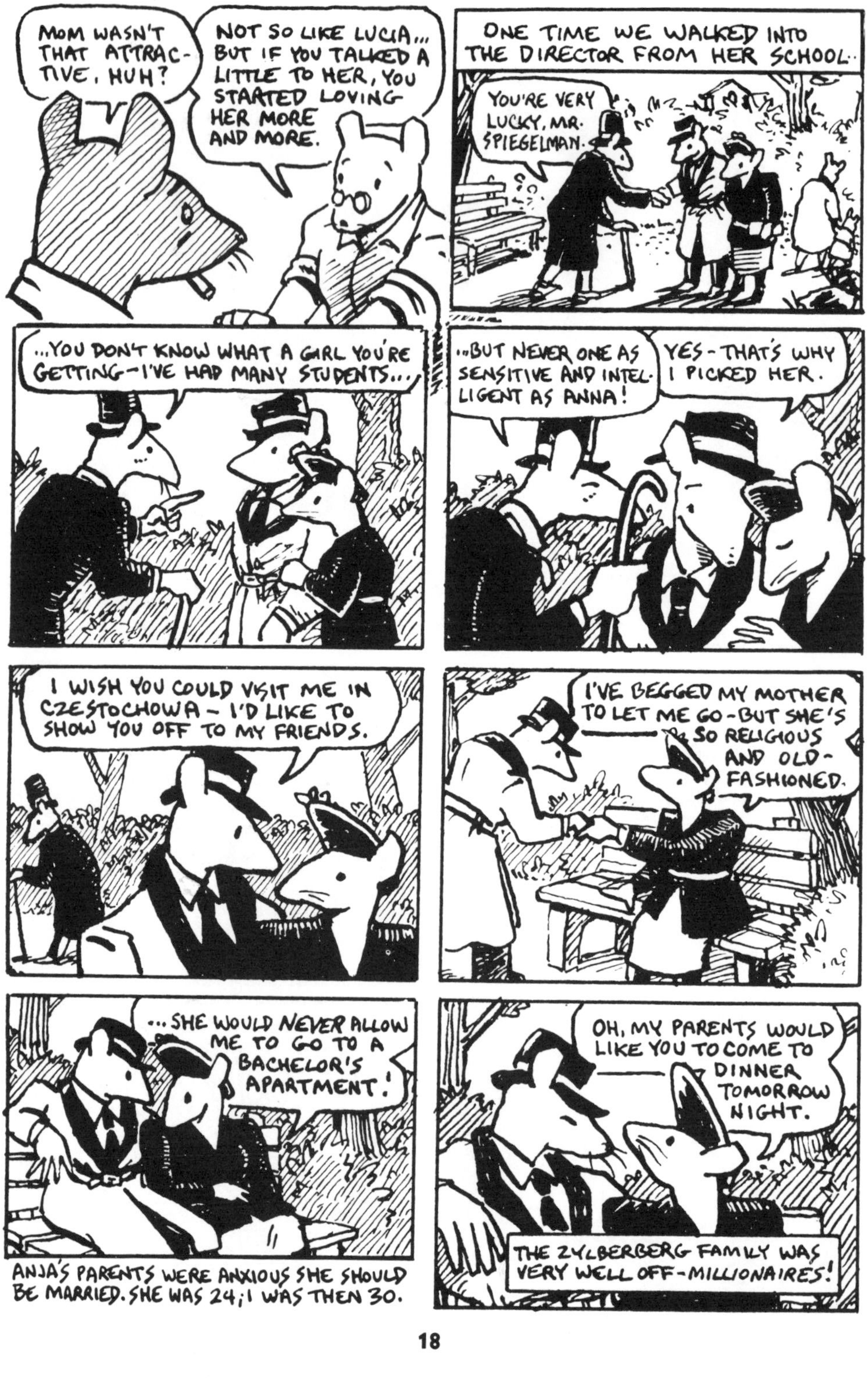
MOM WASN'T THAT ATTRACTIVE, HUH?
NOT SO LIKE LUCIA... BUT IF YOU TALKED A LITTLE TO HER, YOU STARTED LOVING HER MORE AND MORE.
ONE TIME WE WALKED INTO THE DIRECTOR FROM HER SCHOOL.
YOU'RE VERY LUCKY, MR. SPIEGELMAN.
...YOU DON'T KNOW WHAT A GIRL YOU'RE GETTING—I'VE HAD MANY STUDENTS...
...BUT NEVER ONE AS SENSITIVE AND INTELLIGENT AS ANNA!
YES—THAT'S WHY I PICKED HER.
I WISH YOU COULD VISIT ME IN CZESTOCHOWA—I'D LIKE TO SHOW YOU OFF TO MY FRIENDS.
I'VE BEGGED MY MOTHER TO LET ME GO—BUT SHE'S SO RELIGIOUS AND OLD-FASHIONED.
...SHE WOULD NEVER ALLOW ME TO GO TO A BACHELOR'S APARTMENT!
ANJA'S PARENTS WERE ANXIOUS SHE SHOULD BE MARRIED. SHE WAS 24; I WAS THEN 30.
OH, MY PARENTS WOULD LIKE YOU TO COME TO DINNER TOMORROW NIGHT.
THE ZYLBERBERG FAMILY WAS VERY WELL OFF—MILLIONAIRES!

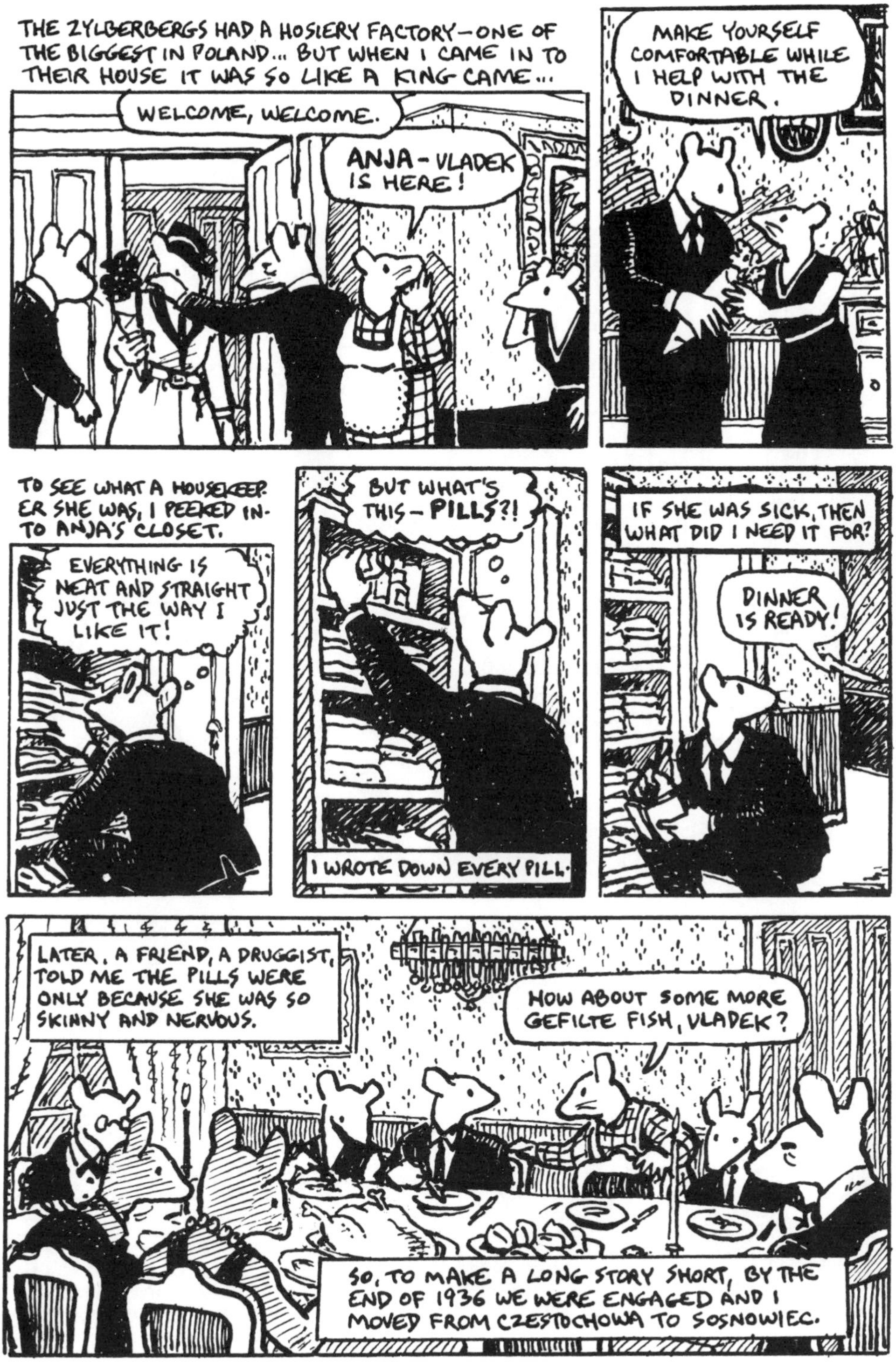
THE ZYLBERBERGS HAD A HOSIERY FACTORY—ONE OF THE BIGGEST IN POLAND... BUT WHEN I CAME IN TO THEIR HOUSE IT WAS SO LIKE A KING CAME...
WELCOME, WELCOME.
ANJA- VLADEK IS HERE!
MAKE YOURSELF COMFORTABLE WHILE I HELP WITH THE DINNER.
TO SEE WHAT A HOUSEKEEPER SHE WAS, I PEEKED INTO ANJA'S CLOSET.
EVERYTHING IS NEAT AND STRAIGHT JUST THE WAY I LIKE IT!
BUT WHAT'S THIS—PILLS?!
I WROTE DOWN EVERY PILL.
IF SHE WAS SICK, THEN WHAT DID I NEED IT FOR?
DINNER IS READY!
LATER, A FRIEND, A DRUGGIST, TOLD ME THE PILLS WERE ONLY BECAUSE SHE WAS SO SKINNY AND NERVOUS.
HOW ABOUT SOME MORE GEFILTE FISH, VLADEK?
SO, TO MAKE A LONG STORY SHORT, BY THE END OF 1936 WE WERE ENGAGED AND I MOVED FROM CZESTOCHOWA TO SOSNOWIEC.

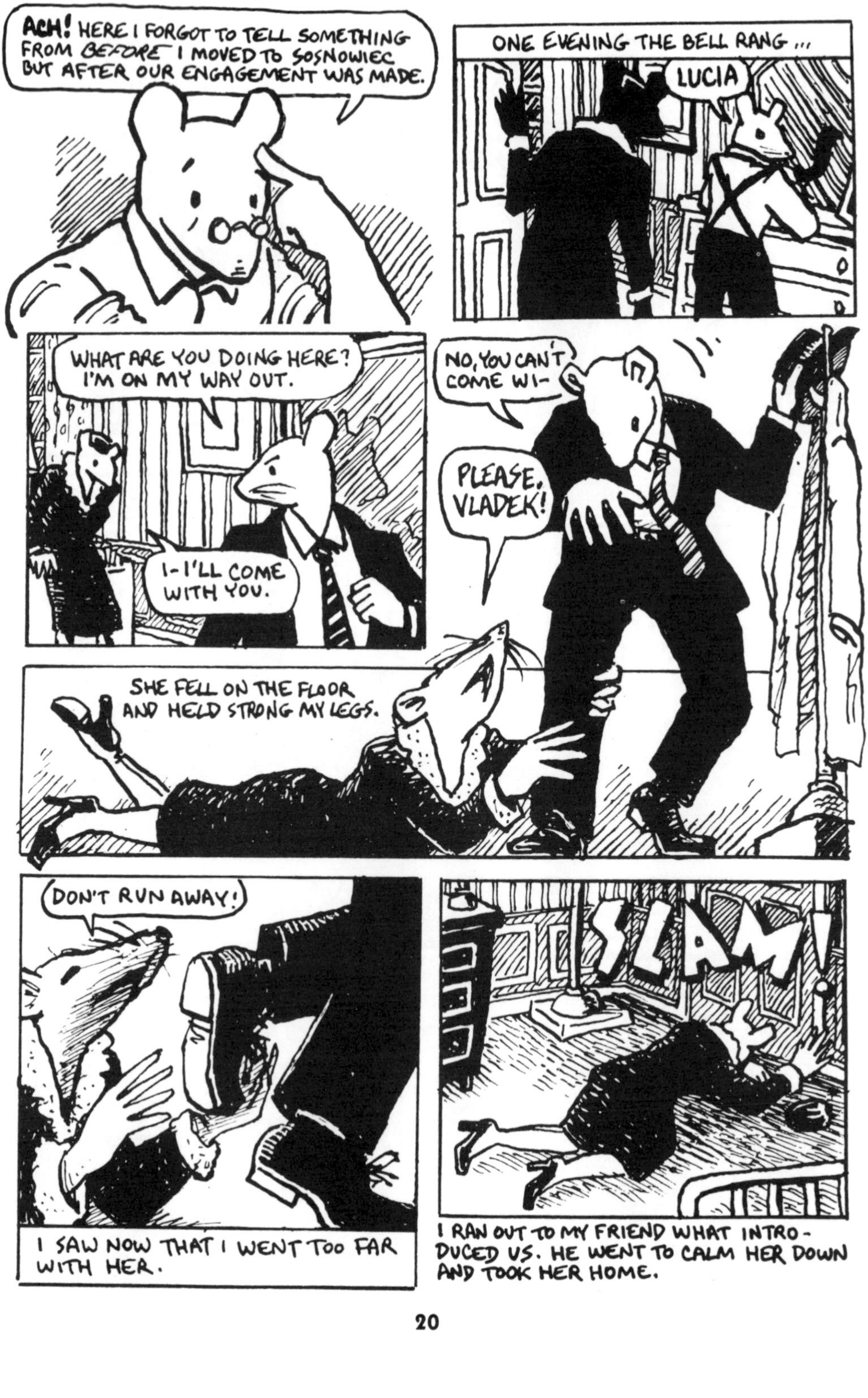
ACH! HERE I FORGOT TO TELL SOMETHING FROM BEFORE I MOVED TO SOSNOWIEC BUT AFTER OUR ENGAGEMENT WAS MADE.
ONE EVENING THE BELL RANG ...
LUCIA
WHAT ARE YOU DOING HERE? I'M ON MY WAY OUT.
I-I'LL COME WITH YOU.
NO, YOU CAN'T COME WI-
PLEASE, VLADEK!
SHE FELL ON THE FLOOR AND HELD STRONG MY LEGS.
DON'T RUN AWAY!
I SAW NOW THAT I WENT TOO FAR WITH HER.
SLAM!
I RAN OUT TO MY FRIEND WHAT INTRO-DUCED US. HE WENT TO CALM HER DOWN AND TOOK HER HOME.

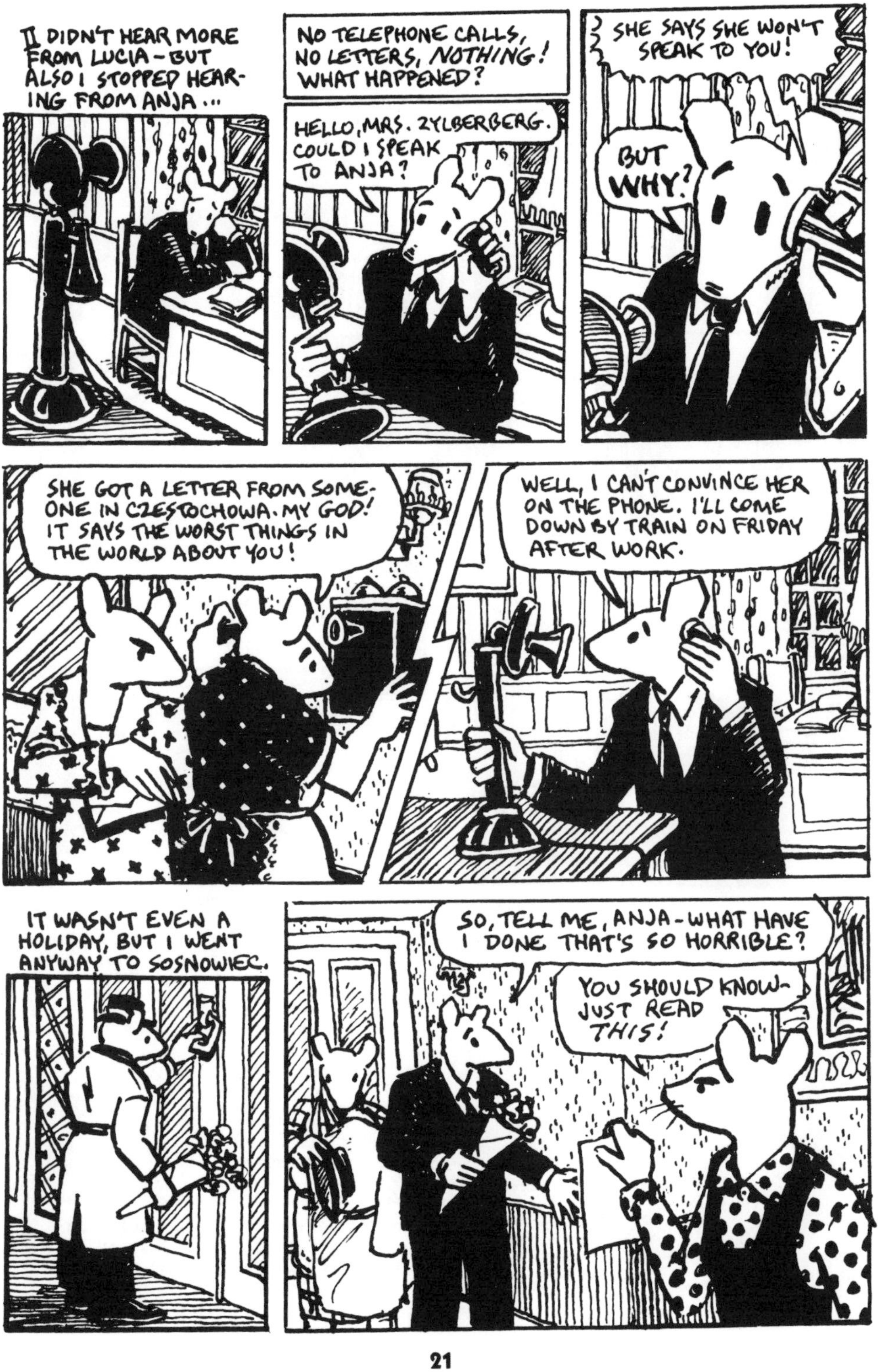
I DIDN'T HEAR MORE FROM LUCIA - BUT ALSO I STOPPED HEARING FROM ANJA ...
NO TELEPHONE CALLS, NO LETTERS, NOTHING! WHAT HAPPENED?
HELLO, MRS. ZYLBERBERG. COULD I SPEAK TO ANJA?
SHE SAYS SHE WON'T SPEAK TO YOU!
BUT WHY?
SHE GOT A LETTER FROM SOMEONE IN CZESTOCHOWA. MY GOD! IT SAYS THE WORST THINGS IN THE WORLD ABOUT YOU!
WELL, I CAN'T CONVINCE HER ON THE PHONE. I'LL COME DOWN BY TRAIN ON FRIDAY AFTER WORK.
IT WASN'T EVEN A HOLIDAY, BUT I WENT ANYWAY TO SOSNOWIEC.
SO, TELL ME, ANJA - WHAT HAVE I DONE THAT'S SO HORRIBLE?
YOU SHOULD KNOW - JUST READ THIS!

22

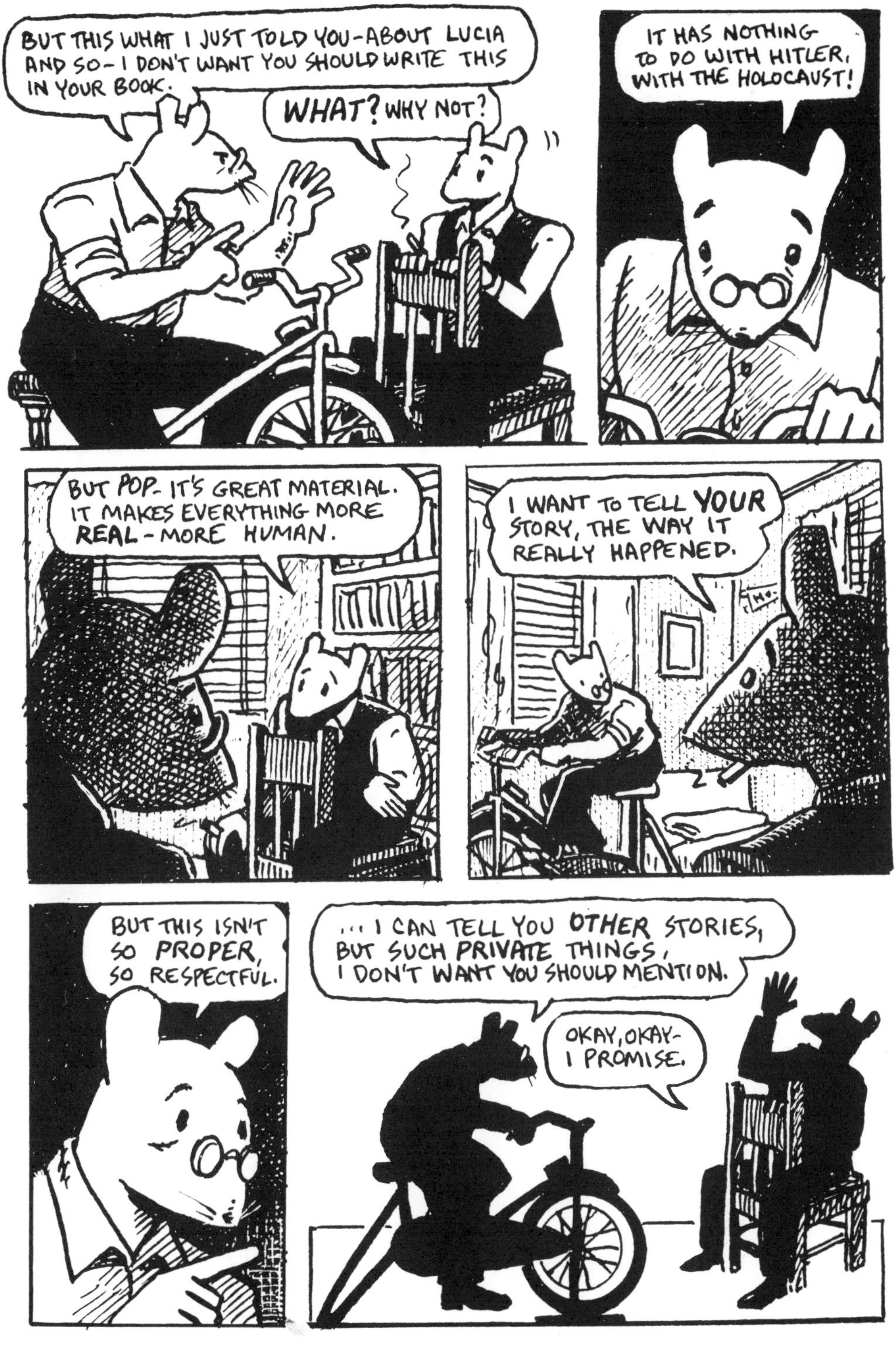
BUT THIS WHAT I JUST TOLD YOU-ABOUT LUCIA AND SO- I DON'T WANT YOU SHOULD WRITE THIS IN YOUR BOOK.
WHAT? WHY NOT?
IT HAS NOTHING TO DO WITH HITLER, WITH THE HOLOCAUST!
BUT POP- IT'S GREAT MATERIAL. IT MAKES EVERYTHING MORE REAL - MORE HUMAN.
I WANT TO TELL YOUR STORY, THE WAY IT REALLY HAPPENED.
BUT THIS ISN'T SO PROPER, SO RESPECTFUL.
... I CAN TELL YOU OTHER STORIES, BUT SUCH PRIVATE THINGS, I DON'T WANT YOU SHOULD MENTION.
OKAY, OKAY- I PROMISE.

# CHAPTER TWO

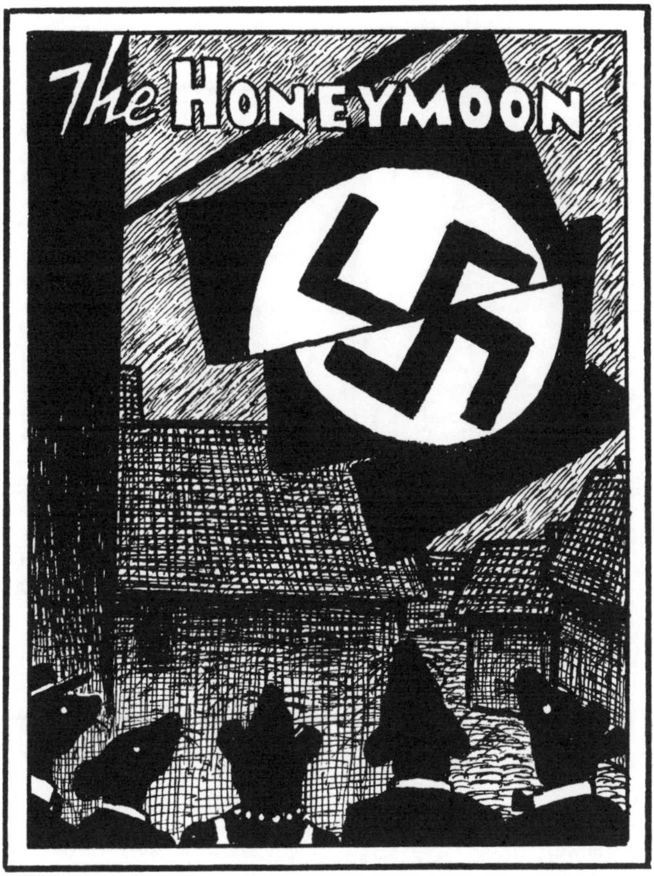
The HONEYMOON

For the next few months I went back to visit my father quite regularly, to hear his story.

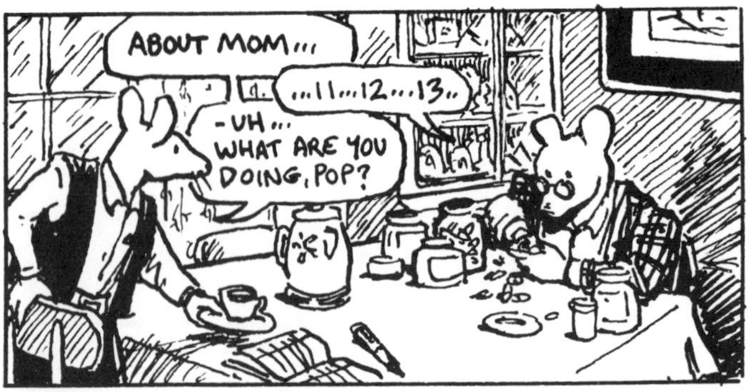
ABOUT MOM...
...11...12...13...
-UH... WHAT ARE YOU DOING, POP?

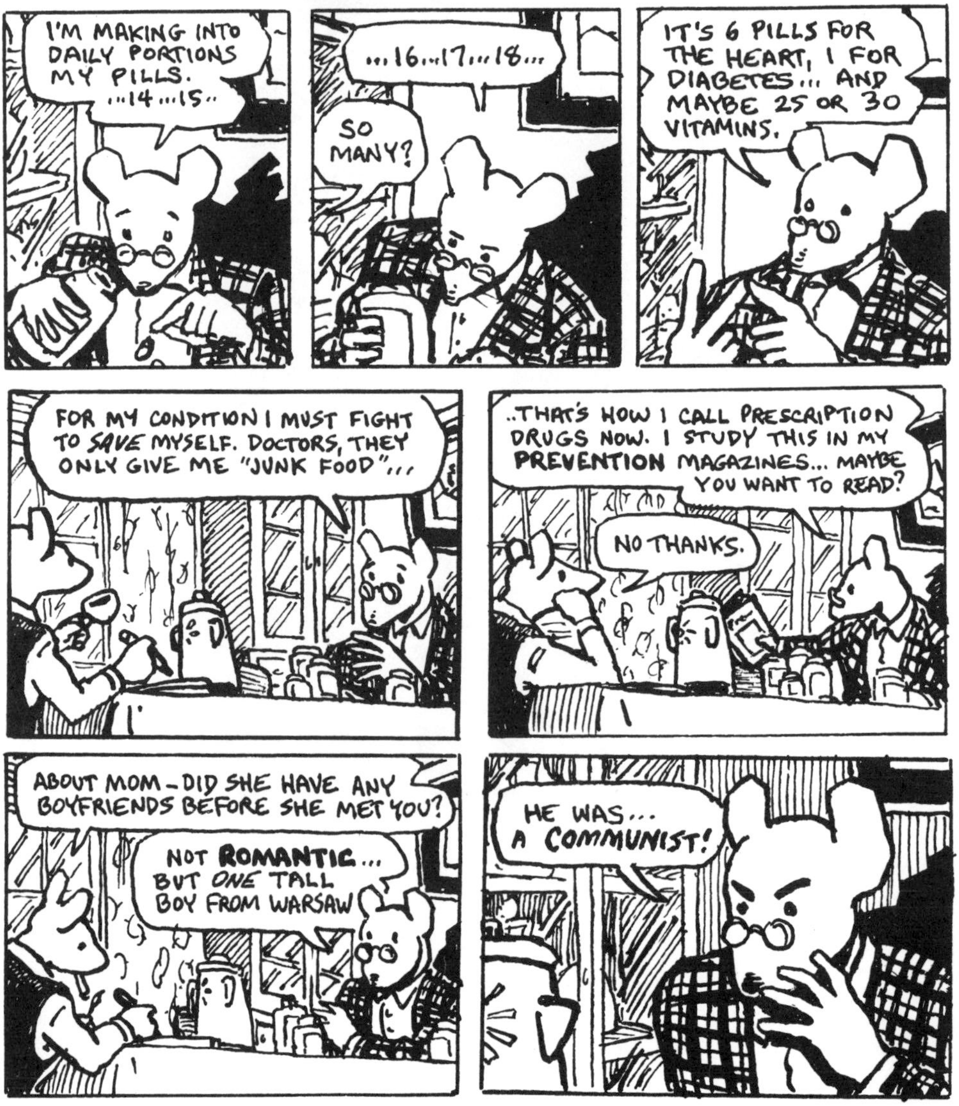
I'M MAKING INTO DAILY PORTIONS MY PILLS. ...14...15...
...16...17...18...
SO MANY?
IT'S 6 PILLS FOR THE HEART, 1 FOR DIABETES... AND MAYBE 25 OR 30 VITAMINS.
FOR MY CONDITION I MUST FIGHT TO *SAVE* MYSELF. DOCTORS, THEY ONLY GIVE ME "JUNK FOOD"...
..THAT'S HOW I CALL PRESCRIPTION DRUGS NOW. I STUDY THIS IN MY **PREVENTION** MAGAZINES... MAYBE YOU WANT TO READ?
NO THANKS.
ABOUT MOM - DID SHE HAVE ANY BOYFRIENDS BEFORE SHE MET YOU?
NOT **ROMANTIC**... BUT *ONE* TALL BOY FROM WARSAW
HE WAS... A **COMMUNIST!**

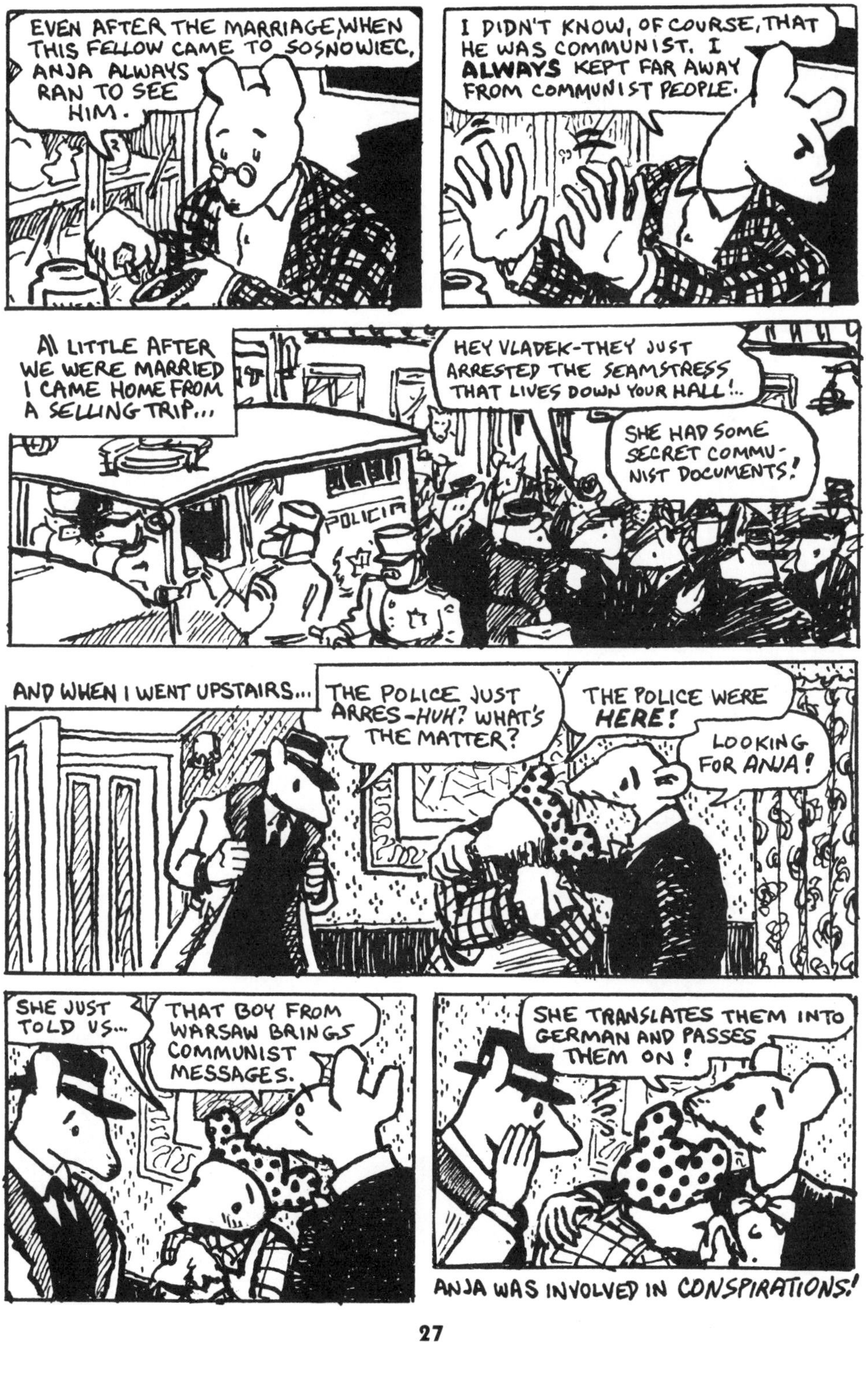
EVEN AFTER THE MARRIAGE, WHEN THIS FELLOW CAME TO SOSNOWIEC, ANJA ALWAYS RAN TO SEE HIM.
I DIDN'T KNOW, OF COURSE, THAT HE WAS COMMUNIST. I **ALWAYS** KEPT FAR AWAY FROM COMMUNIST PEOPLE.
A LITTLE AFTER WE WERE MARRIED I CAME HOME FROM A SELLING TRIP...
HEY VLADEK-THEY JUST ARRESTED THE SEAMSTRESS THAT LIVES DOWN YOUR HALL!..
SHE HAD SOME SECRET COMMUNIST DOCUMENTS!
POLICJA
AND WHEN I WENT UPSTAIRS...
THE POLICE JUST ARRES-*HUH?* WHAT'S THE MATTER?
THE POLICE WERE ***HERE!***
LOOKING FOR *ANJA!*
SHE JUST TOLD US...
THAT BOY FROM WARSAW BRINGS COMMUNIST MESSAGES.
SHE TRANSLATES THEM INTO GERMAN AND PASSES THEM ON!
ANJA WAS INVOLVED IN *CONSPIRATIONS!*

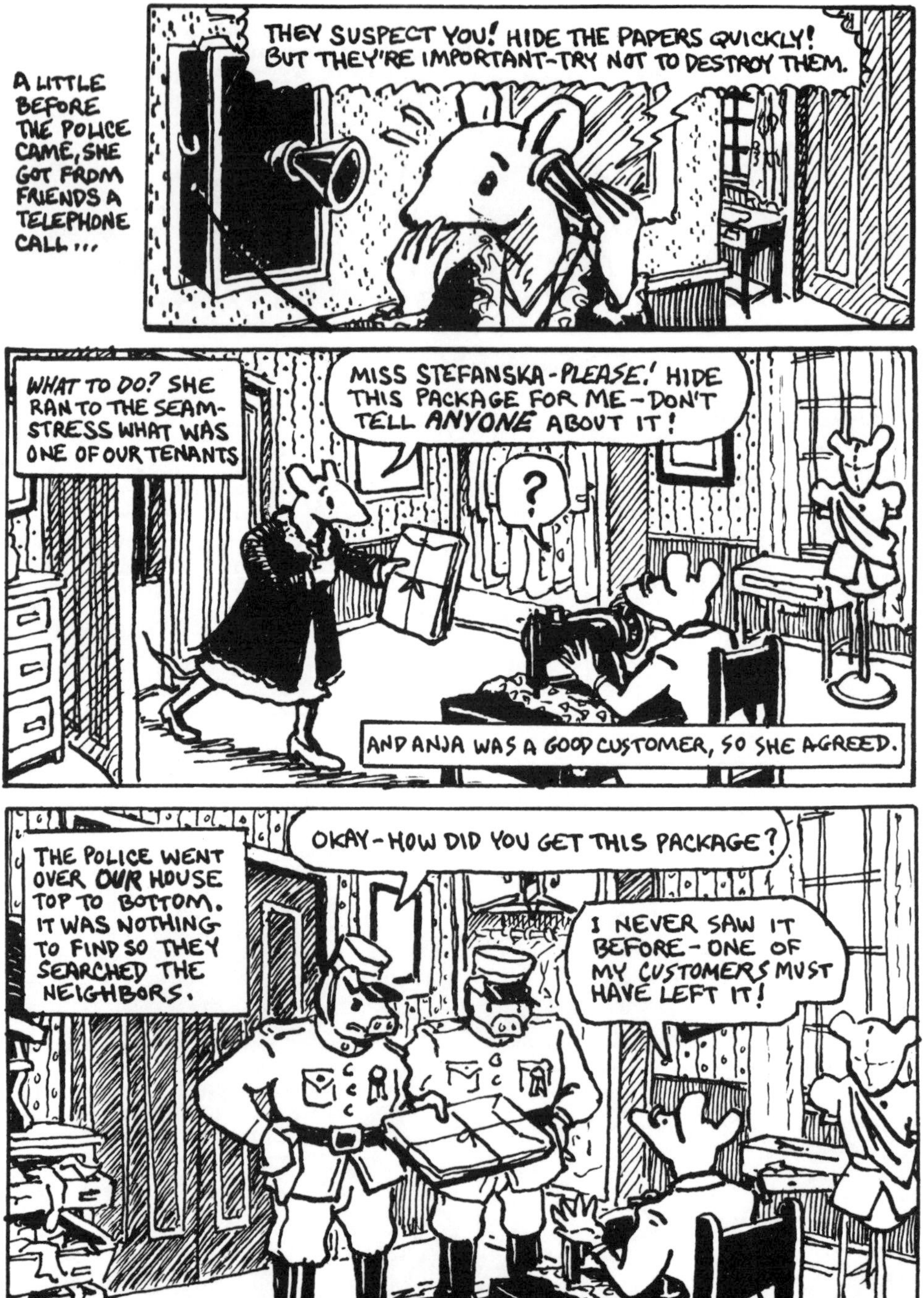
A LITTLE BEFORE THE POLICE CAME, SHE GOT FROM FRIENDS A TELEPHONE CALL...
THEY SUSPECT YOU! HIDE THE PAPERS QUICKLY! BUT THEY'RE IMPORTANT-TRY NOT TO DESTROY THEM.
WHAT TO DO? SHE RAN TO THE SEAMSTRESS WHAT WAS ONE OF OUR TENANTS
MISS STEFANSKA-PLEASE! HIDE THIS PACKAGE FOR ME-DON'T TELL ANYONE ABOUT IT!
?
AND ANJA WAS A GOOD CUSTOMER, SO SHE AGREED.
THE POLICE WENT OVER OUR HOUSE TOP TO BOTTOM. IT WAS NOTHING TO FIND SO THEY SEARCHED THE NEIGHBORS.
OKAY-HOW DID YOU GET THIS PACKAGE?
I NEVER SAW IT BEFORE-ONE OF MY CUSTOMERS MUST HAVE LEFT IT!
ANJA WAS SAFE, BUT THE SEAMSTRESS THEY ARRESTED.

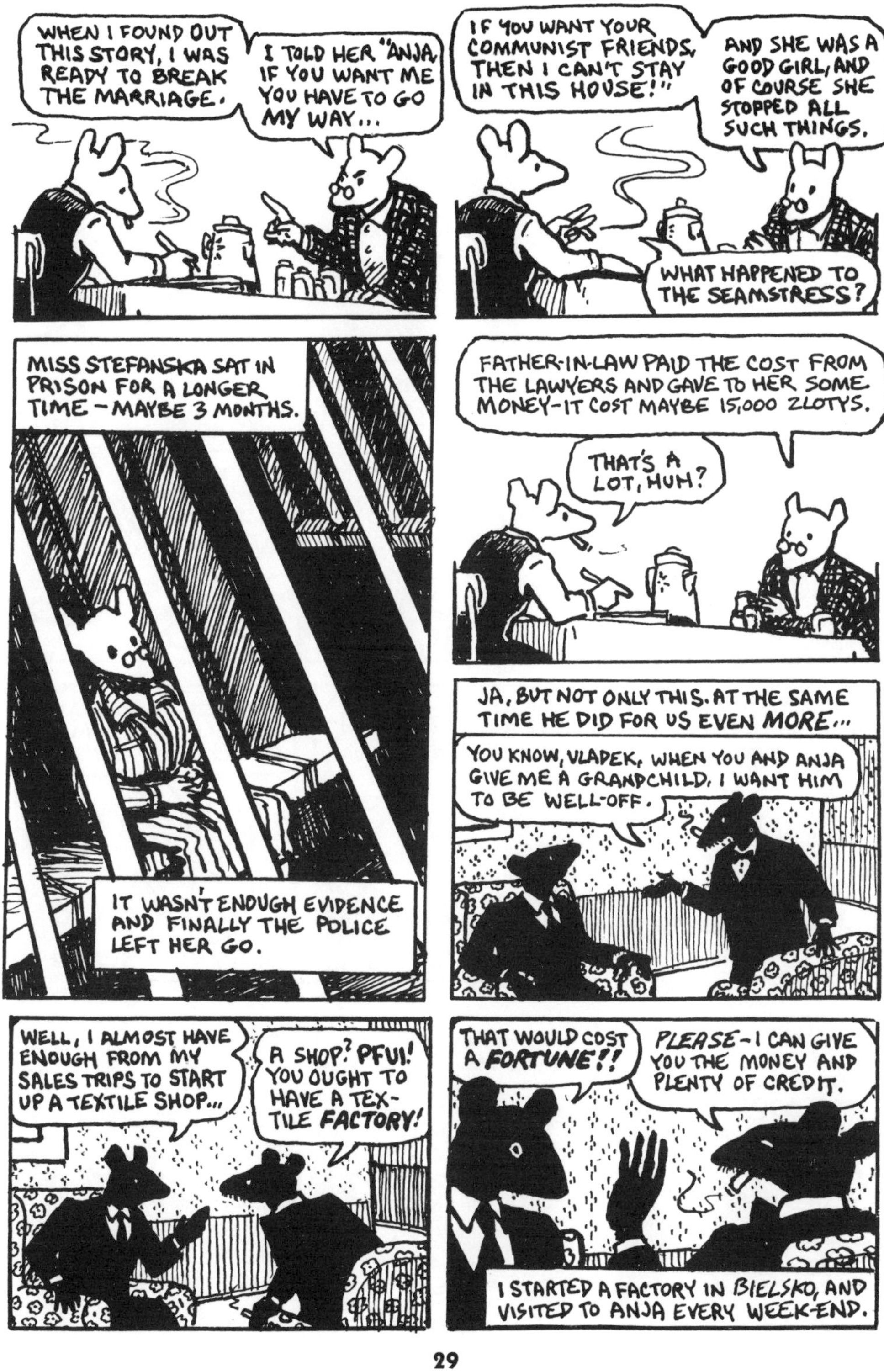
WHEN I FOUND OUT THIS STORY, I WAS READY TO BREAK THE MARRIAGE.
I TOLD HER "ANJA, IF YOU WANT ME YOU HAVE TO GO MY WAY...
IF YOU WANT YOUR COMMUNIST FRIENDS, THEN I CAN'T STAY IN THIS HOUSE!"
AND SHE WAS A GOOD GIRL, AND OF COURSE SHE STOPPED ALL SUCH THINGS.
WHAT HAPPENED TO THE SEAMSTRESS?
MISS STEFANSKA SAT IN PRISON FOR A LONGER TIME - MAYBE 3 MONTHS.
IT WASN'T ENOUGH EVIDENCE AND FINALLY THE POLICE LEFT HER GO.
FATHER-IN-LAW PAID THE COST FROM THE LAWYERS AND GAVE TO HER SOME MONEY-IT COST MAYBE 15,000 ZLOTYS.
THAT'S A LOT, HUH?
JA, BUT NOT ONLY THIS. AT THE SAME TIME HE DID FOR US EVEN MORE...
YOU KNOW, VLADEK, WHEN YOU AND ANJA GIVE ME A GRANDCHILD, I WANT HIM TO BE WELL-OFF.
WELL, I ALMOST HAVE ENOUGH FROM MY SALES TRIPS TO START UP A TEXTILE SHOP...
A SHOP? PFUI! YOU OUGHT TO HAVE A TEX-TILE FACTORY!
THAT WOULD COST A FORTUNE!!
PLEASE - I CAN GIVE YOU THE MONEY AND PLENTY OF CREDIT.
I STARTED A FACTORY IN BIELSKO, AND VISITED TO ANJA EVERY WEEK-END.

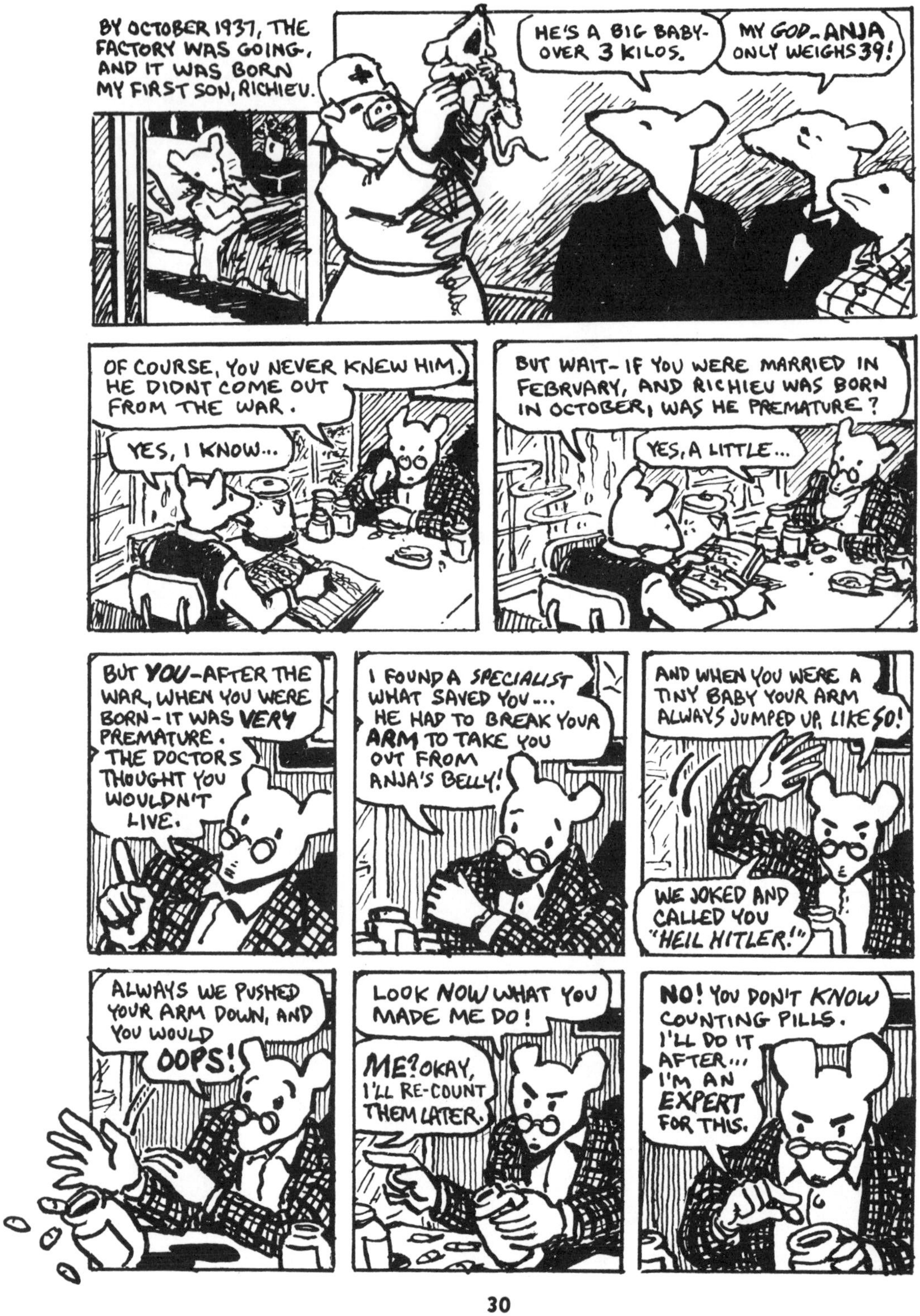
BY OCTOBER 1937, THE FACTORY WAS GOING, AND IT WAS BORN MY FIRST SON, RICHIEU.
HE'S A BIG BABY- OVER 3 KILOS.
MY GOD- ANJA ONLY WEIGHS 39!
OF COURSE, YOU NEVER KNEW HIM. HE DIDNT COME OUT FROM THE WAR.
YES, I KNOW...
BUT WAIT- IF YOU WERE MARRIED IN FEBRUARY, AND RICHIEU WAS BORN IN OCTOBER, WAS HE PREMATURE?
YES, A LITTLE...
BUT YOU- AFTER THE WAR, WHEN YOU WERE BORN- IT WAS VERY PREMATURE. THE DOCTORS THOUGHT YOU WOULDN'T LIVE.
I FOUND A SPECIALIST WHAT SAVED YOU... HE HAD TO BREAK YOUR ARM TO TAKE YOU OUT FROM ANJA'S BELLY!
AND WHEN YOU WERE A TINY BABY YOUR ARM ALWAYS JUMPED UP, LIKE SO!
WE JOKED AND CALLED YOU "HEIL HITLER!"
ALWAYS WE PUSHED YOUR ARM DOWN, AND YOU WOULD
OOPS!
LOOK NOW WHAT YOU MADE ME DO!
ME? OKAY, I'LL RE-COUNT THEM LATER.
NO! YOU DON'T KNOW COUNTING PILLS. I'LL DO IT AFTER... I'M AN EXPERT FOR THIS.

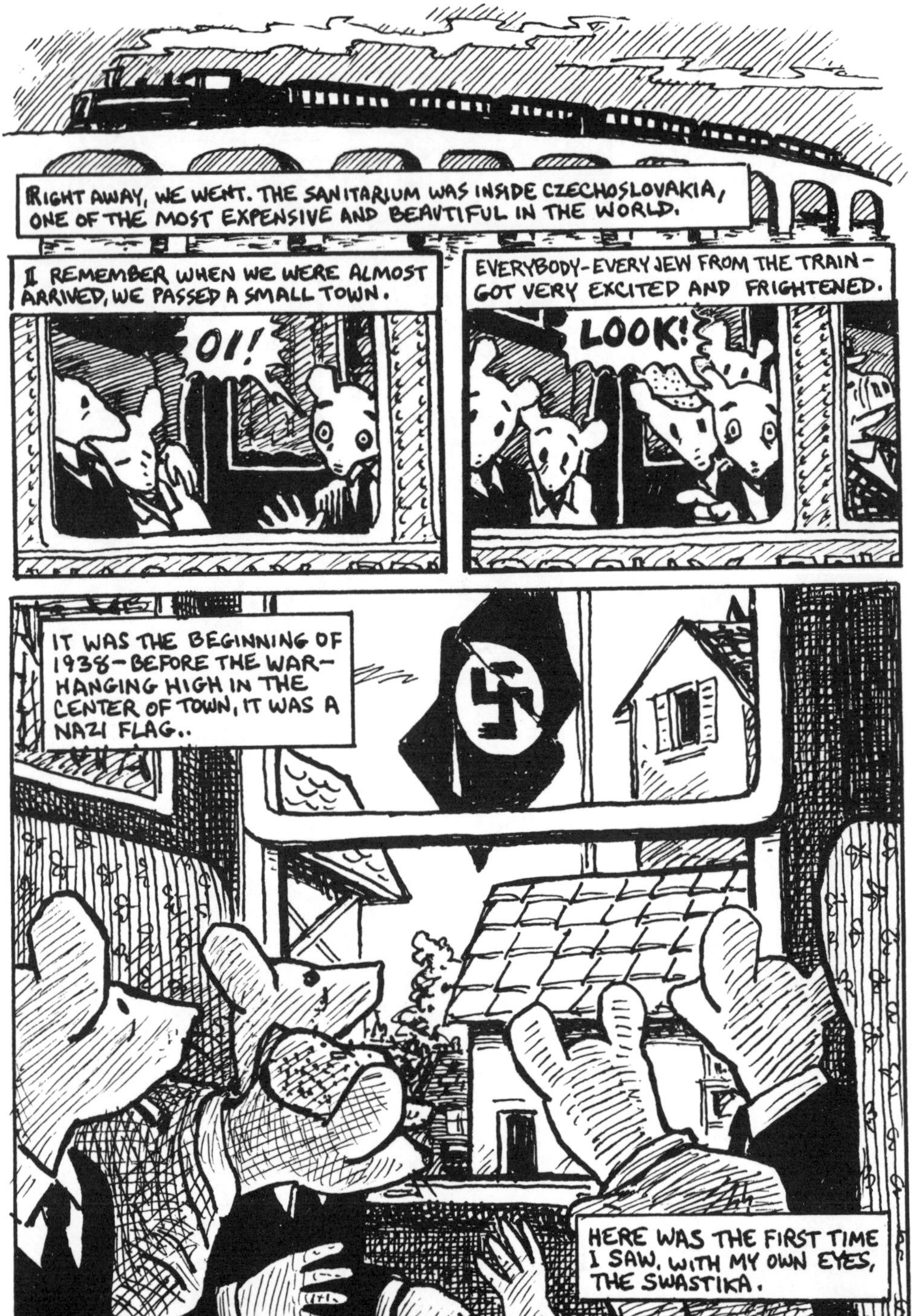

RIGHT AWAY, WE WENT. THE SANITARIUM WAS INSIDE CZECHOSLOVAKIA, ONE OF THE MOST EXPENSIVE AND BEAUTIFUL IN THE WORLD.
I REMEMBER WHEN WE WERE ALMOST ARRIVED, WE PASSED A SMALL TOWN.
OI!
EVERYBODY- EVERY JEW FROM THE TRAIN- GOT VERY EXCITED AND FRIGHTENED.
LOOK!
IT WAS THE BEGINNING OF 1938-BEFORE THE WAR- HANGING HIGH IN THE CENTER OF TOWN, IT WAS A NAZI FLAG..
HERE WAS THE FIRST TIME I SAW, WITH MY OWN EYES, THE SWASTIKA.

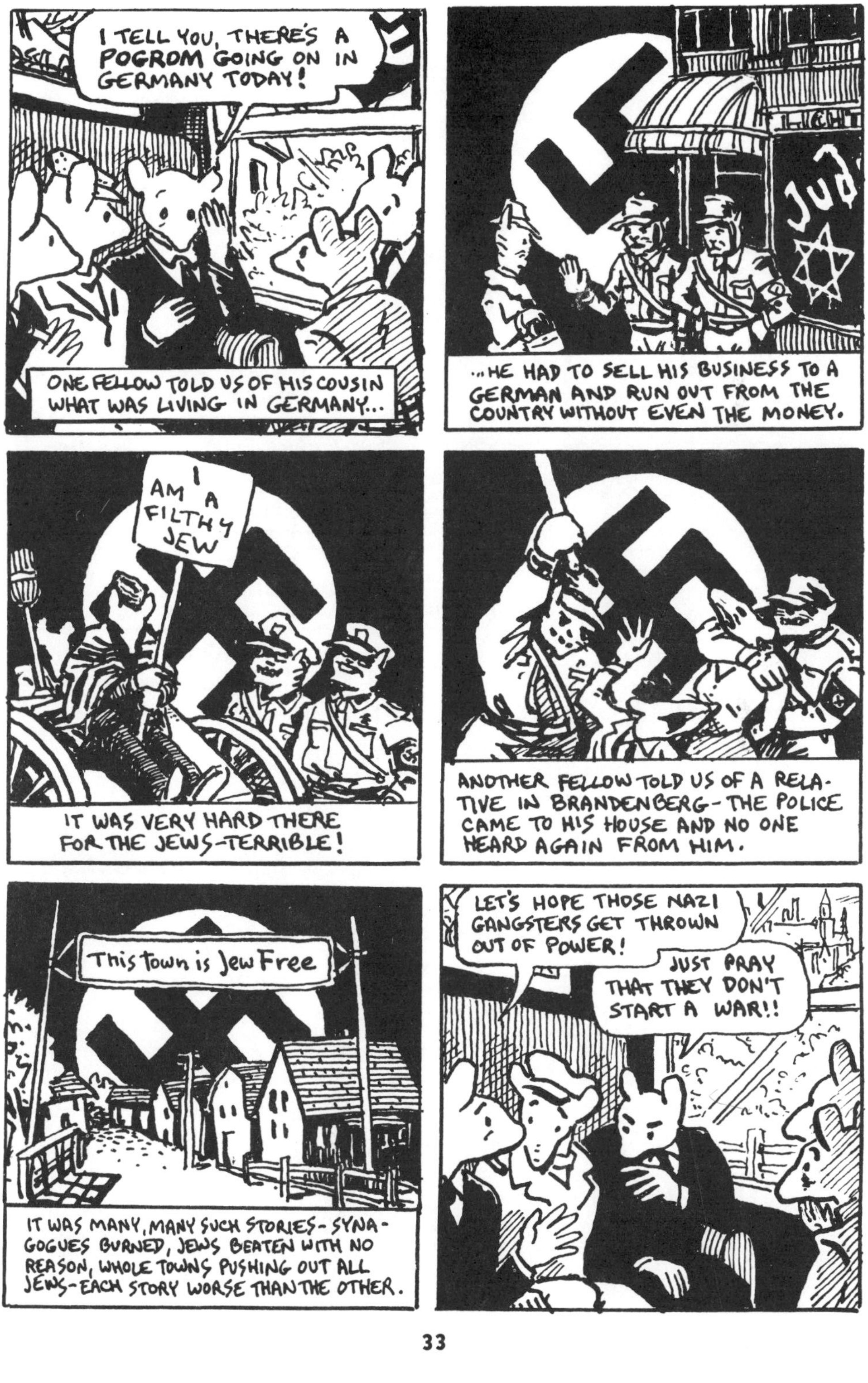

I TELL YOU, THERE'S A POGROM GOING ON IN GERMANY TODAY!
ONE FELLOW TOLD US OF HIS COUSIN WHAT WAS LIVING IN GERMANY...
JUD
...HE HAD TO SELL HIS BUSINESS TO A GERMAN AND RUN OUT FROM THE COUNTRY WITHOUT EVEN THE MONEY.
I AM A FILTHY JEW
IT WAS VERY HARD THERE FOR THE JEWS-TERRIBLE!
ANOTHER FELLOW TOLD US OF A RELATIVE IN BRANDENBERG - THE POLICE CAME TO HIS HOUSE AND NO ONE HEARD AGAIN FROM HIM.
This town is Jew Free
IT WAS MANY, MANY SUCH STORIES - SYNAGOGUES BURNED, JEWS BEATEN WITH NO REASON, WHOLE TOWNS PUSHING OUT ALL JEWS - EACH STORY WORSE THAN THE OTHER.
LET'S HOPE THOSE NAZI GANGSTERS GET THROWN OUT OF POWER!
JUST PRAY THAT THEY DON'T START A WAR!!

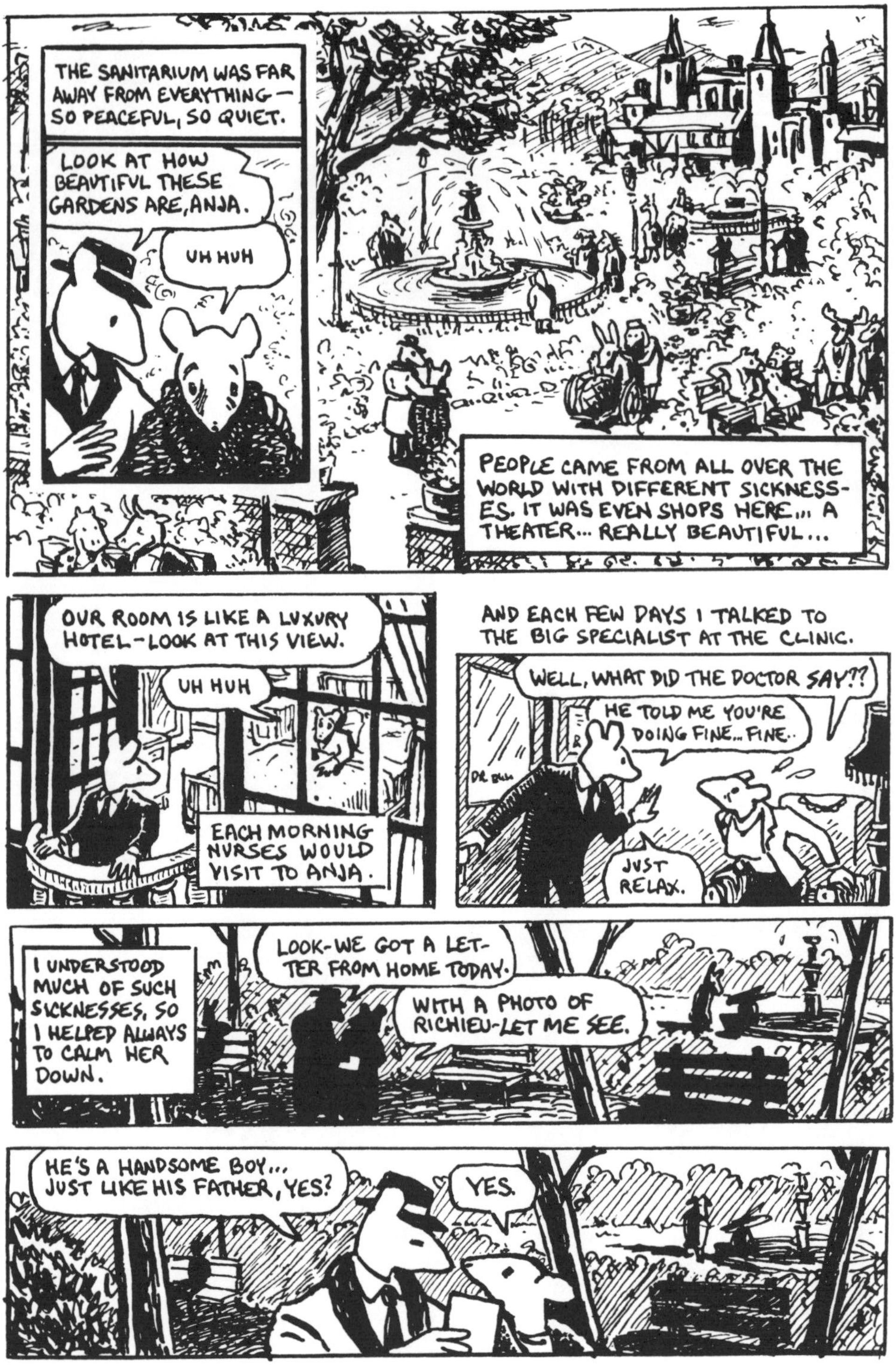
THE SANITARIUM WAS FAR AWAY FROM EVERYTHING—SO PEACEFUL, SO QUIET.
LOOK AT HOW BEAUTIFUL THESE GARDENS ARE, ANJA.
UH HUH
PEOPLE CAME FROM ALL OVER THE WORLD WITH DIFFERENT SICKNESSES. IT WAS EVEN SHOPS HERE... A THEATER... REALLY BEAUTIFUL...
OUR ROOM IS LIKE A LUXURY HOTEL—LOOK AT THIS VIEW.
UH HUH
EACH MORNING NURSES WOULD VISIT TO ANJA.
AND EACH FEW DAYS I TALKED TO THE BIG SPECIALIST AT THE CLINIC.
WELL, WHAT DID THE DOCTOR SAY??
HE TOLD ME YOU'RE DOING FINE... FINE.
JUST RELAX.
I UNDERSTOOD MUCH OF SUCH SICKNESSES, SO I HELPED ALWAYS TO CALM HER DOWN.
LOOK—WE GOT A LETTER FROM HOME TODAY.
WITH A PHOTO OF RICHIEU—LET ME SEE.
HE'S A HANDSOME BOY... JUST LIKE HIS FATHER, YES?
YES.

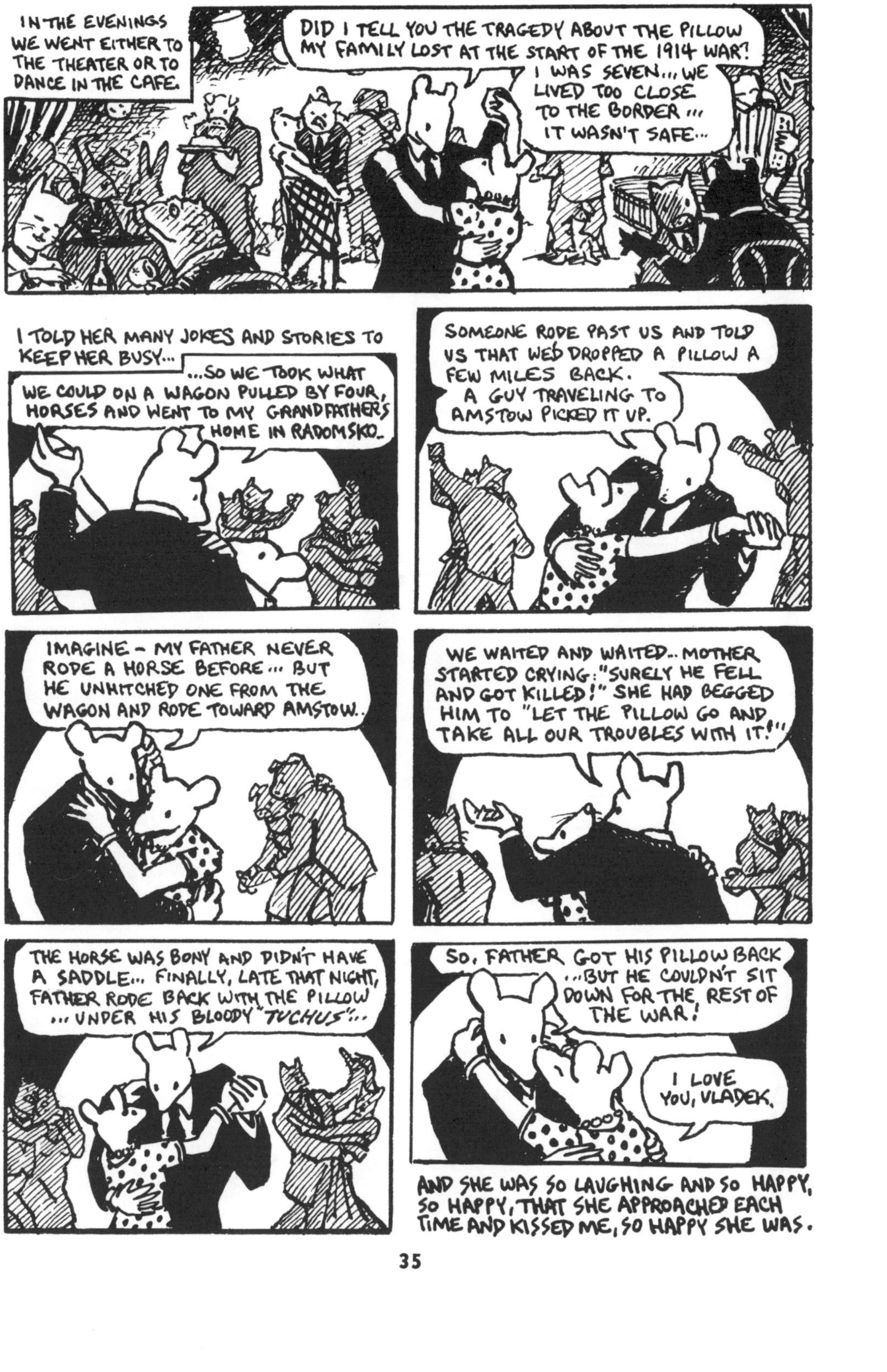
IN THE EVENINGS WE WENT EITHER TO THE THEATER OR TO DANCE IN THE CAFE.
DID I TELL YOU THE TRAGEDY ABOUT THE PILLOW MY FAMILY LOST AT THE START OF THE 1914 WAR?
I WAS SEVEN... WE LIVED TOO CLOSE TO THE BORDER... IT WASN'T SAFE...
I TOLD HER MANY JOKES AND STORIES TO KEEP HER BUSY...
...SO WE TOOK WHAT WE COULD ON A WAGON PULLED BY FOUR HORSES AND WENT TO MY GRANDFATHER'S HOME IN RADOMSKO.
SOMEONE RODE PAST US AND TOLD US THAT WE'D DROPPED A PILLOW A FEW MILES BACK. A GUY TRAVELING TO AMSTOW PICKED IT UP.
IMAGINE - MY FATHER NEVER RODE A HORSE BEFORE... BUT HE UNHITCHED ONE FROM THE WAGON AND RODE TOWARD AMSTOW.
WE WAITED AND WAITED.. MOTHER STARTED CRYING: "SURELY HE FELL AND GOT KILLED!" SHE HAD BEGGED HIM TO "LET THE PILLOW GO AND TAKE ALL OUR TROUBLES WITH IT!"
THE HORSE WAS BONY AND DIDN'T HAVE A SADDLE... FINALLY, LATE THAT NIGHT, FATHER RODE BACK WITH THE PILLOW ...UNDER HIS BLOODY "TUCHUS"...
SO, FATHER GOT HIS PILLOW BACK ...BUT HE COULDN'T SIT DOWN FOR THE REST OF THE WAR!
I LOVE YOU, VLADEK.
AND SHE WAS SO LAUGHING AND SO HAPPY, SO HAPPY, THAT SHE APPROACHED EACH TIME AND KISSED ME, SO HAPPY SHE WAS.

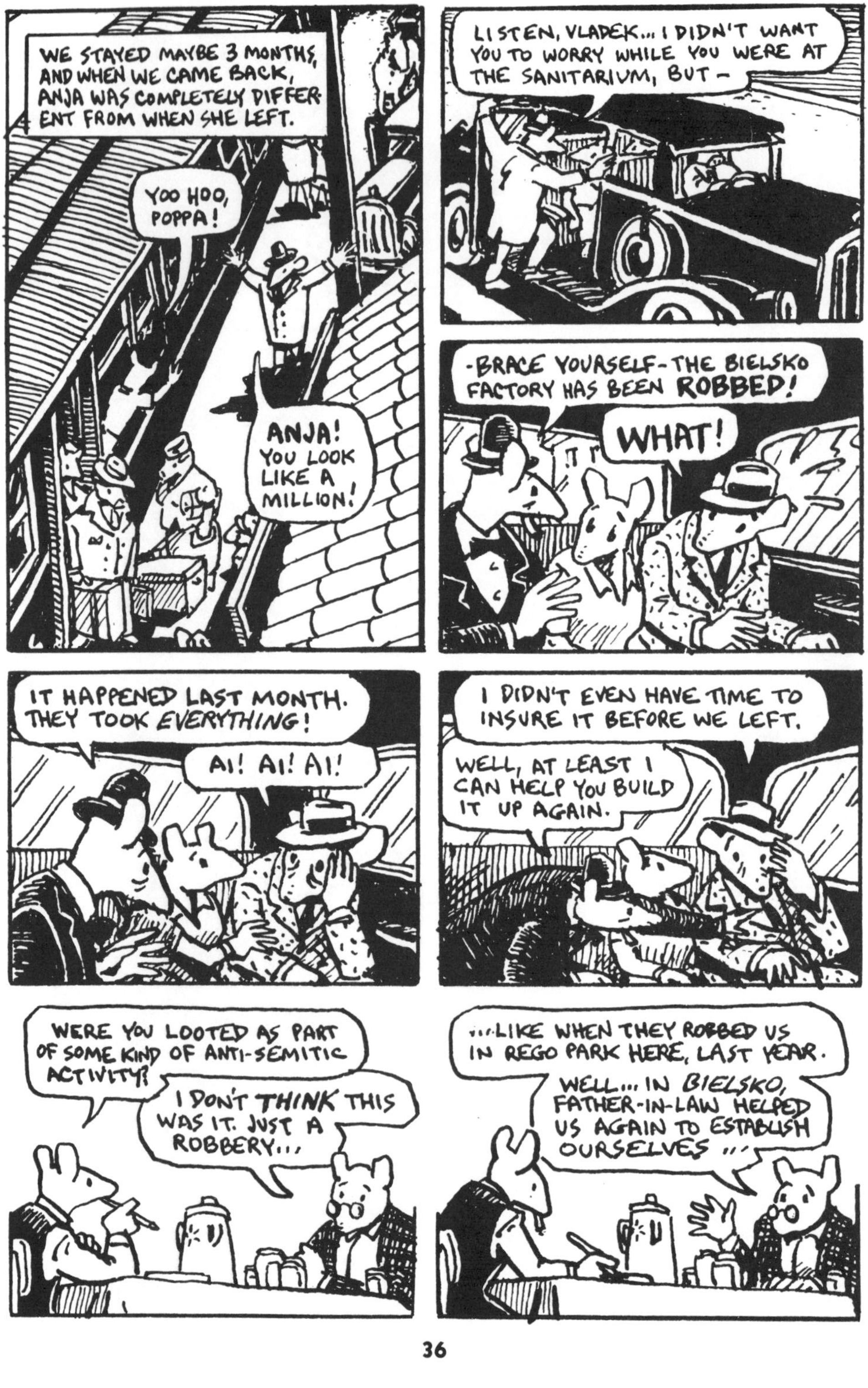
WE STAYED MAYBE 3 MONTHS, AND WHEN WE CAME BACK, ANJA WAS COMPLETELY DIFFERENT FROM WHEN SHE LEFT.
YOO HOO, POPPA!
ANJA! YOU LOOK LIKE A MILLION!
LISTEN, VLADEK... I DIDN'T WANT YOU TO WORRY WHILE YOU WERE AT THE SANITARIUM, BUT -
-BRACE YOURSELF- THE BIELSKO FACTORY HAS BEEN ROBBED!
WHAT!
IT HAPPENED LAST MONTH. THEY TOOK EVERYTHING!
AI! AI! AI!
I DIDN'T EVEN HAVE TIME TO INSURE IT BEFORE WE LEFT.
WELL, AT LEAST I CAN HELP YOU BUILD IT UP AGAIN.
WERE YOU LOOTED AS PART OF SOME KIND OF ANTI-SEMITIC ACTIVITY?
I DON'T THINK THIS WAS IT. JUST A ROBBERY...
...LIKE WHEN THEY ROBBED US IN REGO PARK HERE, LAST YEAR.
WELL... IN BIELSKO, FATHER-IN-LAW HELPED US AGAIN TO ESTABLISH OURSELVES...

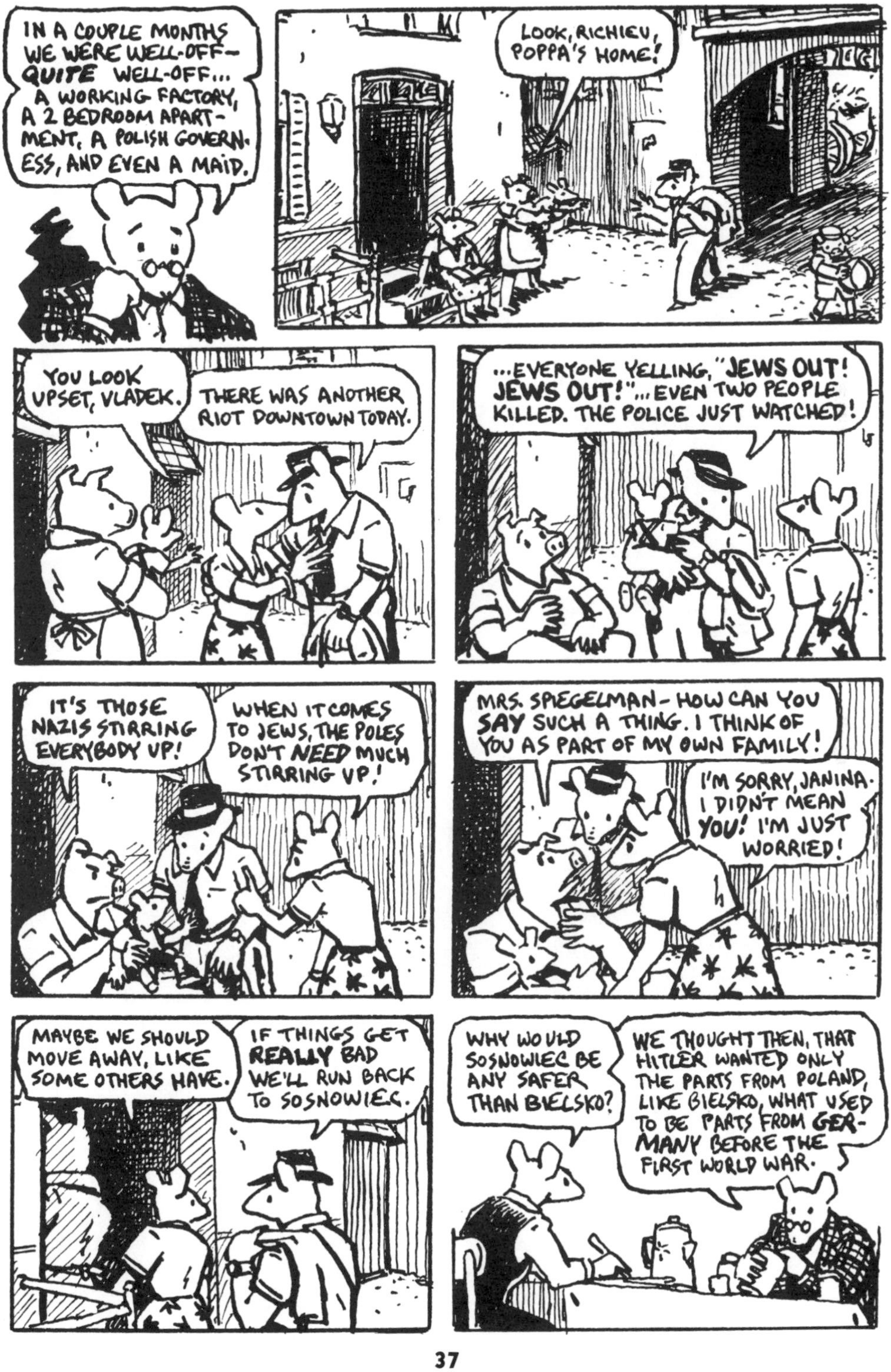
IN A COUPLE MONTHS WE WERE WELL-OFF— QUITE WELL-OFF... A WORKING FACTORY, A 2 BEDROOM APARTMENT, A POLISH GOVERNESS, AND EVEN A MAID.
LOOK, RICHIEU, POPPA'S HOME!
YOU LOOK UPSET, VLADEK.
THERE WAS ANOTHER RIOT DOWNTOWN TODAY.
...EVERYONE YELLING, "JEWS OUT! JEWS OUT!"... EVEN TWO PEOPLE KILLED. THE POLICE JUST WATCHED!
IT'S THOSE NAZIS STIRRING EVERYBODY UP!
WHEN IT COMES TO JEWS, THE POLES DON'T NEED MUCH STIRRING UP!
MRS. SPIEGELMAN- HOW CAN YOU SAY SUCH A THING. I THINK OF YOU AS PART OF MY OWN FAMILY!
I'M SORRY, JANINA. I DIDN'T MEAN YOU! I'M JUST WORRIED!
MAYBE WE SHOULD MOVE AWAY, LIKE SOME OTHERS HAVE.
IF THINGS GET REALLY BAD WE'LL RUN BACK TO SOSNOWIEC.
WHY WOULD SOSNOWIEC BE ANY SAFER THAN BIELSKO?
WE THOUGHT THEN, THAT HITLER WANTED ONLY THE PARTS FROM POLAND, LIKE BIELSKO, WHAT USED TO BE PARTS FROM GERMANY BEFORE THE FIRST WORLD WAR.

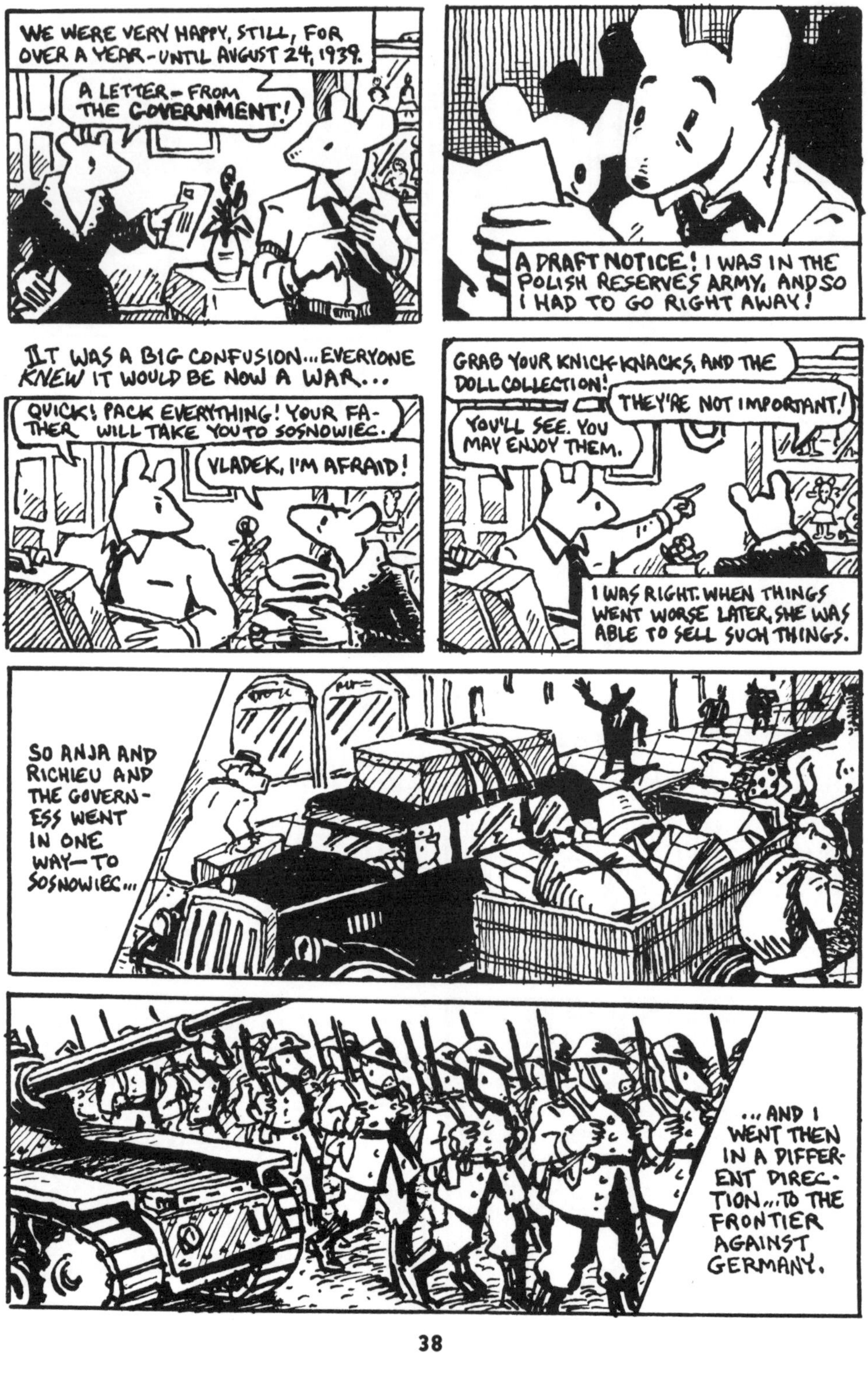
WE WERE VERY HAPPY, STILL, FOR OVER A YEAR - UNTIL AUGUST 24, 1939.
A LETTER - FROM THE GOVERNMENT!
A DRAFT NOTICE! I WAS IN THE POLISH RESERVES ARMY, AND SO I HAD TO GO RIGHT AWAY!
IT WAS A BIG CONFUSION... EVERYONE KNEW IT WOULD BE NOW A WAR...
QUICK! PACK EVERYTHING! YOUR FATHER WILL TAKE YOU TO SOSNOWIEC.
VLADEK, I'M AFRAID!
GRAB YOUR KNICK-KNACKS, AND THE DOLL COLLECTION!
THEY'RE NOT IMPORTANT!
YOU'LL SEE. YOU MAY ENJOY THEM.
I WAS RIGHT. WHEN THINGS WENT WORSE LATER, SHE WAS ABLE TO SELL SUCH THINGS.
SO ANJA AND RICHIEU AND THE GOVERNESS WENT IN ONE WAY— TO SOSNOWIEC...
...AND I WENT THEN IN A DIFFERENT DIRECTION... TO THE FRONTIER AGAINST GERMANY.

39

MY EYE STARTED SO BLEEDING, I HAD TO RUN OUT TO FIND A DOCTOR IN A DIFFERENT HOSPITAL.

THERE ANOTHER SPECIALIST OPERATED RIGHT AWAY! OTHERWISE I COULD HAVE DIED.

SO NOW ITS A GLASS EYE.

HE DID A GOOD JOB, NO? ONE TIME, EVEN, A YOUNG DOCTOR CAME TO MY BED THERE IN THE HOSPITAL...

HE LOOKED WITH A LIGHT A LONG TIME IN MY EYES AND TOLD: "MR. SPIEGELMAN, YOUR LEFT EYE IS PERFECT!...

"...BUT IN YOUR RIGHT EYE IS CATARACTS."

HE DIDN'T KNOW, OF COURSE, THAT THE LEFT EYE IS GLASS...

AND I DIDN'T TELL ANYTHING TO HIM. I DIDN'T WANT TO MAKE HIM AN EMBARRASSMENT.

UH-HUH- YOU TOLD ME ABOUT THAT.

WELL, IT'S ENOUGH FOR TODAY, YES? I'M TIRED AND I MUST COUNT STILL MY PILLS.

OKAY, GOOD IDEA... MY HAND IS SORE FROM WRITING ALL THIS DOWN.

40

# CHAPTER THREE

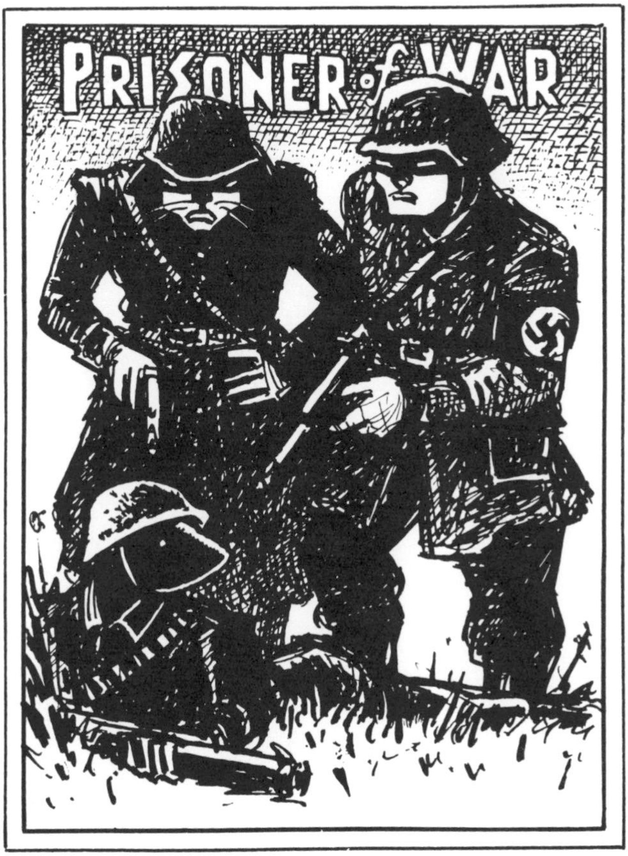
PRISONER of WAR

I visited my father more often in order to get more information about his past..

43

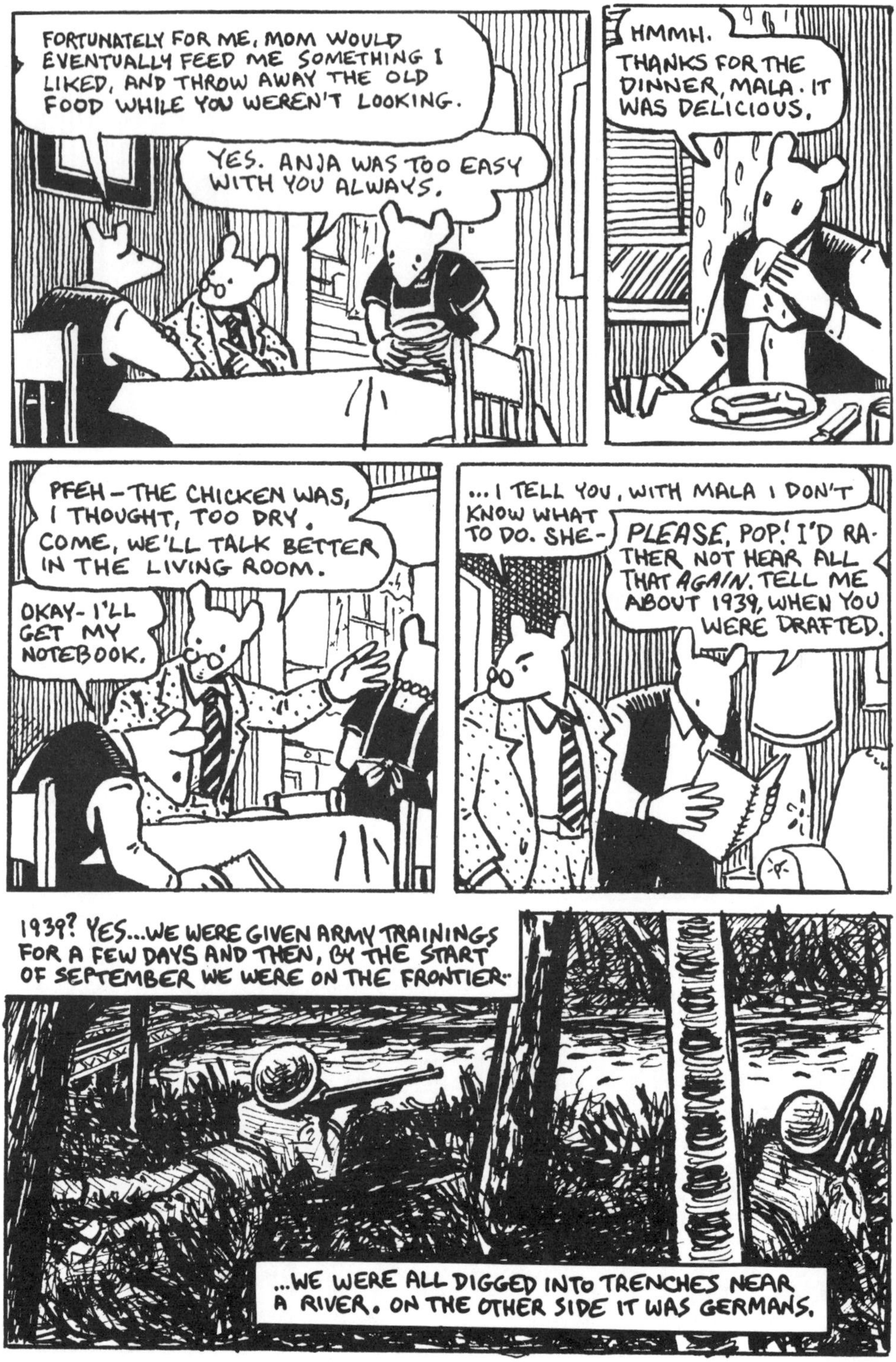
FORTUNATELY FOR ME, MOM WOULD EVENTUALLY FEED ME SOMETHING I LIKED, AND THROW AWAY THE OLD FOOD WHILE YOU WEREN'T LOOKING.
YES. ANJA WAS TOO EASY WITH YOU ALWAYS.
HMMH.
THANKS FOR THE DINNER, MALA. IT WAS DELICIOUS.
PFEH – THE CHICKEN WAS, I THOUGHT, TOO DRY. COME, WE'LL TALK BETTER IN THE LIVING ROOM.
OKAY- I'LL GET MY NOTEBOOK.
...I TELL YOU, WITH MALA I DON'T KNOW WHAT TO DO. SHE-
PLEASE, POP! I'D RATHER NOT HEAR ALL THAT AGAIN. TELL ME ABOUT 1939, WHEN YOU WERE DRAFTED.
1939? YES...WE WERE GIVEN ARMY TRAININGS FOR A FEW DAYS AND THEN, BY THE START OF SEPTEMBER WE WERE ON THE FRONTIER...
...WE WERE ALL DIGGED INTO TRENCHES NEAR A RIVER. ON THE OTHER SIDE IT WAS GERMANS.

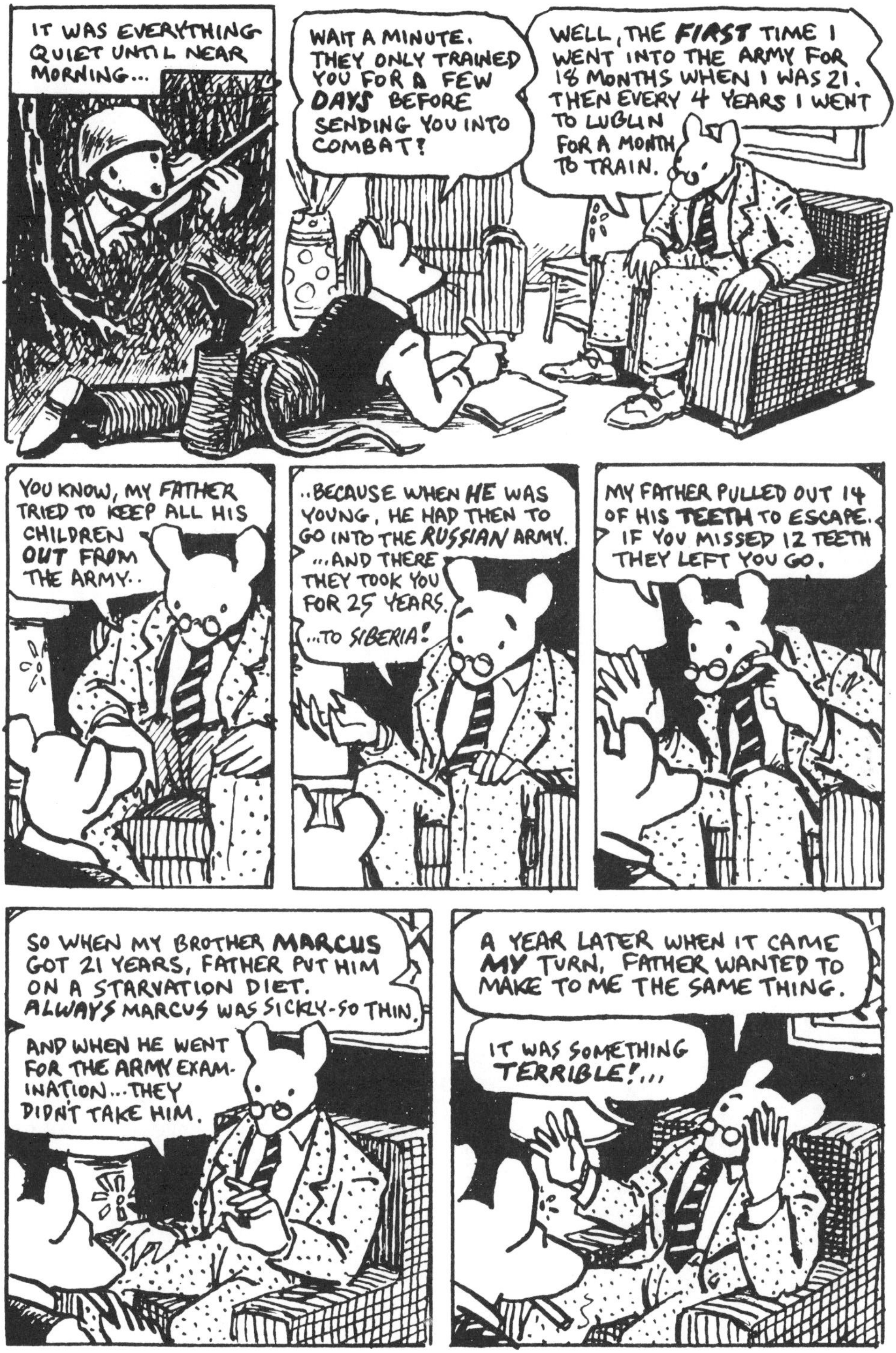
IT WAS EVERYTHING QUIET UNTIL NEAR MORNING...
WAIT A MINUTE. THEY ONLY TRAINED YOU FOR A FEW DAYS BEFORE SENDING YOU INTO COMBAT?
WELL, THE FIRST TIME I WENT INTO THE ARMY FOR 18 MONTHS WHEN I WAS 21. THEN EVERY 4 YEARS I WENT TO LUBLIN FOR A MONTH TO TRAIN.
YOU KNOW, MY FATHER TRIED TO KEEP ALL HIS CHILDREN OUT FROM THE ARMY..
..BECAUSE WHEN HE WAS YOUNG, HE HAD THEN TO GO INTO THE RUSSIAN ARMY.
...AND THERE THEY TOOK YOU FOR 25 YEARS.
...TO SIBERIA!
MY FATHER PULLED OUT 14 OF HIS TEETH TO ESCAPE.
IF YOU MISSED 12 TEETH THEY LEFT YOU GO.
SO WHEN MY BROTHER MARCUS GOT 21 YEARS, FATHER PUT HIM ON A STARVATION DIET. ALWAYS MARCUS WAS SICKLY-SO THIN.
AND WHEN HE WENT FOR THE ARMY EXAMINATION...THEY DIDN'T TAKE HIM.
A YEAR LATER WHEN IT CAME MY TURN, FATHER WANTED TO MAKE TO ME THE SAME THING.
IT WAS SOMETHING TERRIBLE!...

47

48

49

ATTENTION! ALL PRISONERS WILL CARRY OUR DEAD AND WOUNDED TO THE WAITING RED CROSS TRUCKS.

YOU! WHERE DO YOU THINK YOU'RE GOING?

I-I THOUGHT I SAW A BODY OVER BY THE RIVER!

YES. HERE!

I KNEW WHERE THE ONE I SHOT SHOULD BE LAYING.

ER VERBLUTETE! HIS BLOOD RAN OUT! CARRY HIM OVER TO THE TRUCK WITH THE OTHERS.

HIS NAME WAS JAN...

...AND I KNEW THAT I KILLED HIM.

AND I SAID TO MYSELF: "WELL, AT LEAST I DID SOMETHING."

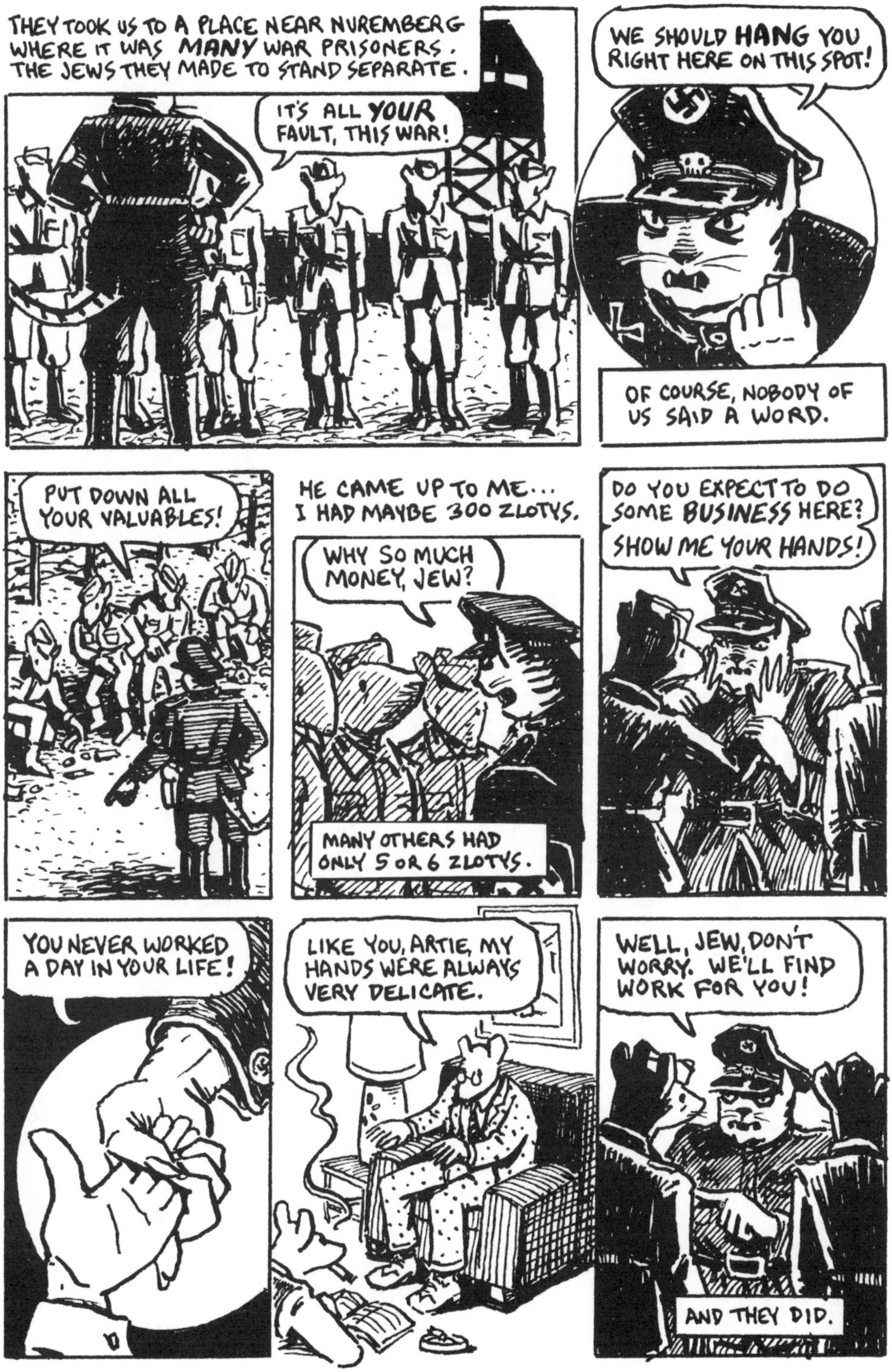

THEY TOOK US TO A PLACE NEAR NUREMBERG WHERE IT WAS MANY WAR PRISONERS. THE JEWS THEY MADE TO STAND SEPARATE.
IT'S ALL YOUR FAULT, THIS WAR!
WE SHOULD HANG YOU RIGHT HERE ON THIS SPOT!
OF COURSE, NOBODY OF US SAID A WORD.
PUT DOWN ALL YOUR VALUABLES!
HE CAME UP TO ME... I HAD MAYBE 300 ZLOTYS.
WHY SO MUCH MONEY, JEW?
MANY OTHERS HAD ONLY 5 OR 6 ZLOTYS.
DO YOU EXPECT TO DO SOME BUSINESS HERE?
SHOW ME YOUR HANDS!
YOU NEVER WORKED A DAY IN YOUR LIFE!
LIKE YOU, ARTIE, MY HANDS WERE ALWAYS VERY DELICATE.
WELL, JEW, DON'T WORRY. WE'LL FIND WORK FOR YOU!
AND THEY DID.

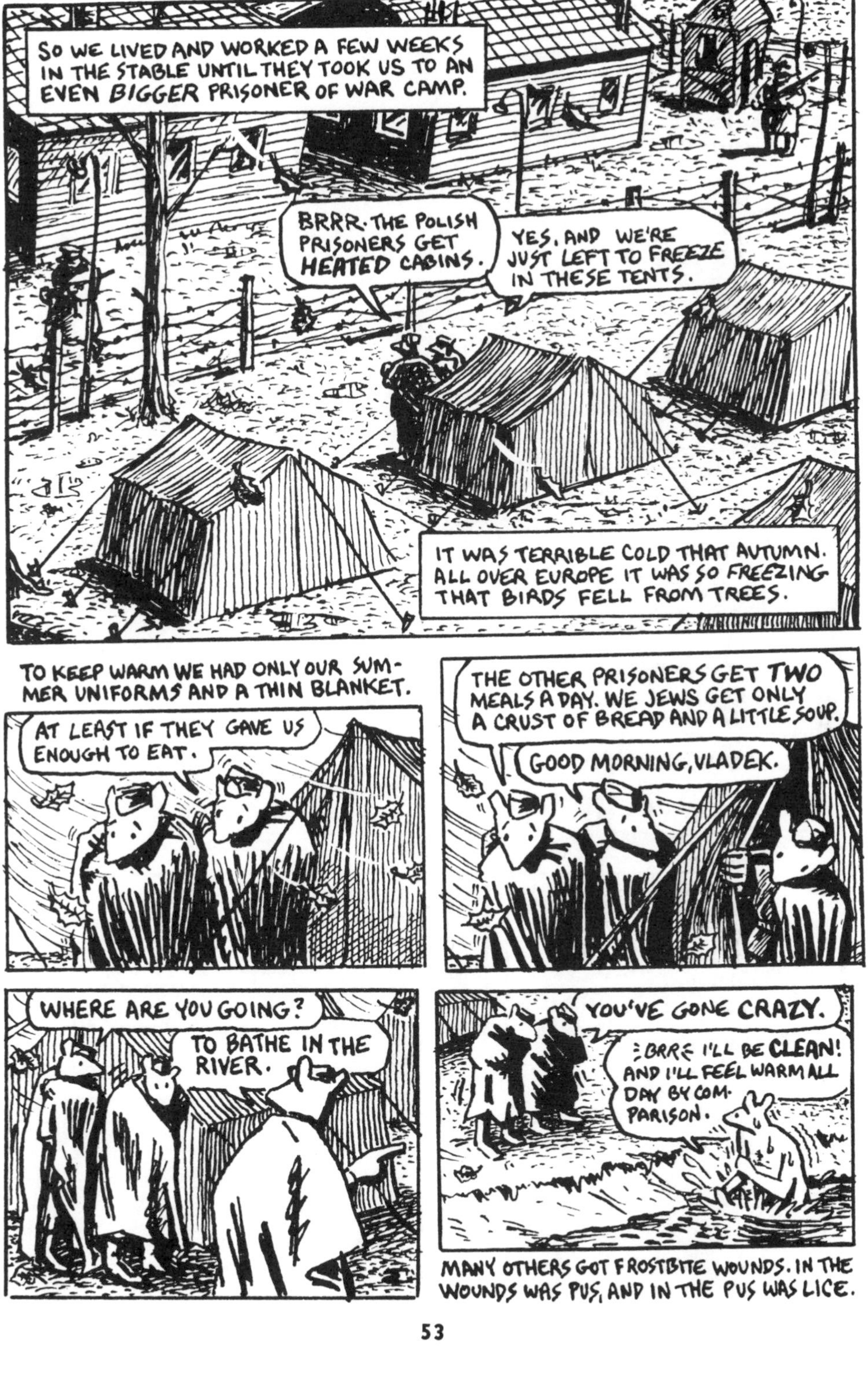
SO WE LIVED AND WORKED A FEW WEEKS IN THE STABLE UNTIL THEY TOOK US TO AN EVEN *BIGGER* PRISONER OF WAR CAMP.
BRRR. THE POLISH PRISONERS GET **HEATED** CABINS.
YES. AND WE'RE JUST LEFT TO FREEZE IN THESE TENTS.
IT WAS TERRIBLE COLD THAT AUTUMN. ALL OVER EUROPE IT WAS SO FREEZING THAT BIRDS FELL FROM TREES.
TO KEEP WARM WE HAD ONLY OUR SUMMER UNIFORMS AND A THIN BLANKET.
AT LEAST IF THEY GAVE US ENOUGH TO EAT.
THE OTHER PRISONERS GET *TWO* MEALS A DAY. WE JEWS GET ONLY A CRUST OF BREAD AND A LITTLE SOUP.
GOOD MORNING, VLADEK.
WHERE ARE YOU GOING?
TO BATHE IN THE RIVER.
YOU'VE GONE **CRAZY**.
BRR I'LL BE **CLEAN**! AND I'LL FEEL WARM ALL DAY BY COMPARISON.
MANY OTHERS GOT FROSTBITE WOUNDS. IN THE WOUNDS WAS PUS, AND IN THE PUS WAS LICE.

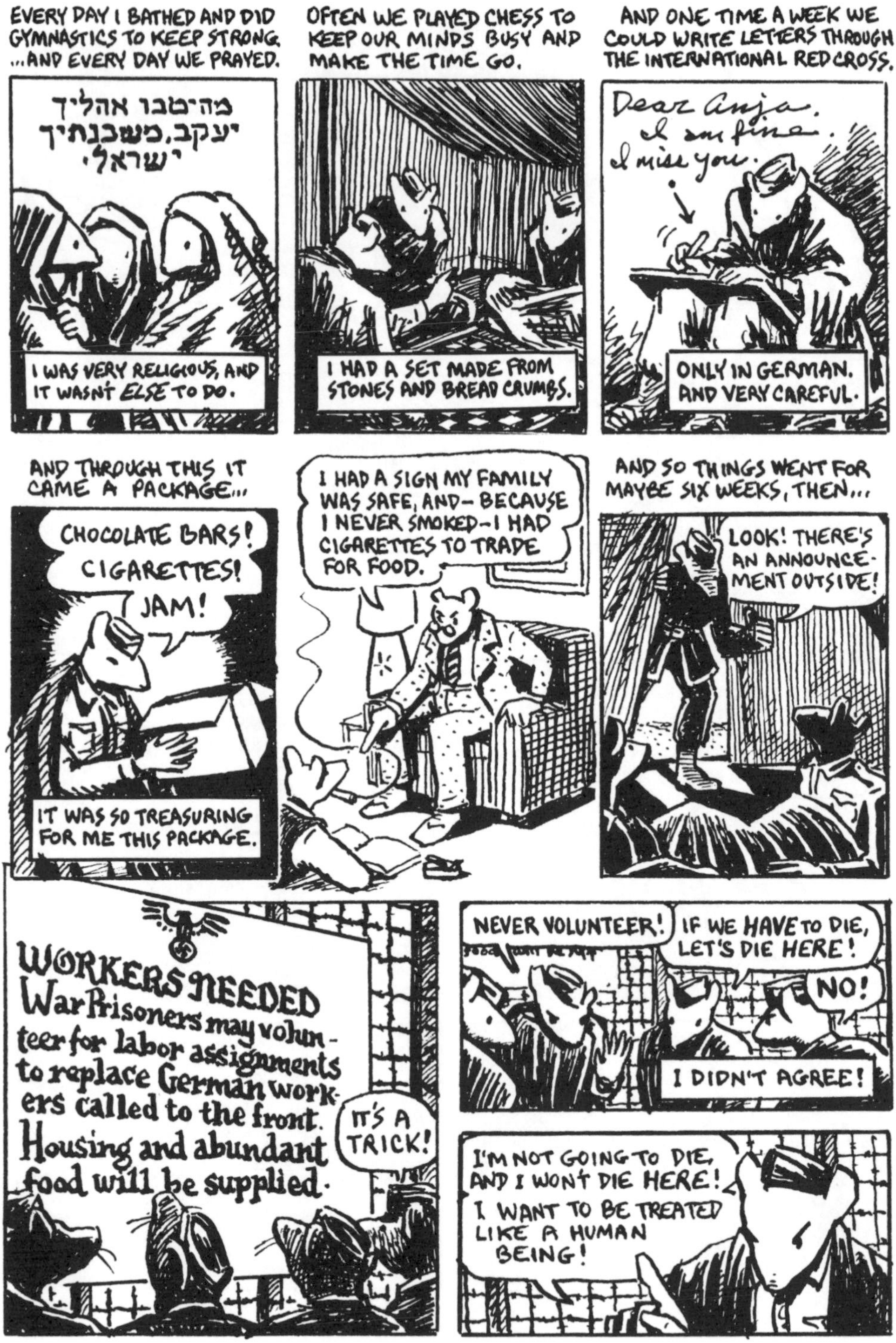

EVERY DAY I BATHED AND DID GYMNASTICS TO KEEP STRONG. ...AND EVERY DAY WE PRAYED.
מה-טבו אהליך יעקב. משכנתיך ישראל.
I WAS VERY RELIGIOUS, AND IT WASN'T ELSE TO DO.
OFTEN WE PLAYED CHESS TO KEEP OUR MINDS BUSY AND MAKE THE TIME GO.
I HAD A SET MADE FROM STONES AND BREAD CRUMBS.
AND ONE TIME A WEEK WE COULD WRITE LETTERS THROUGH THE INTERNATIONAL RED CROSS.
Dear Anja. I am fine. I miss you.
ONLY IN GERMAN. AND VERY CAREFUL.
AND THROUGH THIS IT CAME A PACKAGE...
CHOCOLATE BARS! CIGARETTES!
JAM!
IT WAS SO TREASURING FOR ME THIS PACKAGE.
I HAD A SIGN MY FAMILY WAS SAFE, AND– BECAUSE I NEVER SMOKED– I HAD CIGARETTES TO TRADE FOR FOOD.
AND SO THINGS WENT FOR MAYBE SIX WEEKS, THEN...
LOOK! THERE'S AN ANNOUNCEMENT OUTSIDE!
WORKERS NEEDED
War Prisoners may volunteer for labor assignments to replace German workers called to the front. Housing and abundant food will be supplied.
IT'S A TRICK!
NEVER VOLUNTEER!
IF WE HAVE TO DIE, LET'S DIE HERE!
NO!
I DIDN'T AGREE!
I'M NOT GOING TO DIE, AND I WON'T DIE HERE!
I WANT TO BE TREATED LIKE A HUMAN BEING!

55

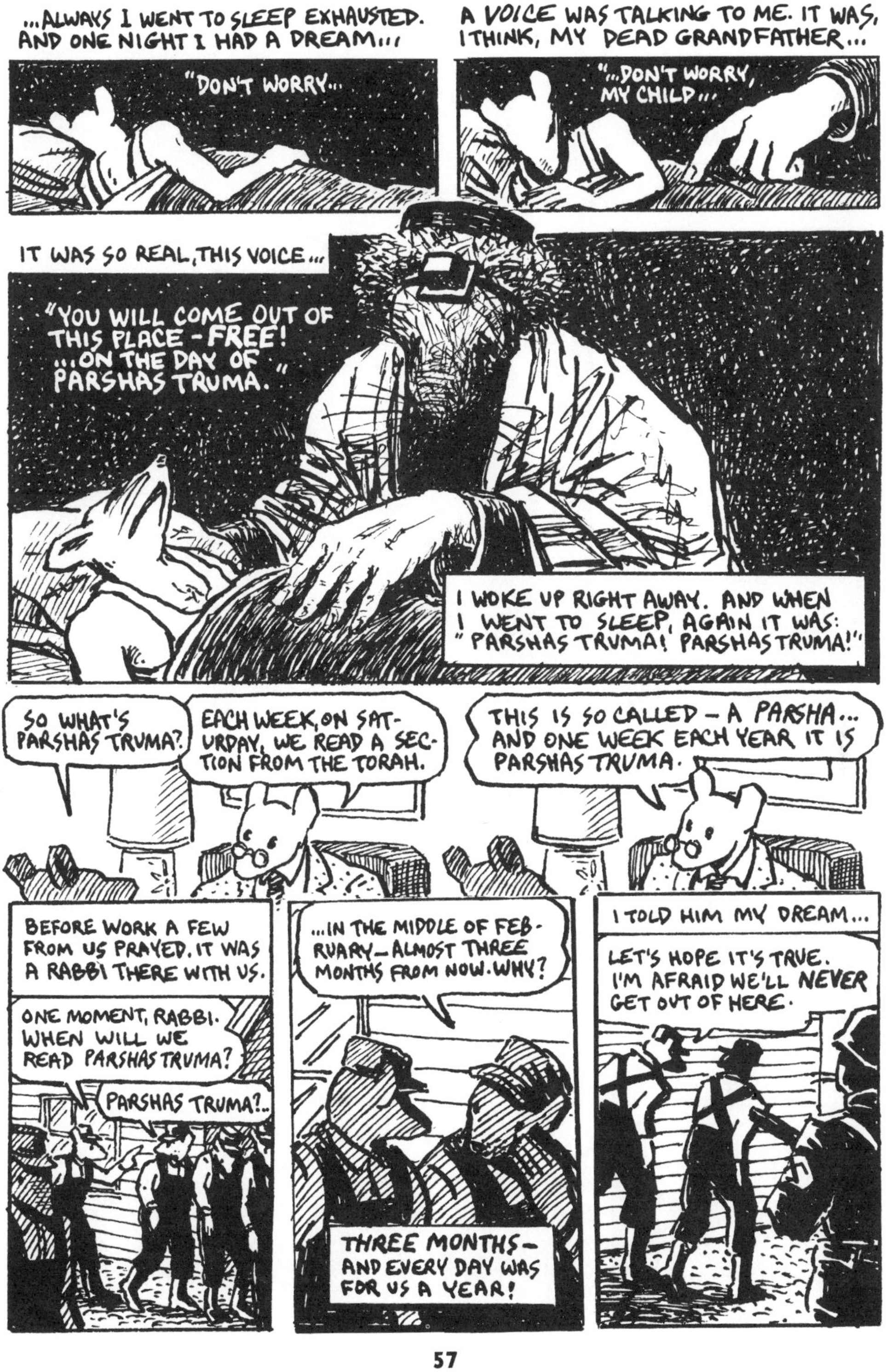
...ALWAYS I WENT TO SLEEP EXHAUSTED. AND ONE NIGHT I HAD A DREAM...
"DON'T WORRY...
A VOICE WAS TALKING TO ME. IT WAS, I THINK, MY DEAD GRANDFATHER...
"...DON'T WORRY, MY CHILD...
IT WAS SO REAL, THIS VOICE...
"YOU WILL COME OUT OF THIS PLACE - FREE! ...ON THE DAY OF PARSHAS TRUMA."
I WOKE UP RIGHT AWAY. AND WHEN I WENT TO SLEEP, AGAIN IT WAS: "PARSHAS TRUMA! PARSHAS TRUMA!"
SO WHAT'S PARSHAS TRUMA?
EACH WEEK, ON SATURDAY, WE READ A SECTION FROM THE TORAH.
THIS IS SO CALLED - A PARSHA... AND ONE WEEK EACH YEAR IT IS PARSHAS TRUMA.
BEFORE WORK A FEW FROM US PRAYED. IT WAS A RABBI THERE WITH US.
ONE MOMENT, RABBI. WHEN WILL WE READ PARSHAS TRUMA?
PARSHAS TRUMA?..
...IN THE MIDDLE OF FEBRUARY - ALMOST THREE MONTHS FROM NOW. WHY?
THREE MONTHS - AND EVERY DAY WAS FOR US A YEAR!
I TOLD HIM MY DREAM...
LET'S HOPE IT'S TRUE. I'M AFRAID WE'LL NEVER GET OUT OF HERE.

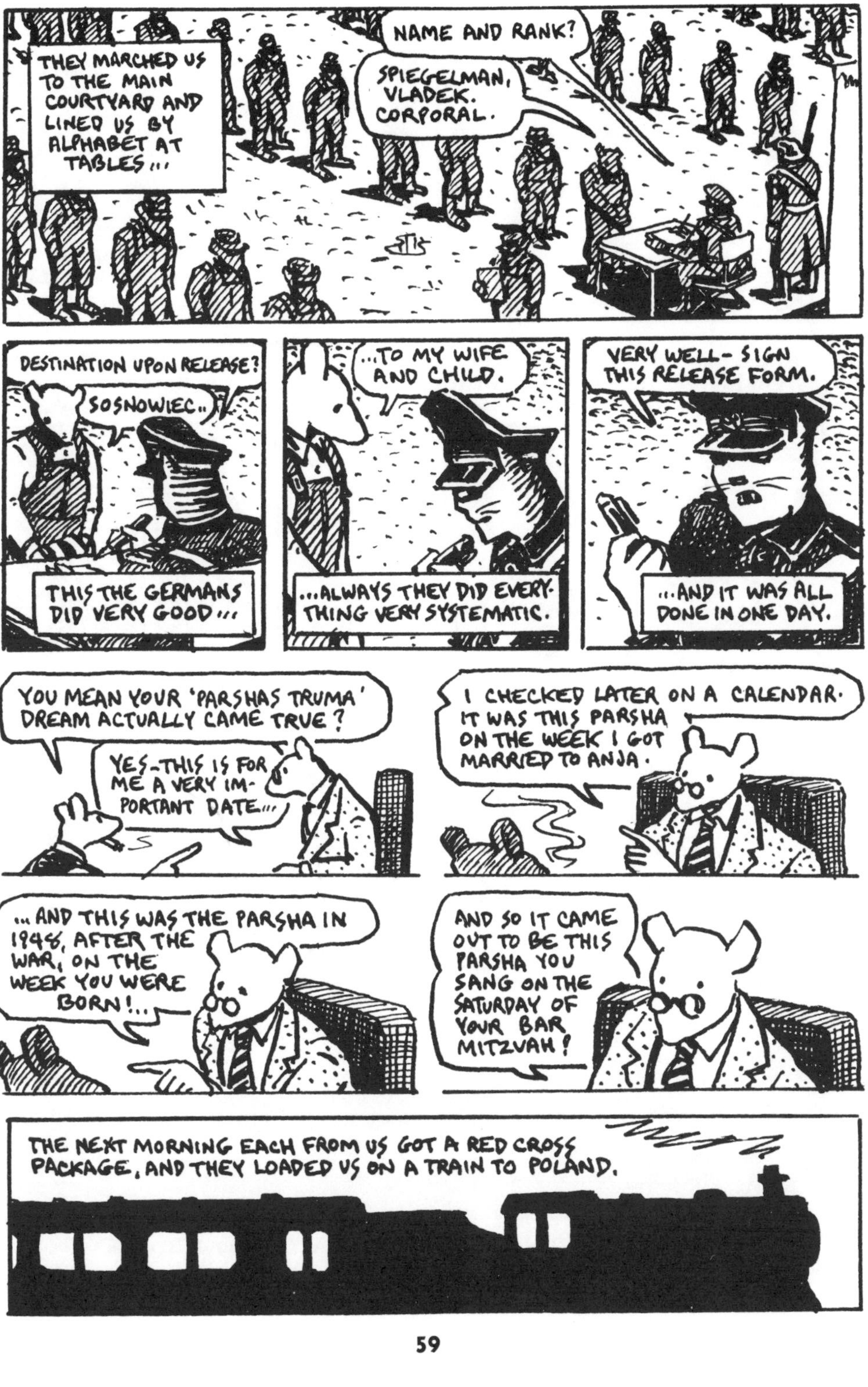
THEY MARCHED US TO THE MAIN COURTYARD AND LINED US BY ALPHABET AT TABLES...
NAME AND RANK?
SPIEGELMAN, VLADEK. CORPORAL.
DESTINATION UPON RELEASE?
SOSNOWIEC..
THIS THE GERMANS DID VERY GOOD...
...TO MY WIFE AND CHILD.
...ALWAYS THEY DID EVERYTHING VERY SYSTEMATIC.
VERY WELL- SIGN THIS RELEASE FORM.
...AND IT WAS ALL DONE IN ONE DAY.
YOU MEAN YOUR 'PARSHAS TRUMA' DREAM ACTUALLY CAME TRUE?
YES-THIS IS FOR ME A VERY IMPORTANT DATE...
I CHECKED LATER ON A CALENDAR. IT WAS THIS PARSHA ON THE WEEK I GOT MARRIED TO ANJA.
...AND THIS WAS THE PARSHA IN 1948, AFTER THE WAR, ON THE WEEK YOU WERE BORN!...
AND SO IT CAME OUT TO BE THIS PARSHA YOU SANG ON THE SATURDAY OF YOUR BAR MITZVAH!
THE NEXT MORNING EACH FROM US GOT A RED CROSS PACKAGE, AND THEY LOADED US ON A TRAIN TO POLAND.

DURING THE JOURNEY I SAT WITH THE RABBI.

SO, MY SON. NOW I SEE YOU ARE A "ROH-EH HANOLED," ONE WHO SEES WHAT THE FUTURE WILL BRING.

HEY! THIS TRAIN SEEMS TO BE *PASSING* SOSNOWIEC!

WHEN THEY DIDN'T STOP THE TRAIN I BECAME VERY WORRIED.

YOU SEE, THE NAZIS DIVIDED POLAND INTO PIECES: **PROTECTORATE** AND **REICH**, WITH A GUARDED BORDER BETWEEN.

THE TRAIN WENT COMPLETELY *PAST* MY PART OF POLAND—THE **REICH**—AND STOPPED ONLY IN THE PROTECTORATE.

THOSE WITH PAPERS FOR KRAKOW—OUT!

BALTIC SEA

LITHUANIA

E. PRUSSIA

(annexed to Russia)

P O L A N D

WARSAW

LUBLIN

SOSNOWIEC

KRAKOW

SLOVAKIA

HUNGARY

RUMANIA

GERMANY

SOVIET UNION

REICH: Annexed to Germany.

PROTECTORATE: German controlled Government.

AND, WHEN IT STOPPED IN WARSAW, THE RABBI GOT OUT.

I'LL WRITE TO YOU.

BUT I NEVER HEARD AGAIN FROM HIM. IT CAME SUCH A MISERY IN WARSAW, ALMOST NONE SURVIVED.

AND THE TRAIN WAS A LONG WAY PAST SOSNOWIEC. THEY TOOK ME UP, UP, VERY FAR—MAYBE 300 MILES—UNTIL WE CAME TO LUBLIN. THERE THEY UNLOADED ALL OF US FROM THE REICH.

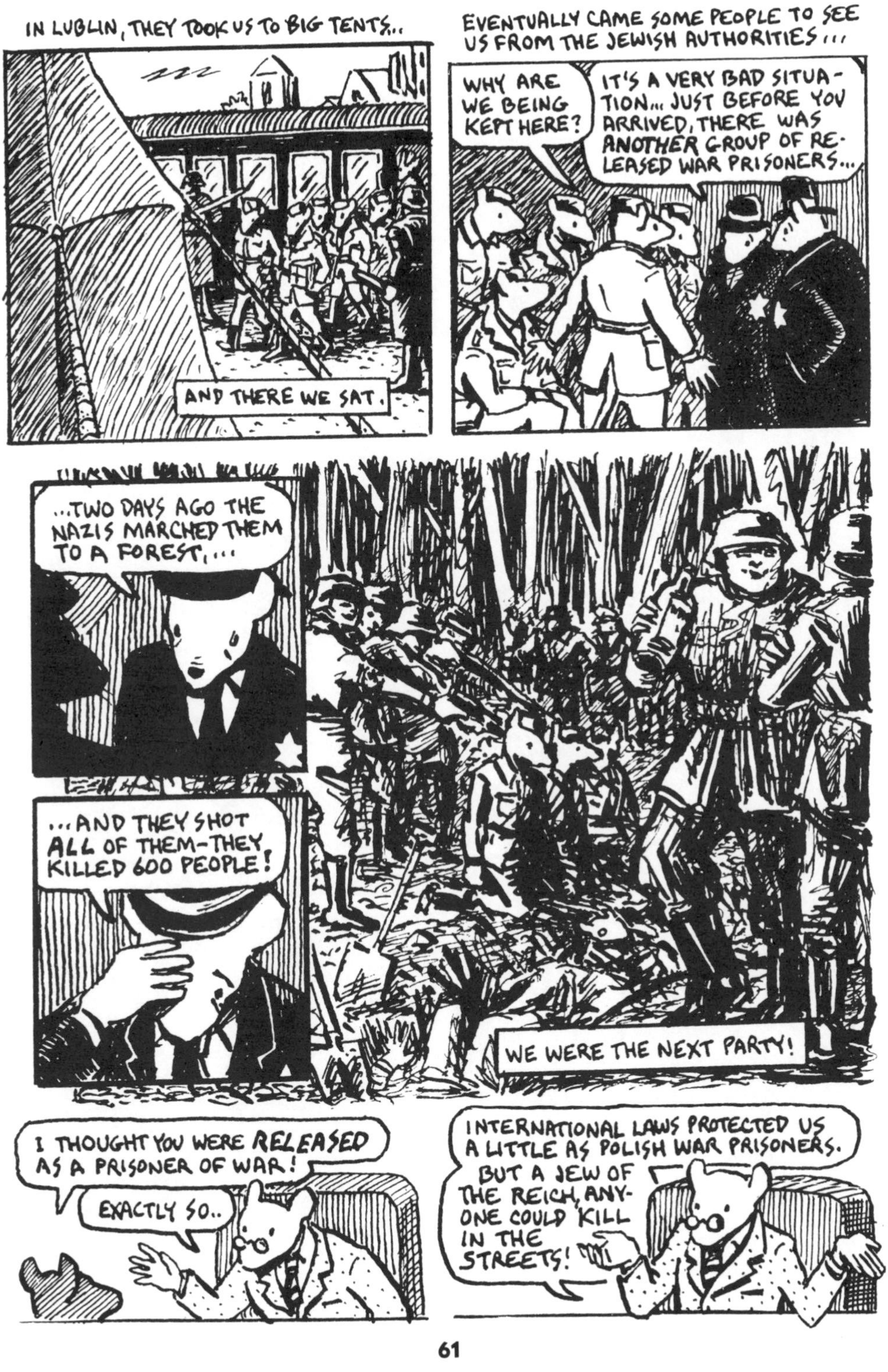
IN LUBLIN, THEY TOOK US TO BIG TENTS..
AND THERE WE SAT.
EVENTUALLY CAME SOME PEOPLE TO SEE US FROM THE JEWISH AUTHORITIES...
WHY ARE WE BEING KEPT HERE?
IT'S A VERY BAD SITUATION... JUST BEFORE YOU ARRIVED, THERE WAS ANOTHER GROUP OF RELEASED WAR PRISONERS...
...TWO DAYS AGO THE NAZIS MARCHED THEM TO A FOREST, ...
...AND THEY SHOT ALL OF THEM-THEY KILLED 600 PEOPLE!
WE WERE THE NEXT PARTY!
I THOUGHT YOU WERE RELEASED AS A PRISONER OF WAR!
EXACTLY SO..
INTERNATIONAL LAWS PROTECTED US A LITTLE AS POLISH WAR PRISONERS.
BUT A JEW OF THE REICH, ANYONE COULD KILL IN THE STREETS!

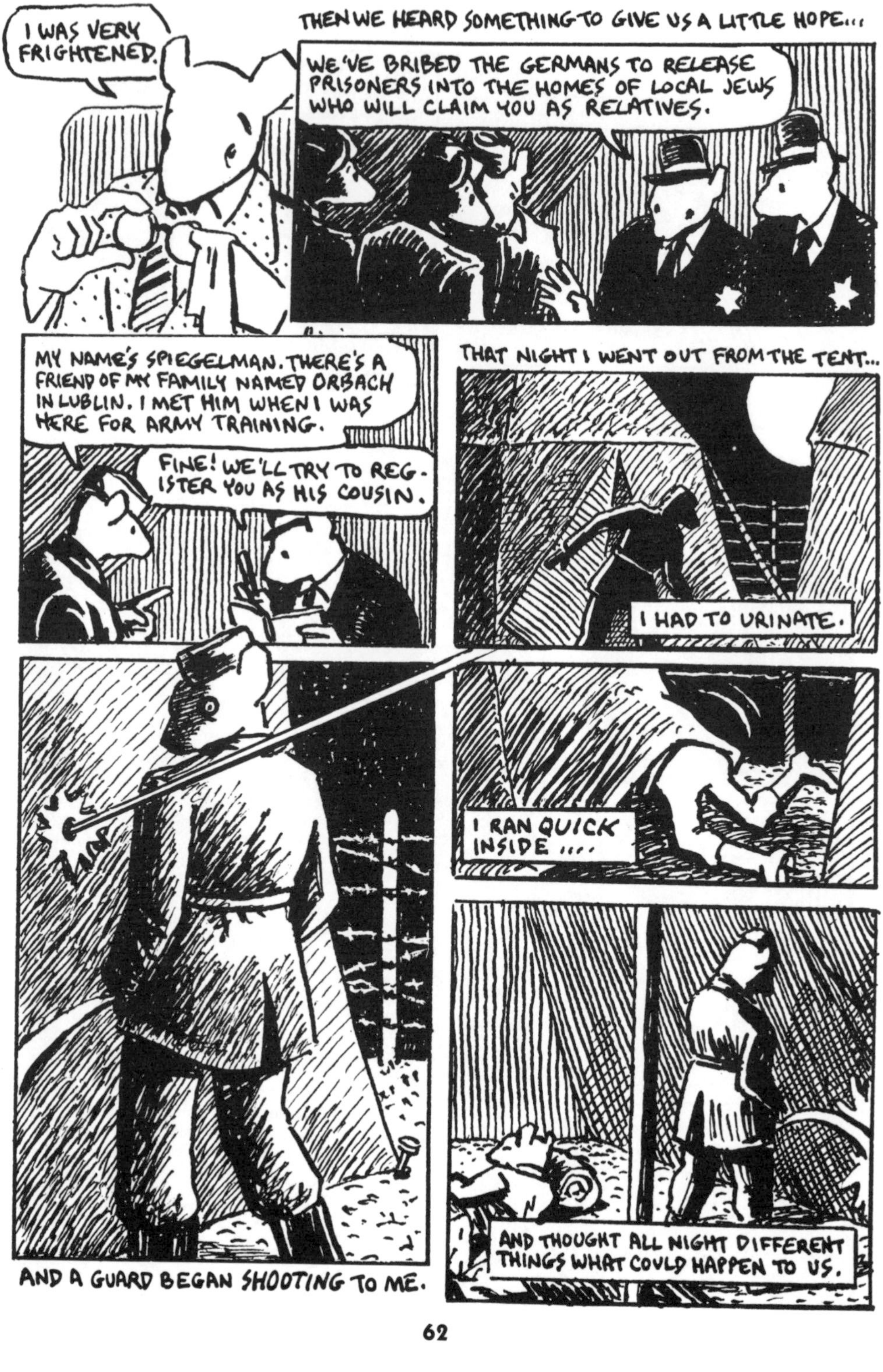
I WAS VERY FRIGHTENED.
THEN WE HEARD SOMETHING TO GIVE US A LITTLE HOPE...
WE'VE BRIBED THE GERMANS TO RELEASE PRISONERS INTO THE HOMES OF LOCAL JEWS WHO WILL CLAIM YOU AS RELATIVES.
MY NAME'S SPIEGELMAN. THERE'S A FRIEND OF MY FAMILY NAMED ORBACH IN LUBLIN. I MET HIM WHEN I WAS HERE FOR ARMY TRAINING.
FINE! WE'LL TRY TO REG-ISTER YOU AS HIS COUSIN.
THAT NIGHT I WENT OUT FROM THE TENT...
I HAD TO URINATE.
AND A GUARD BEGAN SHOOTING TO ME.
I RAN QUICK INSIDE ....
AND THOUGHT ALL NIGHT DIFFERENT THINGS WHAT COULD HAPPEN TO US.

THEN, AS SOON AS IT WAS LIGHT...

SPIEGELMAN!.. SPIEGELMAN!..

VLADEK!

ORBACH! AM I GLAD TO SEE YOU!

AND IN TEN MINUTES, I WAS FREE!

ORBACH WAS A FRIEND FROM MY UNCLE—HE HAD TWO BEAUTIFUL DAUGHTERS NEAR TO MY AGE.

I'M SORRY WE CAN'T OFFER YOU A BETTER MEAL, VLADEK—BUT THE JEWS OF LUBLIN GET VERY FEW FOOD COUPONS.

ONE MOMENT, GIRLS—I HAVE A GIFT FOR EACH OF YOU...

OH MY GOD! CHOCOLATE!

THESE I SAVED FROM A RED CROSS PACKAGE. ALWAYS I SAVED... JUST IN CASE!

EVENTUALLY, WHEN I CAME AGAIN TO SOSNO-WIEC, WE SENT THEM FOOD PACKAGES...

... WE WERE FOR A WHILE A LITTLE BETTER OFF... AND THEY WROTE BACK VERY HAPPY HOW IT HELPED SURVIVE THEM...

...THEN THEY WROTE THAT THE GERMANS WERE KEEPING THE PACKAGES. AND THEN THEY STOPPED TO WRITE. FINISHED.

WITH ORBACHS' I STAYED A FEW DAYS RECUPERATING. BUT I WAS RESTLESS. HOW COULD I MANAGE TO SNEAK ACROSS THE BORDER TO MY FAMILY?

TRAINS WERE STILL GOING FROM PROTECTORATE TO REICH. ONLY, ONE NEEDED LEGAL PAPERS. OF COURSE, THIS I DIDN'T HAVE ...

...BUT ANYWAY I GOT ON THE TRAIN IN THE DIRECTION I WANTED.

I APPROACHED TO THE TRAIN MAN, A POLE...

MAY I TALK TO YOU FOR A MOMENT?

SURE, SOLDIER.

I STILL HAD ON MY ARMY UNIFORM, AND I DIDN'T LET KNOW I WAS A JEW.

YOU'RE A POLE LIKE ME, SO I CAN TRUST YOU...THE STINKING NAZIS HAD ME IN A WAR PRISON...I JUST ESCAPED.

THE POLES WERE VERY BITTER ON THE GERMANS, SO IT WAS GOOD TO SPEAK BAD OF THEM.

I'M TRYING TO GET TO SOSNOWIEC - BACK TO MY FAMILY.

DON'T WORRY... WHEN WE GET TO THE BORDER, HIDE IN HERE.

AND SO THE TRAIN MAN HELPED ME COME BACK TO MY SIDE OF POLAND.

...WHAT I THOUGHT I MIGHT NEVER SEE AGAIN.

OY GEVALT! IT'S VLADEK!

I WALKED FIRST OVER TO MY PARENTS' HOUSE...

69

# CHAPTER FOUR

73

75

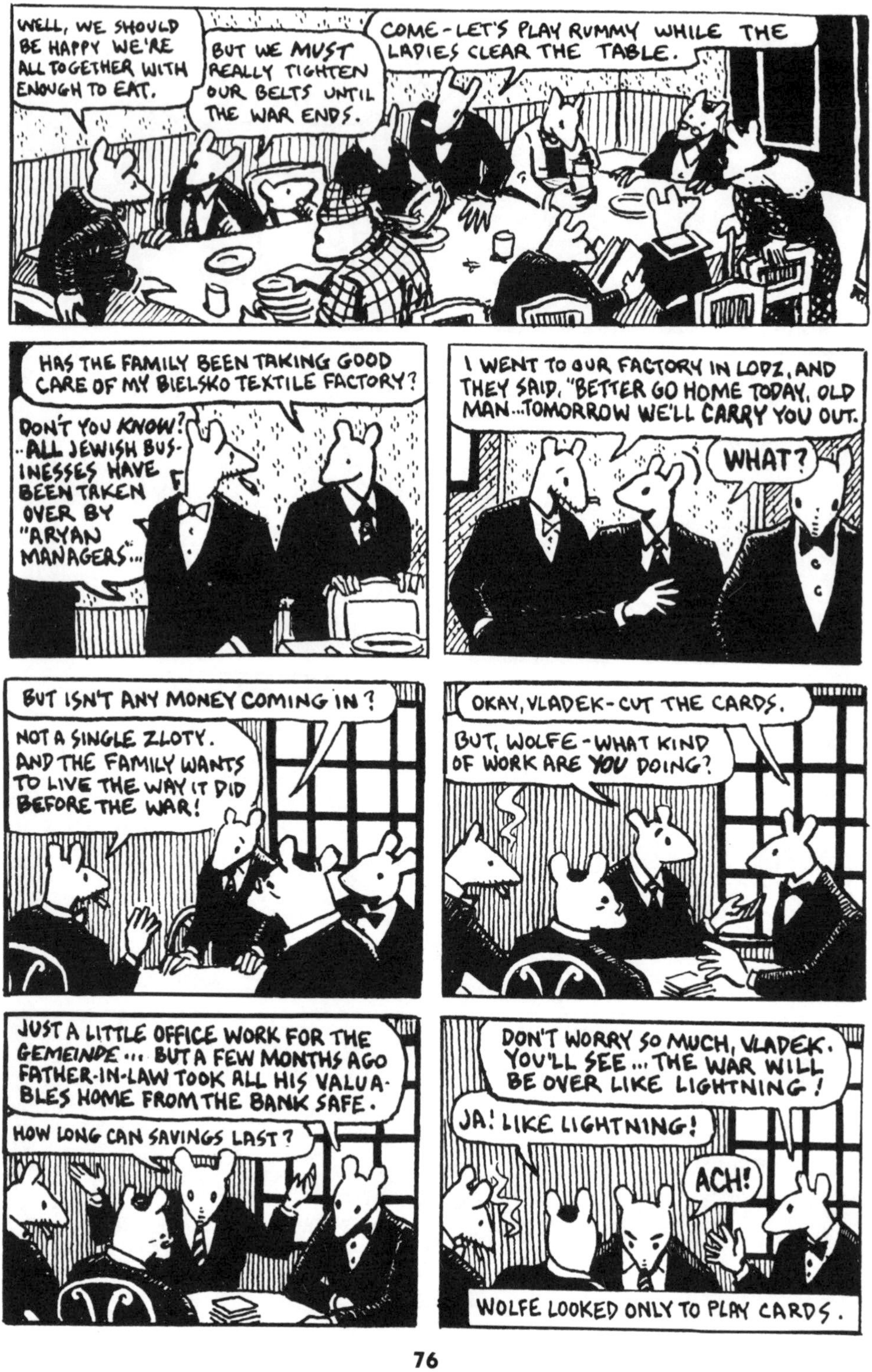
WELL, WE SHOULD BE HAPPY WE'RE ALL TOGETHER WITH ENOUGH TO EAT.
BUT WE MUST REALLY TIGHTEN OUR BELTS UNTIL THE WAR ENDS.
COME - LET'S PLAY RUMMY WHILE THE LADIES CLEAR THE TABLE.
HAS THE FAMILY BEEN TAKING GOOD CARE OF MY BIELSKO TEXTILE FACTORY?
DON'T YOU KNOW? .. ALL JEWISH BUSINESSES HAVE BEEN TAKEN OVER BY "ARYAN MANAGERS"...
I WENT TO OUR FACTORY IN LODZ, AND THEY SAID, "BETTER GO HOME TODAY, OLD MAN...TOMORROW WE'LL CARRY YOU OUT."
WHAT?
BUT ISN'T ANY MONEY COMING IN?
NOT A SINGLE ZLOTY. AND THE FAMILY WANTS TO LIVE THE WAY IT DID BEFORE THE WAR!
OKAY, VLADEK - CUT THE CARDS.
BUT, WOLFE - WHAT KIND OF WORK ARE YOU DOING?
JUST A LITTLE OFFICE WORK FOR THE GEMEINDE ... BUT A FEW MONTHS AGO FATHER-IN-LAW TOOK ALL HIS VALUABLES HOME FROM THE BANK SAFE.
HOW LONG CAN SAVINGS LAST?
DON'T WORRY SO MUCH, VLADEK. YOU'LL SEE ... THE WAR WILL BE OVER LIKE LIGHTNING!
JA! LIKE LIGHTNING!
ACH!
WOLFE LOOKED ONLY TO PLAY CARDS.

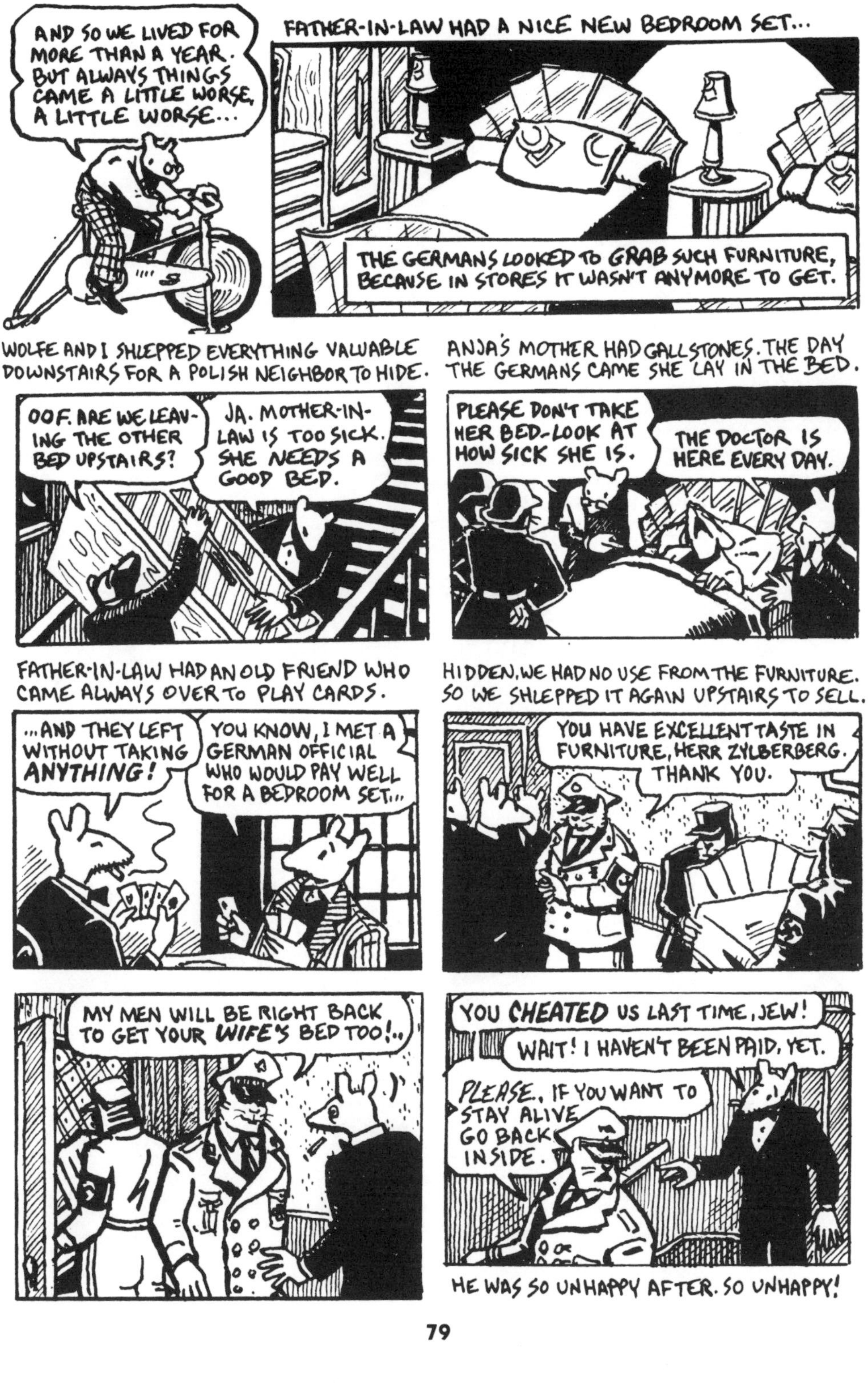
AND SO WE LIVED FOR MORE THAN A YEAR. BUT ALWAYS THINGS CAME A LITTLE WORSE, A LITTLE WORSE...
FATHER-IN-LAW HAD A NICE NEW BEDROOM SET...
THE GERMANS LOOKED TO GRAB SUCH FURNITURE, BECAUSE IN STORES IT WASN'T ANYMORE TO GET.
WOLFE AND I SHLEPPED EVERYTHING VALUABLE DOWNSTAIRS FOR A POLISH NEIGHBOR TO HIDE.
OOF. ARE WE LEAVING THE OTHER BED UPSTAIRS?
JA. MOTHER-IN-LAW IS TOO SICK. SHE NEEDS A GOOD BED.
ANJA'S MOTHER HAD GALLSTONES. THE DAY THE GERMANS CAME SHE LAY IN THE BED.
PLEASE DON'T TAKE HER BED-LOOK AT HOW SICK SHE IS.
THE DOCTOR IS HERE EVERY DAY.
FATHER-IN-LAW HAD AN OLD FRIEND WHO CAME ALWAYS OVER TO PLAY CARDS.
...AND THEY LEFT WITHOUT TAKING ANYTHING!
YOU KNOW, I MET A GERMAN OFFICIAL WHO WOULD PAY WELL FOR A BEDROOM SET...
HIDDEN, WE HAD NO USE FROM THE FURNITURE. SO WE SHLEPPED IT AGAIN UPSTAIRS TO SELL.
YOU HAVE EXCELLENT TASTE IN FURNITURE, HERR ZYLBERBERG.
THANK YOU.
MY MEN WILL BE RIGHT BACK TO GET YOUR WIFE'S BED TOO!..
YOU CHEATED US LAST TIME, JEW!
WAIT! I HAVEN'T BEEN PAID, YET.
PLEASE., IF YOU WANT TO STAY ALIVE GO BACK INSIDE.
HE WAS SO UNHAPPY AFTER. SO UNHAPPY!

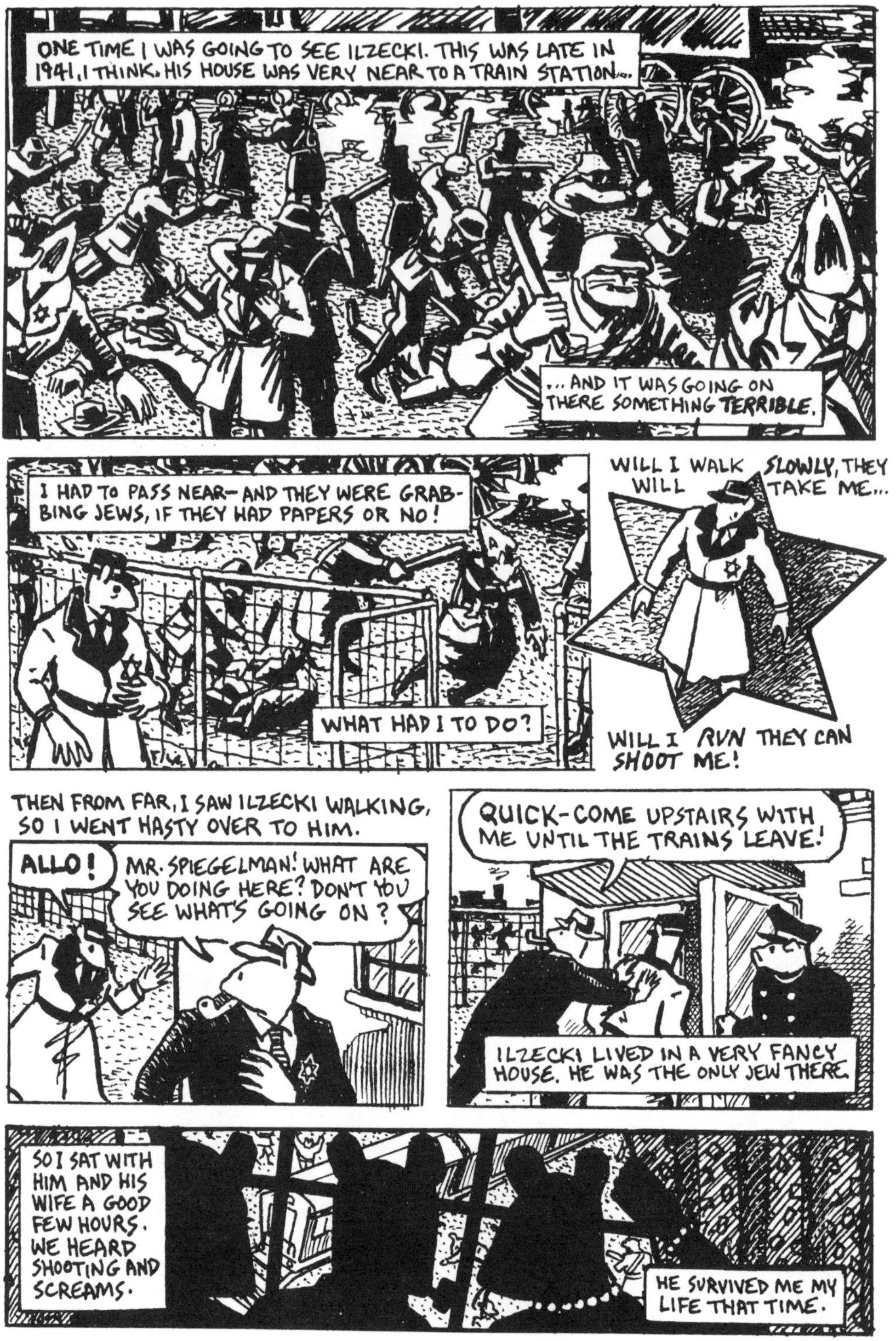
ONE TIME I WAS GOING TO SEE ILZECKI. THIS WAS LATE IN 1941, I THINK. HIS HOUSE WAS VERY NEAR TO A TRAIN STATION...
...AND IT WAS GOING ON THERE SOMETHING TERRIBLE.
I HAD TO PASS NEAR– AND THEY WERE GRABBING JEWS, IF THEY HAD PAPERS OR NO!
WHAT HAD I TO DO?
WILL I WALK SLOWLY, THEY WILL TAKE ME...
WILL I RUN THEY CAN SHOOT ME!
THEN FROM FAR, I SAW ILZECKI WALKING, SO I WENT HASTY OVER TO HIM.
ALLO!
MR. SPIEGELMAN! WHAT ARE YOU DOING HERE? DON'T YOU SEE WHAT'S GOING ON?
QUICK– COME UPSTAIRS WITH ME UNTIL THE TRAINS LEAVE!
ILZECKI LIVED IN A VERY FANCY HOUSE. HE WAS THE ONLY JEW THERE.
SO I SAT WITH HIM AND HIS WIFE A GOOD FEW HOURS. WE HEARD SHOOTING AND SCREAMS.
HE SURVIVED ME MY LIFE THAT TIME.

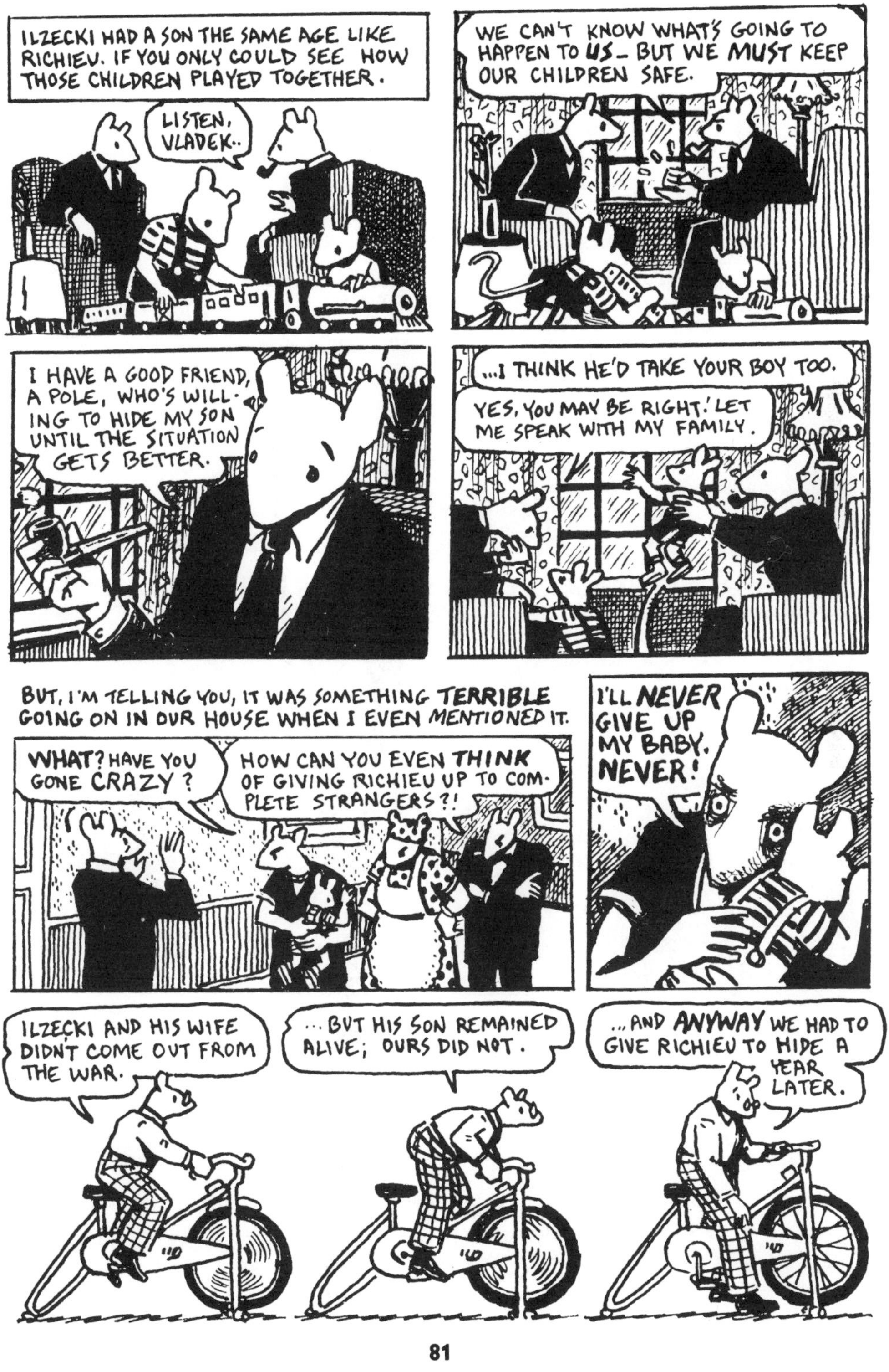
ILZECKI HAD A SON THE SAME AGE LIKE RICHIEU. IF YOU ONLY COULD SEE HOW THOSE CHILDREN PLAYED TOGETHER.
LISTEN, VLADEK..
WE CAN'T KNOW WHAT'S GOING TO HAPPEN TO US — BUT WE MUST KEEP OUR CHILDREN SAFE.
I HAVE A GOOD FRIEND, A POLE, WHO'S WILLING TO HIDE MY SON UNTIL THE SITUATION GETS BETTER.
...I THINK HE'D TAKE YOUR BOY TOO.
YES, YOU MAY BE RIGHT! LET ME SPEAK WITH MY FAMILY.
BUT, I'M TELLING YOU, IT WAS SOMETHING TERRIBLE GOING ON IN OUR HOUSE WHEN I EVEN MENTIONED IT.
WHAT? HAVE YOU GONE CRAZY?
HOW CAN YOU EVEN THINK OF GIVING RICHIEU UP TO COMPLETE STRANGERS?!
I'LL NEVER GIVE UP MY BABY. NEVER!
ILZECKI AND HIS WIFE DIDN'T COME OUT FROM THE WAR.
... BUT HIS SON REMAINED ALIVE; OURS DID NOT.
...AND ANYWAY WE HAD TO GIVE RICHIEU TO HIDE A YEAR LATER.

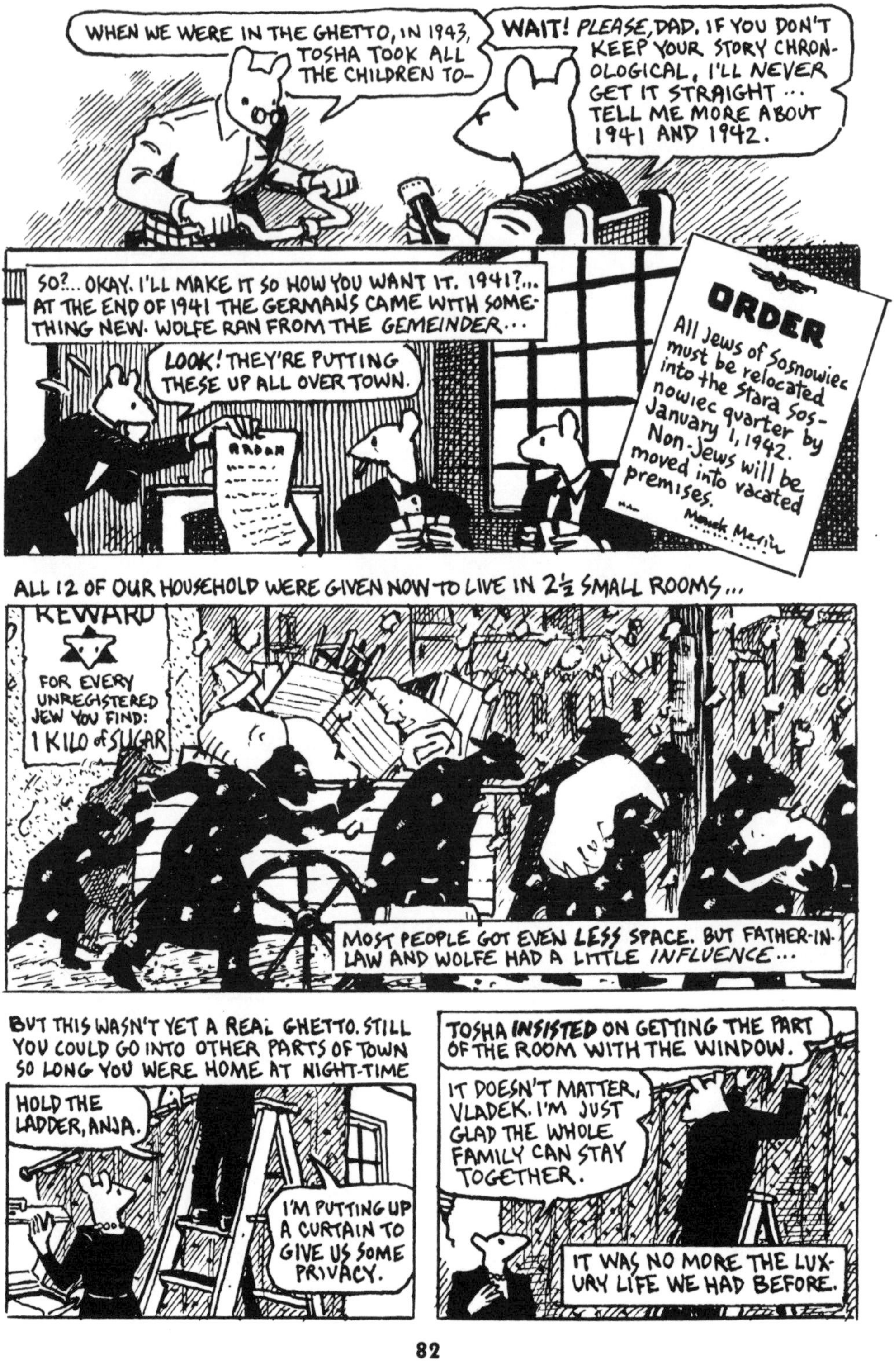

WHEN WE WERE IN THE GHETTO, IN 1943, TOSHA TOOK ALL THE CHILDREN TO-
WAIT! PLEASE, DAD. IF YOU DON'T KEEP YOUR STORY CHRONOLOGICAL, I'LL NEVER GET IT STRAIGHT... TELL ME MORE ABOUT 1941 AND 1942.
SO?... OKAY. I'LL MAKE IT SO HOW YOU WANT IT. 1941?... AT THE END OF 1941 THE GERMANS CAME WITH SOMETHING NEW. WOLFE RAN FROM THE GEMEINDER...
LOOK! THEY'RE PUTTING THESE UP ALL OVER TOWN.
ORDER
All Jews of Sosnowiec must be relocated into the Stara Sosnowiec quarter by January 1, 1942. Non-Jews will be moved into vacated premises.
ALL 12 OF OUR HOUSEHOLD WERE GIVEN NOW TO LIVE IN 2½ SMALL ROOMS...
REWARD
FOR EVERY UNREGISTERED JEW YOU FIND: 1 KILO of SUGAR
MOST PEOPLE GOT EVEN LESS SPACE. BUT FATHER-IN-LAW AND WOLFE HAD A LITTLE INFLUENCE...
BUT THIS WASN'T YET A REAL GHETTO. STILL YOU COULD GO INTO OTHER PARTS OF TOWN SO LONG YOU WERE HOME AT NIGHT-TIME
HOLD THE LADDER, ANJA.
I'M PUTTING UP A CURTAIN TO GIVE US SOME PRIVACY.
TOSHA INSISTED ON GETTING THE PART OF THE ROOM WITH THE WINDOW.
IT DOESN'T MATTER, VLADEK. I'M JUST GLAD THE WHOLE FAMILY CAN STAY TOGETHER.
IT WAS NO MORE THE LUXURY LIFE WE HAD BEFORE.

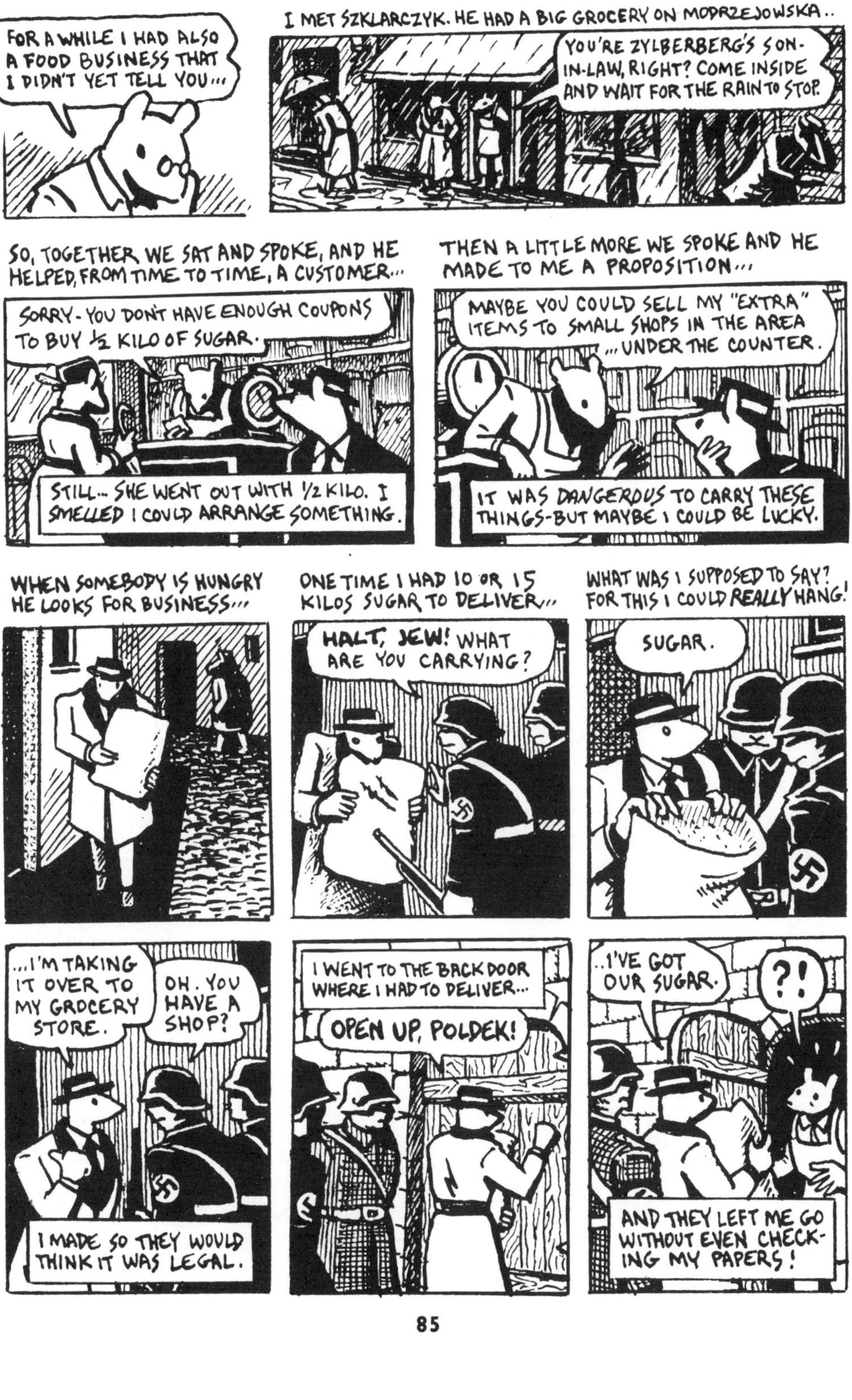

FOR A WHILE I HAD ALSO A FOOD BUSINESS THAT I DIDN'T YET TELL YOU...
I MET SZKLARCZYK. HE HAD A BIG GROCERY ON MODRZEJOWSKA..
YOU'RE ZYLBERBERG'S SON-IN-LAW, RIGHT? COME INSIDE AND WAIT FOR THE RAIN TO STOP.
SO, TOGETHER WE SAT AND SPOKE, AND HE HELPED, FROM TIME TO TIME, A CUSTOMER...
SORRY - YOU DON'T HAVE ENOUGH COUPONS TO BUY ½ KILO OF SUGAR.
STILL... SHE WENT OUT WITH 1/2 KILO. I SMELLED I COULD ARRANGE SOMETHING.
THEN A LITTLE MORE WE SPOKE AND HE MADE TO ME A PROPOSITION...
MAYBE YOU COULD SELL MY "EXTRA" ITEMS TO SMALL SHOPS IN THE AREA ...UNDER THE COUNTER.
IT WAS DANGEROUS TO CARRY THESE THINGS - BUT MAYBE I COULD BE LUCKY.
WHEN SOMEBODY IS HUNGRY HE LOOKS FOR BUSINESS...
ONE TIME I HAD 10 OR 15 KILOS SUGAR TO DELIVER...
HALT, JEW! WHAT ARE YOU CARRYING?
WHAT WAS I SUPPOSED TO SAY? FOR THIS I COULD REALLY HANG!
SUGAR.
...I'M TAKING IT OVER TO MY GROCERY STORE.
OH. YOU HAVE A SHOP?
I MADE SO THEY WOULD THINK IT WAS LEGAL.
I WENT TO THE BACK DOOR WHERE I HAD TO DELIVER...
OPEN UP, POLDEK!
..I'VE GOT OUR SUGAR.
?!
AND THEY LEFT ME GO WITHOUT EVEN CHECKING MY PAPERS!

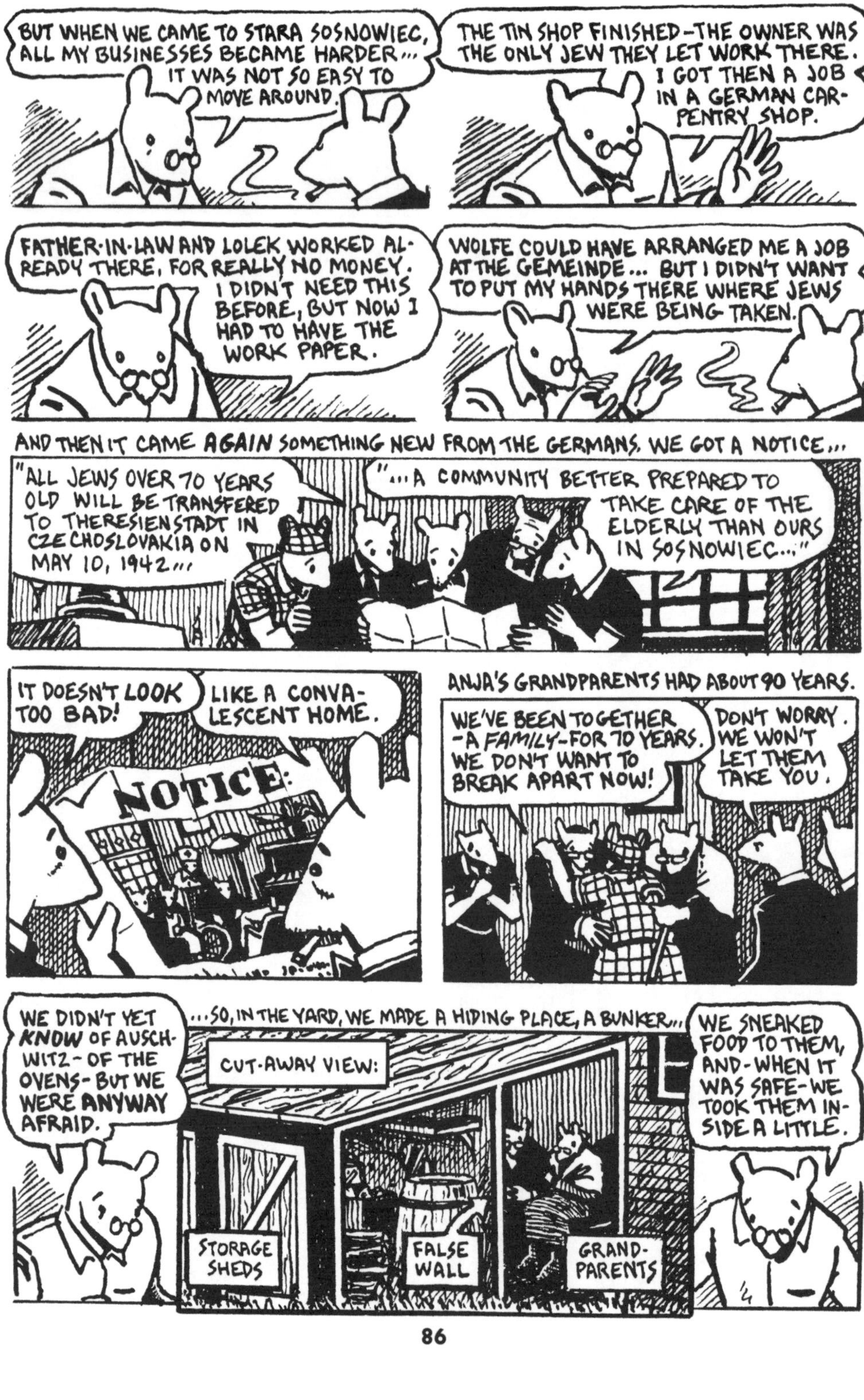

BUT WHEN WE CAME TO STARA SOSNOWIEC, ALL MY BUSINESSES BECAME HARDER... IT WAS NOT SO EASY TO MOVE AROUND.
THE TIN SHOP FINISHED-THE OWNER WAS THE ONLY JEW THEY LET WORK THERE. I GOT THEN A JOB IN A GERMAN CARPENTRY SHOP.
FATHER-IN-LAW AND LOLEK WORKED ALREADY THERE, FOR REALLY NO MONEY. I DIDN'T NEED THIS BEFORE, BUT NOW I HAD TO HAVE THE WORK PAPER.
WOLFE COULD HAVE ARRANGED ME A JOB AT THE GEMEINDE... BUT I DIDN'T WANT TO PUT MY HANDS THERE WHERE JEWS WERE BEING TAKEN.
AND THEN IT CAME AGAIN SOMETHING NEW FROM THE GERMANS. WE GOT A NOTICE...
"ALL JEWS OVER 70 YEARS OLD WILL BE TRANSFERED TO THERESIENSTADT IN CZECHOSLOVAKIA ON MAY 10, 1942...
"...A COMMUNITY BETTER PREPARED TO TAKE CARE OF THE ELDERLY THAN OURS IN SOSNOWIEC..."
IT DOESN'T LOOK TOO BAD!
LIKE A CONVALESCENT HOME.
NOTICE:
ANJA'S GRANDPARENTS HAD ABOUT 90 YEARS.
WE'VE BEEN TOGETHER -A FAMILY- FOR 70 YEARS. WE DON'T WANT TO BREAK APART NOW!
DON'T WORRY. WE WON'T LET THEM TAKE YOU.
WE DIDN'T YET KNOW OF AUSCHWITZ- OF THE OVENS- BUT WE WERE ANYWAY AFRAID.
...SO, IN THE YARD, WE MADE A HIDING PLACE, A BUNKER...
CUT-AWAY VIEW:
STORAGE SHEDS
FALSE WALL
GRAND-PARENTS
WE SNEAKED FOOD TO THEM, AND-WHEN IT WAS SAFE-WE TOOK THEM INSIDE A LITTLE.

SEVERAL TIMES CAME THE JEWISH POLICE TO OUR HOUSE...

OUR RECORDS SHOW THAT MR. AND MRS. KARMIO LIVE HERE. THEY HAVEN'T REGISTERED FOR TRANSFER.

YES - MY WIFE'S PARENTS - THEY LEFT WITHOUT A WORD A MONTH AGO.

JEWISH POLICE?

YES - WITH BIG STICKS.

SOME JEWS THOUGHT IN THIS WAY: IF THEY GAVE TO THE GERMANS A FEW JEWS, THEY COULD SAVE THE REST.

AND AT LEAST THEY COULD SAVE THEMSELVES.

AND A MONTH AFTER, THEY AGAIN CAME TO FATHER-IN-LAW.

MR. ZYLBERBERG, YOU AND YOUR WIFE MUST COME WITH US.

IF THE KARMIOS DON'T TURN UP IN 3 DAYS YOU TWO WILL BE SENT IN THEIR PLACE!

HE HAD STILL A LITTLE "PROTECTION" FROM THE GEMEIN-DE, SO THEY TOOK ONLY HIM AWAY - NOT HIS WIFE.

HE SAT A FEW DAYS THERE, THEN HE SENT TO US A NOTE

HE WROTE THAT WE HAD TO GIVE OVER THE GRANDPARENTS. EVEN IF THEY TOOK ONLY HIM AWAY NOW, NEXT THEY WOULD GRAB HIS WIFE, AND THEN THE REST OF THE FAMILY.

SO, WHAT HAPPENED?

WHAT HAPPENED? WE HAD TO DELIVER THEM!

THEY THOUGHT IT WAS TO THERESIENSTADT THEY WERE GOING.

LET US KNOW IF YOU NEED ANYTHING!

BUT THEY WENT RIGHT AWAY TO AUSCHWITZ, TO THE GAS.

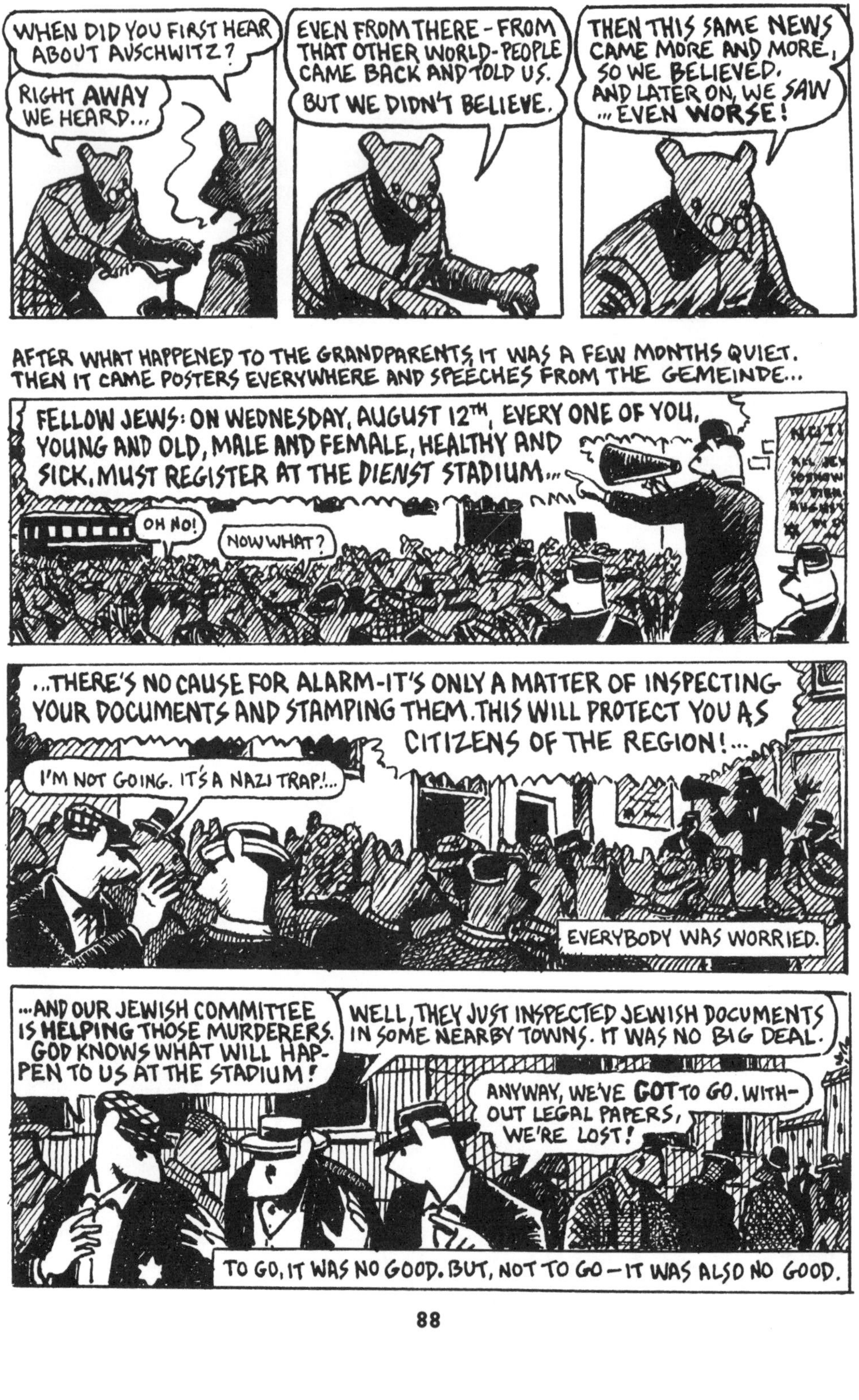
WHEN DID YOU FIRST HEAR ABOUT AUSCHWITZ?
RIGHT AWAY WE HEARD...
EVEN FROM THERE - FROM THAT OTHER WORLD - PEOPLE CAME BACK AND TOLD US.
BUT WE DIDN'T BELIEVE.
THEN THIS SAME NEWS CAME MORE AND MORE, SO WE BELIEVED. AND LATER ON, WE SAW ...EVEN WORSE!
AFTER WHAT HAPPENED TO THE GRANDPARENTS, IT WAS A FEW MONTHS QUIET. THEN IT CAME POSTERS EVERYWHERE AND SPEECHES FROM THE GEMEINDE...
FELLOW JEWS: ON WEDNESDAY, AUGUST 12TH, EVERY ONE OF YOU, YOUNG AND OLD, MALE AND FEMALE, HEALTHY AND SICK, MUST REGISTER AT THE DIENST STADIUM...
OH NO!
NOW WHAT?
...THERE'S NO CAUSE FOR ALARM - IT'S ONLY A MATTER OF INSPECTING YOUR DOCUMENTS AND STAMPING THEM. THIS WILL PROTECT YOU AS CITIZENS OF THE REGION!...
I'M NOT GOING. IT'S A NAZI TRAP!...
EVERYBODY WAS WORRIED.
...AND OUR JEWISH COMMITTEE IS HELPING THOSE MURDERERS. GOD KNOWS WHAT WILL HAPPEN TO US AT THE STADIUM!
WELL, THEY JUST INSPECTED JEWISH DOCUMENTS IN SOME NEARBY TOWNS. IT WAS NO BIG DEAL.
ANYWAY, WE'VE GOT TO GO. WITHOUT LEGAL PAPERS, WE'RE LOST!
TO GO, IT WAS NO GOOD. BUT, NOT TO GO - IT WAS ALSO NO GOOD.

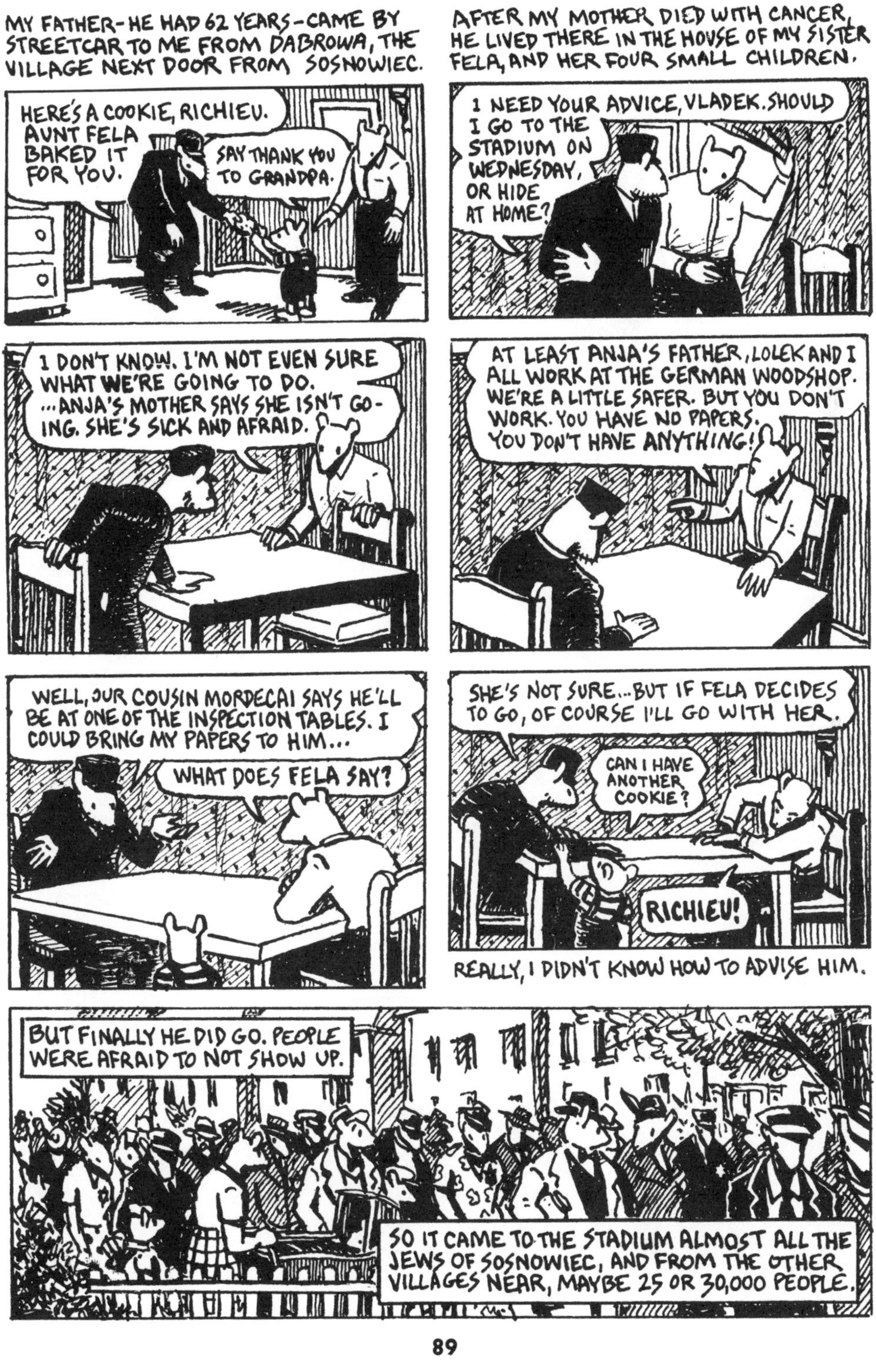
MY FATHER- HE HAD 62 YEARS - CAME BY STREETCAR TO ME FROM DABROWA, THE VILLAGE NEXT DOOR FROM SOSNOWIEC.
HERE'S A COOKIE, RICHIEU. AUNT FELA BAKED IT FOR YOU.
SAY THANK YOU TO GRANDPA.
AFTER MY MOTHER DIED WITH CANCER, HE LIVED THERE IN THE HOUSE OF MY SISTER FELA, AND HER FOUR SMALL CHILDREN.
I NEED YOUR ADVICE, VLADEK. SHOULD I GO TO THE STADIUM ON WEDNESDAY, OR HIDE AT HOME?
I DON'T KNOW. I'M NOT EVEN SURE WHAT WE'RE GOING TO DO. ...ANJA'S MOTHER SAYS SHE ISN'T GOING. SHE'S SICK AND AFRAID.
AT LEAST ANJA'S FATHER, LOLEK AND I ALL WORK AT THE GERMAN WOODSHOP. WE'RE A LITTLE SAFER. BUT YOU DON'T WORK. YOU HAVE NO PAPERS. YOU DON'T HAVE ANYTHING!
WELL, OUR COUSIN MORDECAI SAYS HE'LL BE AT ONE OF THE INSPECTION TABLES. I COULD BRING MY PAPERS TO HIM...
WHAT DOES FELA SAY?
SHE'S NOT SURE...BUT IF FELA DECIDES TO GO, OF COURSE I'LL GO WITH HER.
CAN I HAVE ANOTHER COOKIE?
RICHIEU!
REALLY, I DIDN'T KNOW HOW TO ADVISE HIM.
BUT FINALLY HE DID GO. PEOPLE WERE AFRAID TO NOT SHOW UP.
SO IT CAME TO THE STADIUM ALMOST ALL THE JEWS OF SOSNOWIEC, AND FROM THE OTHER VILLAGES NEAR, MAYBE 25 OR 30,000 PEOPLE.

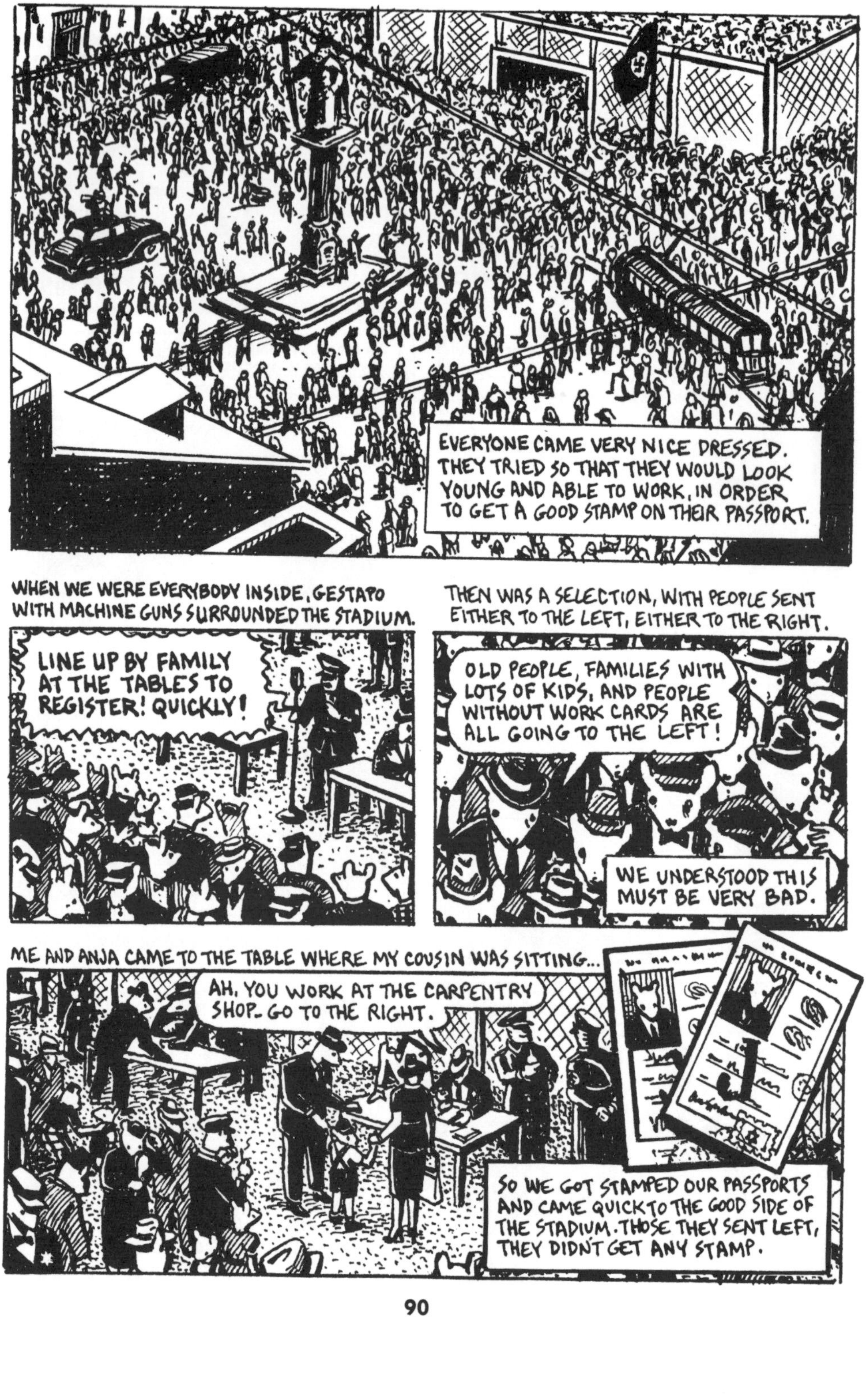
EVERYONE CAME VERY NICE DRESSED. THEY TRIED SO THAT THEY WOULD LOOK YOUNG AND ABLE TO WORK, IN ORDER TO GET A GOOD STAMP ON THEIR PASSPORT.
WHEN WE WERE EVERYBODY INSIDE, GESTAPO WITH MACHINE GUNS SURROUNDED THE STADIUM.
LINE UP BY FAMILY AT THE TABLES TO REGISTER! QUICKLY!
THEN WAS A SELECTION, WITH PEOPLE SENT EITHER TO THE LEFT, EITHER TO THE RIGHT.
OLD PEOPLE, FAMILIES WITH LOTS OF KIDS, AND PEOPLE WITHOUT WORK CARDS ARE ALL GOING TO THE LEFT!
WE UNDERSTOOD THIS MUST BE VERY BAD.
ME AND ANJA CAME TO THE TABLE WHERE MY COUSIN WAS SITTING...
AH, YOU WORK AT THE CARPENTRY SHOP. GO TO THE RIGHT.
SO WE GOT STAMPED OUR PASSPORTS AND CAME QUICK TO THE GOOD SIDE OF THE STADIUM. THOSE THEY SENT LEFT, THEY DIDN'T GET ANY STAMP.

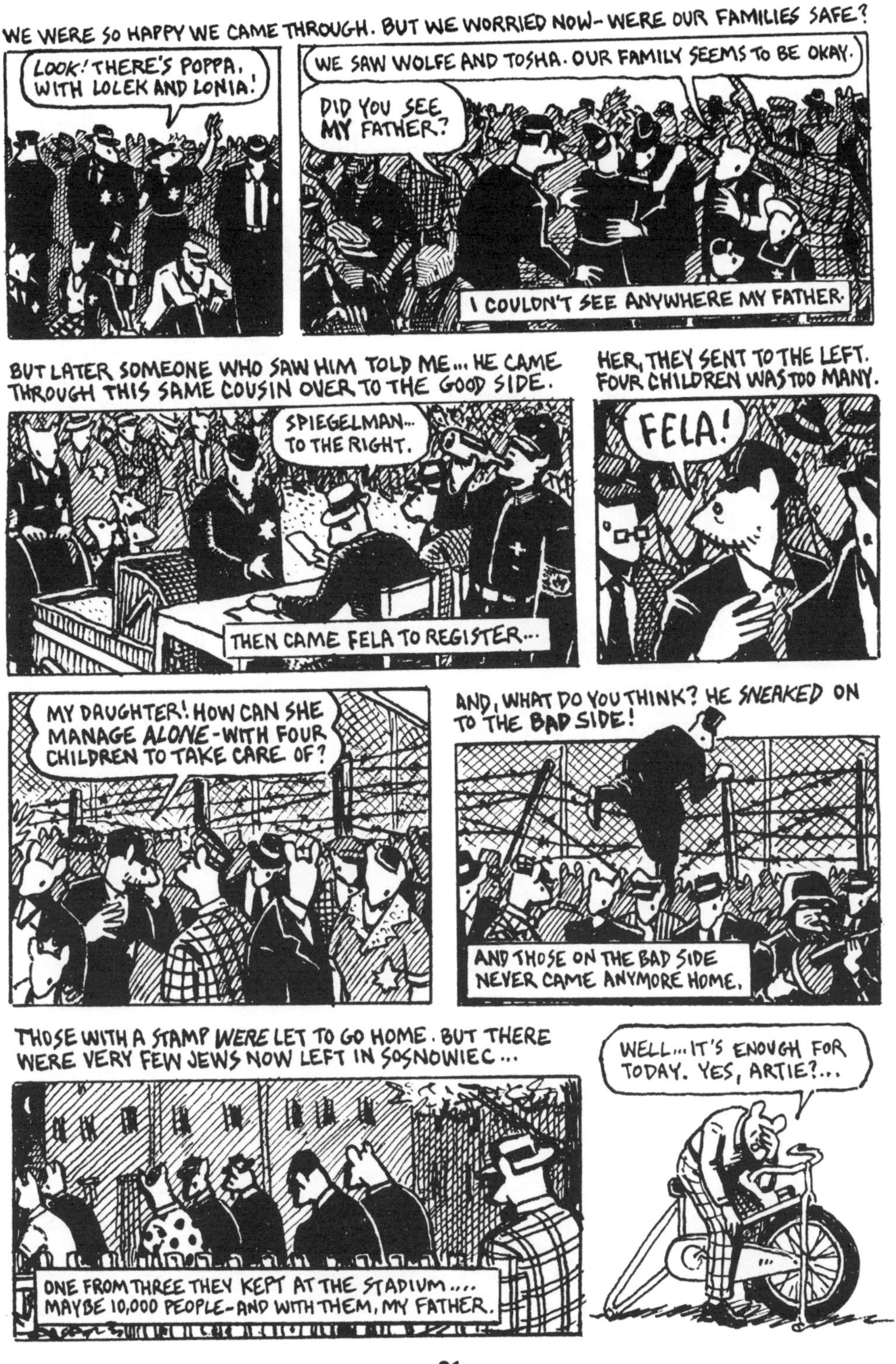
WE WERE SO HAPPY WE CAME THROUGH. BUT WE WORRIED NOW- WERE OUR FAMILIES SAFE?
LOOK! THERE'S POPPA, WITH LOLEK AND LONIA!
WE SAW WOLFE AND TOSHA. OUR FAMILY SEEMS TO BE OKAY.
DID YOU SEE MY FATHER?
I COULDN'T SEE ANYWHERE MY FATHER.
BUT LATER SOMEONE WHO SAW HIM TOLD ME... HE CAME THROUGH THIS SAME COUSIN OVER TO THE GOOD SIDE.
SPIEGELMAN... TO THE RIGHT.
THEN CAME FELA TO REGISTER...
HER, THEY SENT TO THE LEFT. FOUR CHILDREN WAS TOO MANY.
FELA!
MY DAUGHTER! HOW CAN SHE MANAGE ALONE-WITH FOUR CHILDREN TO TAKE CARE OF?
AND, WHAT DO YOU THINK? HE SNEAKED ON TO THE BAD SIDE!
AND THOSE ON THE BAD SIDE NEVER CAME ANYMORE HOME.
THOSE WITH A STAMP WERE LET TO GO HOME. BUT THERE WERE VERY FEW JEWS NOW LEFT IN SOSNOWIEC...
ONE FROM THREE THEY KEPT AT THE STADIUM.... MAYBE 10,000 PEOPLE- AND WITH THEM, MY FATHER.
WELL... IT'S ENOUGH FOR TODAY. YES, ARTIE?...

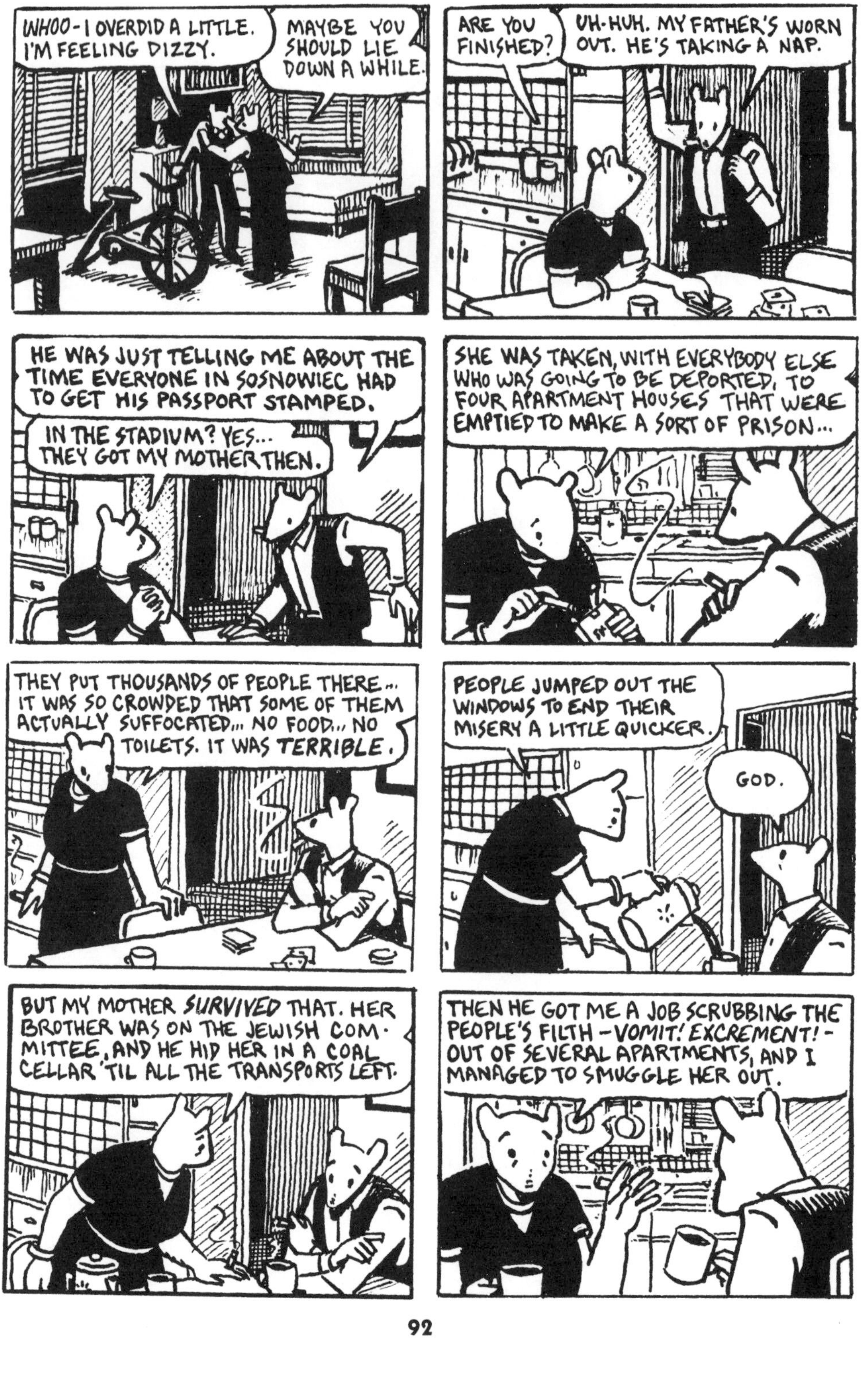
WHOO-I OVERDID A LITTLE. I'M FEELING DIZZY.
MAYBE YOU SHOULD LIE DOWN A WHILE.
ARE YOU FINISHED?
UH-HUH. MY FATHER'S WORN OUT. HE'S TAKING A NAP.
HE WAS JUST TELLING ME ABOUT THE TIME EVERYONE IN SOSNOWIEC HAD TO GET HIS PASSPORT STAMPED.
IN THE STADIUM? YES... THEY GOT MY MOTHER THEN.
SHE WAS TAKEN, WITH EVERYBODY ELSE WHO WAS GOING TO BE DEPORTED, TO FOUR APARTMENT HOUSES THAT WERE EMPTIED TO MAKE A SORT OF PRISON...
THEY PUT THOUSANDS OF PEOPLE THERE... IT WAS SO CROWDED THAT SOME OF THEM ACTUALLY SUFFOCATED... NO FOOD... NO TOILETS. IT WAS TERRIBLE.
PEOPLE JUMPED OUT THE WINDOWS TO END THEIR MISERY A LITTLE QUICKER.
GOD.
BUT MY MOTHER SURVIVED THAT. HER BROTHER WAS ON THE JEWISH COM-MITTEE, AND HE HID HER IN A COAL CELLAR 'TIL ALL THE TRANSPORTS LEFT.
THEN HE GOT ME A JOB SCRUBBING THE PEOPLE'S FILTH - VOMIT! EXCREMENT! - OUT OF SEVERAL APARTMENTS, AND I MANAGED TO SMUGGLE HER OUT.

93

# CHAPTER FIVE

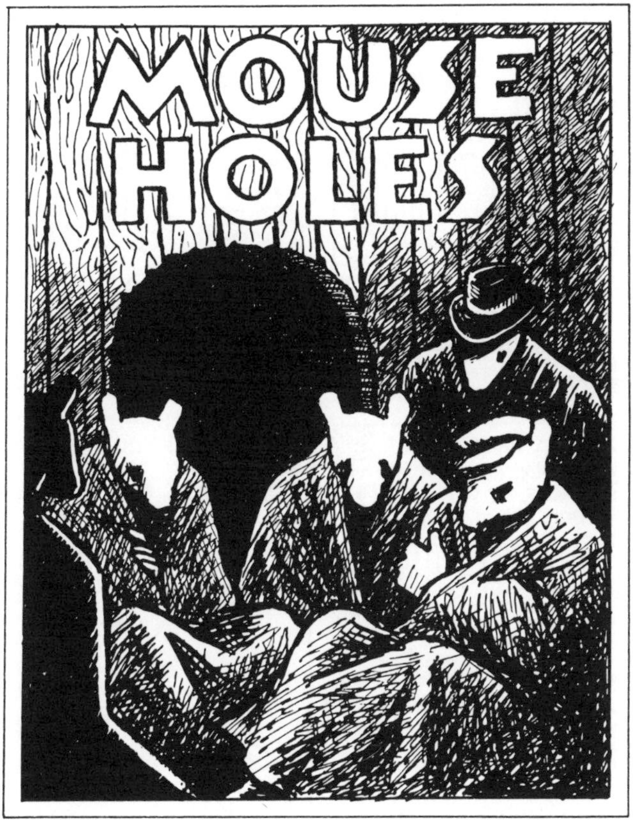
MOUSE
HOLES

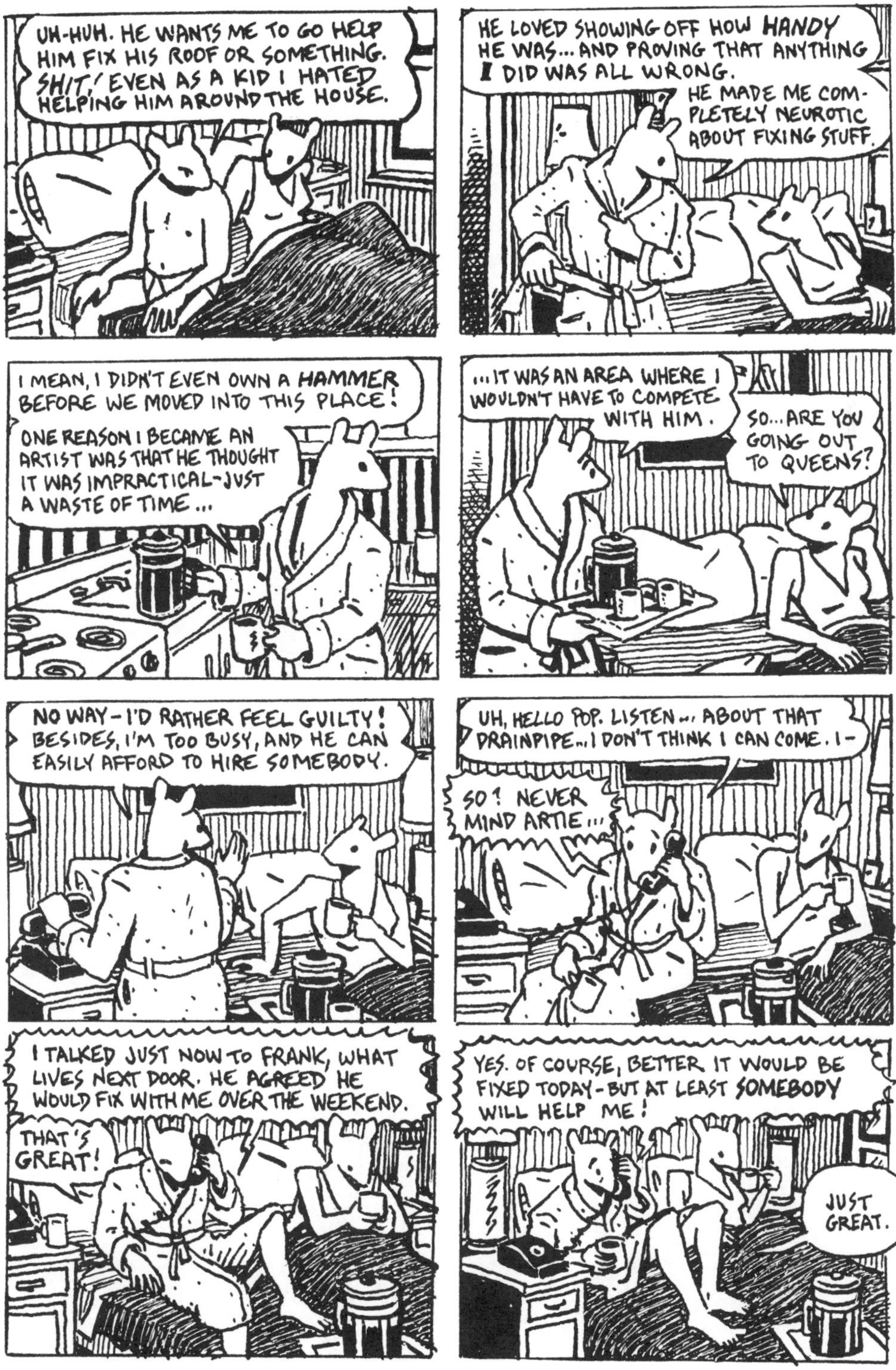
UH-HUH. HE WANTS ME TO GO HELP HIM FIX HIS ROOF OR SOMETHING. SHIT! EVEN AS A KID I HATED HELPING HIM AROUND THE HOUSE.
HE LOVED SHOWING OFF HOW HANDY HE WAS... AND PROVING THAT ANYTHING I DID WAS ALL WRONG.
HE MADE ME COMPLETELY NEUROTIC ABOUT FIXING STUFF.
I MEAN, I DIDN'T EVEN OWN A HAMMER BEFORE WE MOVED INTO THIS PLACE!
ONE REASON I BECAME AN ARTIST WAS THAT HE THOUGHT IT WAS IMPRACTICAL- JUST A WASTE OF TIME ...
...IT WAS AN AREA WHERE I WOULDN'T HAVE TO COMPETE WITH HIM.
SO... ARE YOU GOING OUT TO QUEENS?
NO WAY- I'D RATHER FEEL GUILTY! BESIDES, I'M TOO BUSY, AND HE CAN EASILY AFFORD TO HIRE SOMEBODY.
UH, HELLO POP. LISTEN... ABOUT THAT DRAINPIPE... I DON'T THINK I CAN COME. I-
SO? NEVER MIND ARTIE...
I TALKED JUST NOW TO FRANK, WHAT LIVES NEXT DOOR. HE AGREED HE WOULD FIX WITH ME OVER THE WEEKEND.
THAT'S GREAT!
YES. OF COURSE, BETTER IT WOULD BE FIXED TODAY- BUT AT LEAST SOMEBODY WILL HELP ME!
JUST GREAT.

About a week later, early afternoon...

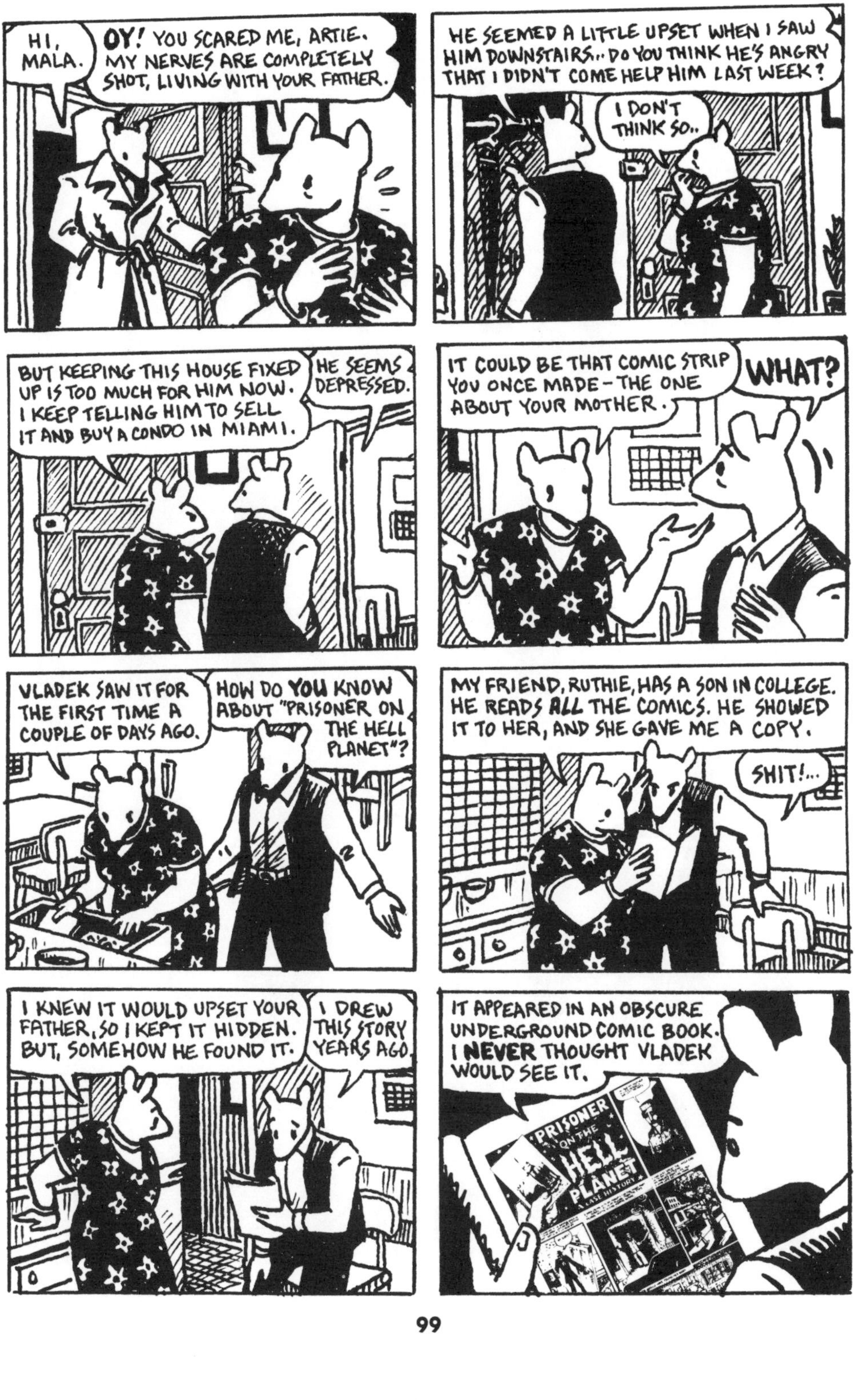
HI, MALA.
OY! YOU SCARED ME, ARTIE. MY NERVES ARE COMPLETELY SHOT, LIVING WITH YOUR FATHER.
HE SEEMED A LITTLE UPSET WHEN I SAW HIM DOWNSTAIRS.. DO YOU THINK HE'S ANGRY THAT I DIDN'T COME HELP HIM LAST WEEK?
I DON'T THINK SO..
BUT KEEPING THIS HOUSE FIXED UP IS TOO MUCH FOR HIM NOW. I KEEP TELLING HIM TO SELL IT AND BUY A CONDO IN MIAMI.
HE SEEMS DEPRESSED.
IT COULD BE THAT COMIC STRIP YOU ONCE MADE - THE ONE ABOUT YOUR MOTHER.
WHAT?
VLADEK SAW IT FOR THE FIRST TIME A COUPLE OF DAYS AGO.
HOW DO YOU KNOW ABOUT "PRISONER ON THE HELL PLANET"?
MY FRIEND, RUTHIE, HAS A SON IN COLLEGE. HE READS ALL THE COMICS. HE SHOWED IT TO HER, AND SHE GAVE ME A COPY.
SHIT!...
I KNEW IT WOULD UPSET YOUR FATHER, SO I KEPT IT HIDDEN. BUT, SOMEHOW HE FOUND IT.
I DREW THIS STORY YEARS AGO.
IT APPEARED IN AN OBSCURE UNDERGROUND COMIC BOOK. I NEVER THOUGHT VLADEK WOULD SEE IT.
PRISONER ON THE HELL PLANET
A CASE HISTORY

© art spiegelman, 1972

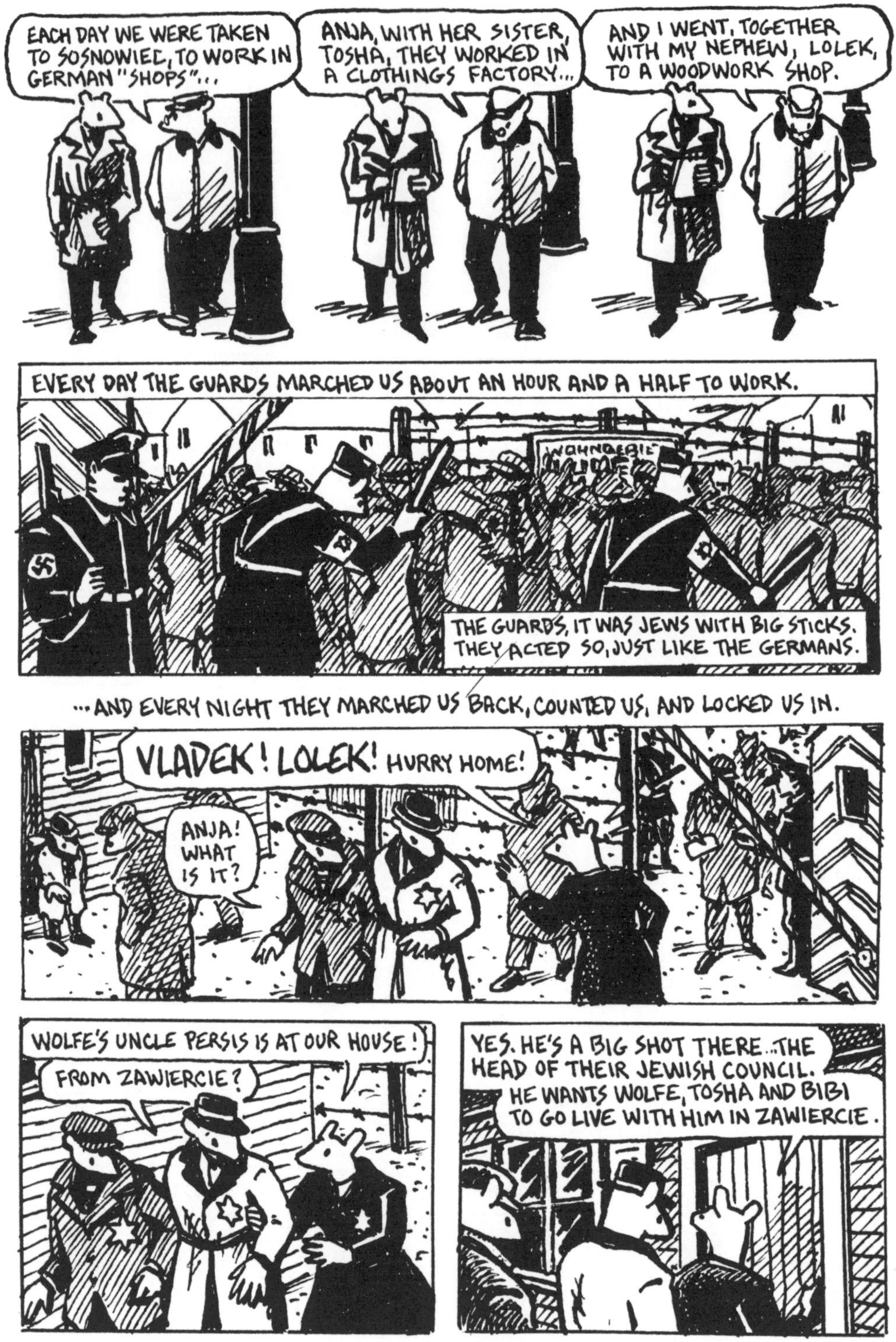
EACH DAY WE WERE TAKEN TO SOSNOWIEC, TO WORK IN GERMAN "SHOPS"...
ANJA, WITH HER SISTER, TOSHA, THEY WORKED IN A CLOTHINGS FACTORY...
AND I WENT, TOGETHER WITH MY NEPHEW, LOLEK, TO A WOODWORK SHOP.
EVERY DAY THE GUARDS MARCHED US ABOUT AN HOUR AND A HALF TO WORK.
THE GUARDS, IT WAS JEWS WITH BIG STICKS. THEY ACTED SO, JUST LIKE THE GERMANS.
...AND EVERY NIGHT THEY MARCHED US BACK, COUNTED US, AND LOCKED US IN.
VLADEK! LOLEK! HURRY HOME!
ANJA! WHAT IS IT?
WOLFE'S UNCLE PERSIS IS AT OUR HOUSE!
FROM ZAWIERCIE?
YES. HE'S A BIG SHOT THERE...THE HEAD OF THEIR JEWISH COUNCIL.
HE WANTS WOLFE, TOSHA AND BIBI TO GO LIVE WITH HIM IN ZAWIERCIE.

...YOU'VE ALL HEARD THE STORIES ABOUT AUSCHWITZ. HORRIBLE UNBELIEVABLE STORIES.

THEY **CAN'T** BE TRUE!

ONE THING IS CERTAIN— AS BAD AS THINGS ARE IN THE GHETTO, BEING DE-PORTED IS EVEN WORSE.

**PLEASE!** IT'S BAD LUCK TO EVEN **SPEAK** OF IT!

LOOK. YOU DON'T HAVE MUCH INFLUENCE HERE. IN ZAWIERCIE I HAVE SOME INFLUENCE WITH THE GERMANS... I CAN BRIBE THEM.

MY 90-YEAR-OLD FATHER STILL LIVES WITH ME...WHENEVER THERE'S A ROUND-UP, AN S.S. MAN GUARDS HIM TO KEEP HIM SAFE!

NINETY! THIS WAS 1943! IT WASN'T **LEFT** ANY OTHER JEWS WHAT HAD NINETY YEARS!

PERSIS WAS REALLY A FINE MAN—NOT SO LIKE MONIEK MERIN, THE HEAD OF **OUR** GHETTO, WHO LOOKED ONLY OUT FOR HIMSELF. ...PERSIS TRIED REALLY TO HELP HIS JEWS.

I CAN MANAGE PAPERS TO TAKE WOLFE, TOSHA AND BIBI—AND MAYBE LITTLE LONIA AND RICHIEU IF YOU'LL LET ME.

YES. THEY'D BE BETTER OFF.

YOU SEE? I WANTED TO SEND RICHIEU SOMEPLACE SAFE A **YEAR** AGO— WITH ILZECKI'S CHILD!

THINGS ARE EVEN WORSE NOW, VLADEK. WE HAVE NO CHOICE!

**NO!** WE MUST ALL STAY TOGETHER! WE'VE MADE IT THIS FAR. GOD WILL STILL HELP US!

MATKA! BE **REALISTIC!**

ANJA'S MOTHER DIDN'T LIKE TO LOOK AT THE FACTS. BUT FINALLY EVEN SHE AGREED,

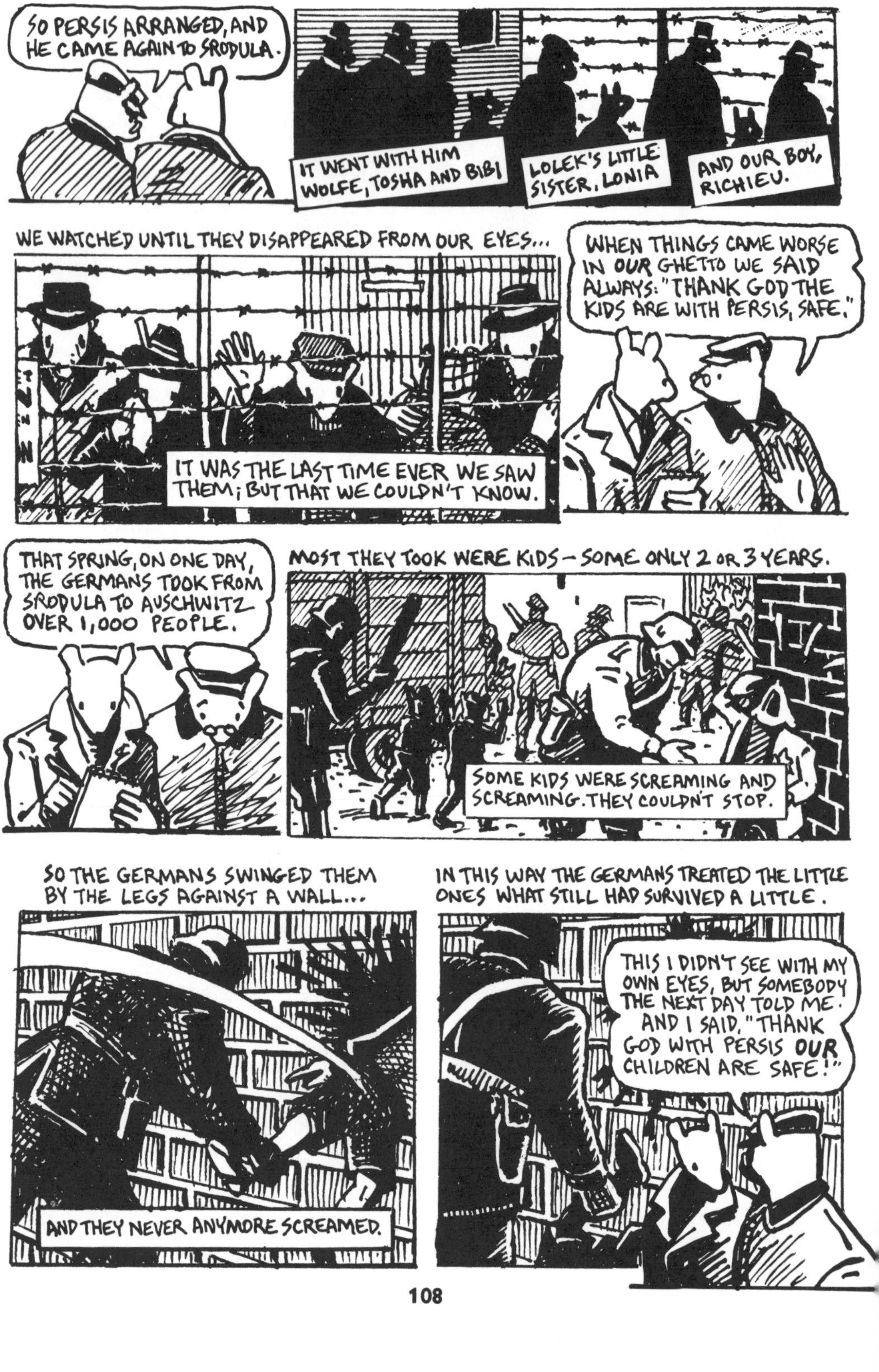
SO PERSIS ARRANGED, AND HE CAME AGAIN TO SRODULA.
IT WENT WITH HIM WOLFE, TOSHA AND BIBI
LOLEK'S LITTLE SISTER, LONIA
AND OUR BOY, RICHIEU.
WE WATCHED UNTIL THEY DISAPPEARED FROM OUR EYES...
IT WAS THE LAST TIME EVER WE SAW THEM; BUT THAT WE COULDN'T KNOW.
WHEN THINGS CAME WORSE IN OUR GHETTO WE SAID ALWAYS: "THANK GOD THE KIDS ARE WITH PERSIS, SAFE."
THAT SPRING, ON ONE DAY, THE GERMANS TOOK FROM SRODULA TO AUSCHWITZ OVER 1,000 PEOPLE.
MOST THEY TOOK WERE KIDS – SOME ONLY 2 OR 3 YEARS.
SOME KIDS WERE SCREAMING AND SCREAMING. THEY COULDN'T STOP.
SO THE GERMANS SWINGED THEM BY THE LEGS AGAINST A WALL...
AND THEY NEVER ANYMORE SCREAMED.
IN THIS WAY THE GERMANS TREATED THE LITTLE ONES WHAT STILL HAD SURVIVED A LITTLE.
THIS I DIDN'T SEE WITH MY OWN EYES, BUT SOMEBODY THE NEXT DAY TOLD ME. AND I SAID, "THANK GOD WITH PERSIS OUR CHILDREN ARE SAFE!"

109

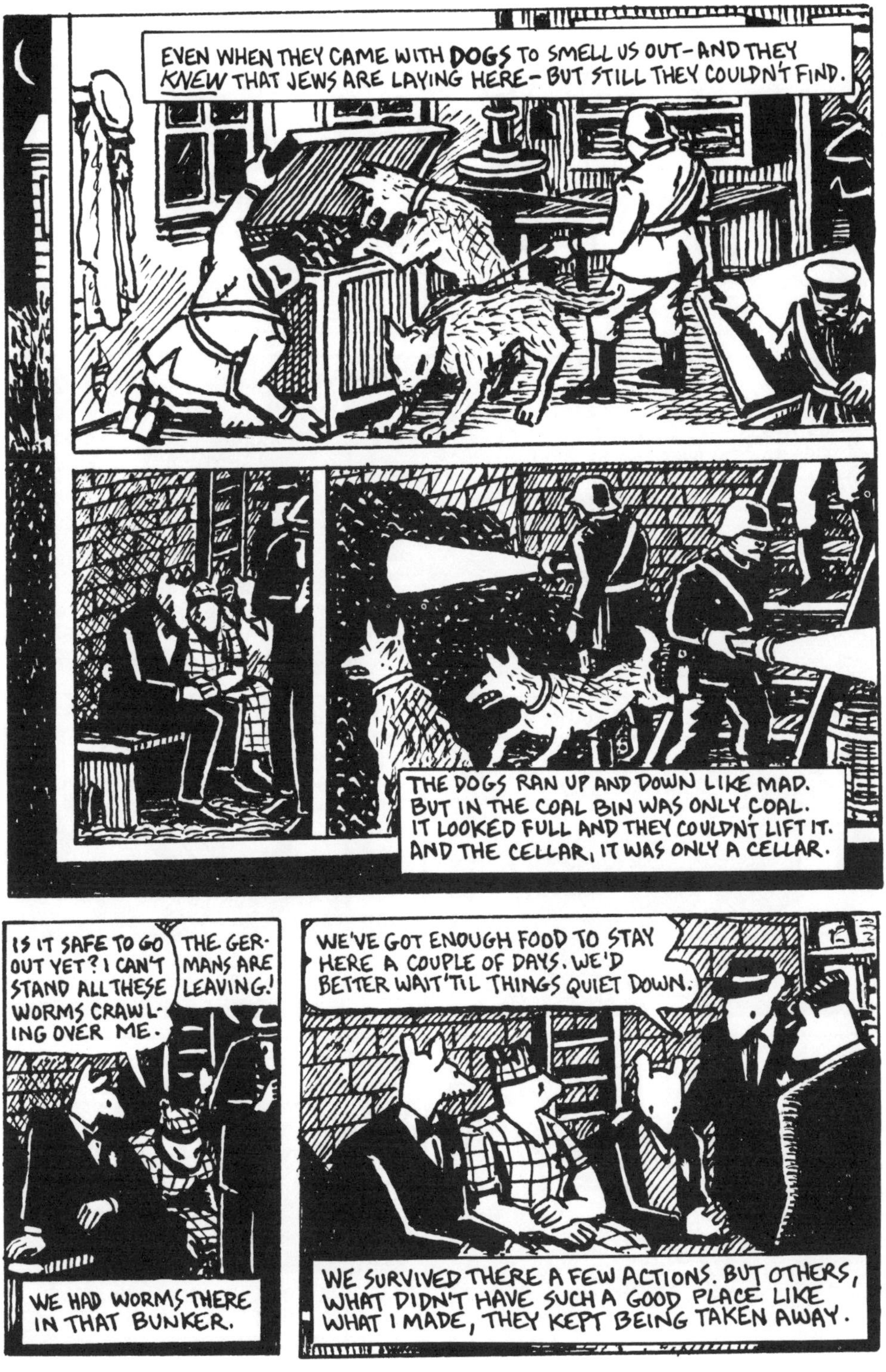

EVEN WHEN THEY CAME WITH DOGS TO SMELL US OUT-AND THEY KNEW THAT JEWS ARE LAYING HERE-BUT STILL THEY COULDN'T FIND.
THE DOGS RAN UP AND DOWN LIKE MAD. BUT IN THE COAL BIN WAS ONLY COAL. IT LOOKED FULL AND THEY COULDN'T LIFT IT. AND THE CELLAR, IT WAS ONLY A CELLAR.
IS IT SAFE TO GO OUT YET? I CAN'T STAND ALL THESE WORMS CRAWLING OVER ME.
THE GERMANS ARE LEAVING!
WE HAD WORMS THERE IN THAT BUNKER.
WE'VE GOT ENOUGH FOOD TO STAY HERE A COUPLE OF DAYS. WE'D BETTER WAIT 'TIL THINGS QUIET DOWN.
WE SURVIVED THERE A FEW ACTIONS. BUT OTHERS, WHAT DIDN'T HAVE SUCH A GOOD PLACE LIKE WHAT I MADE, THEY KEPT BEING TAKEN AWAY.

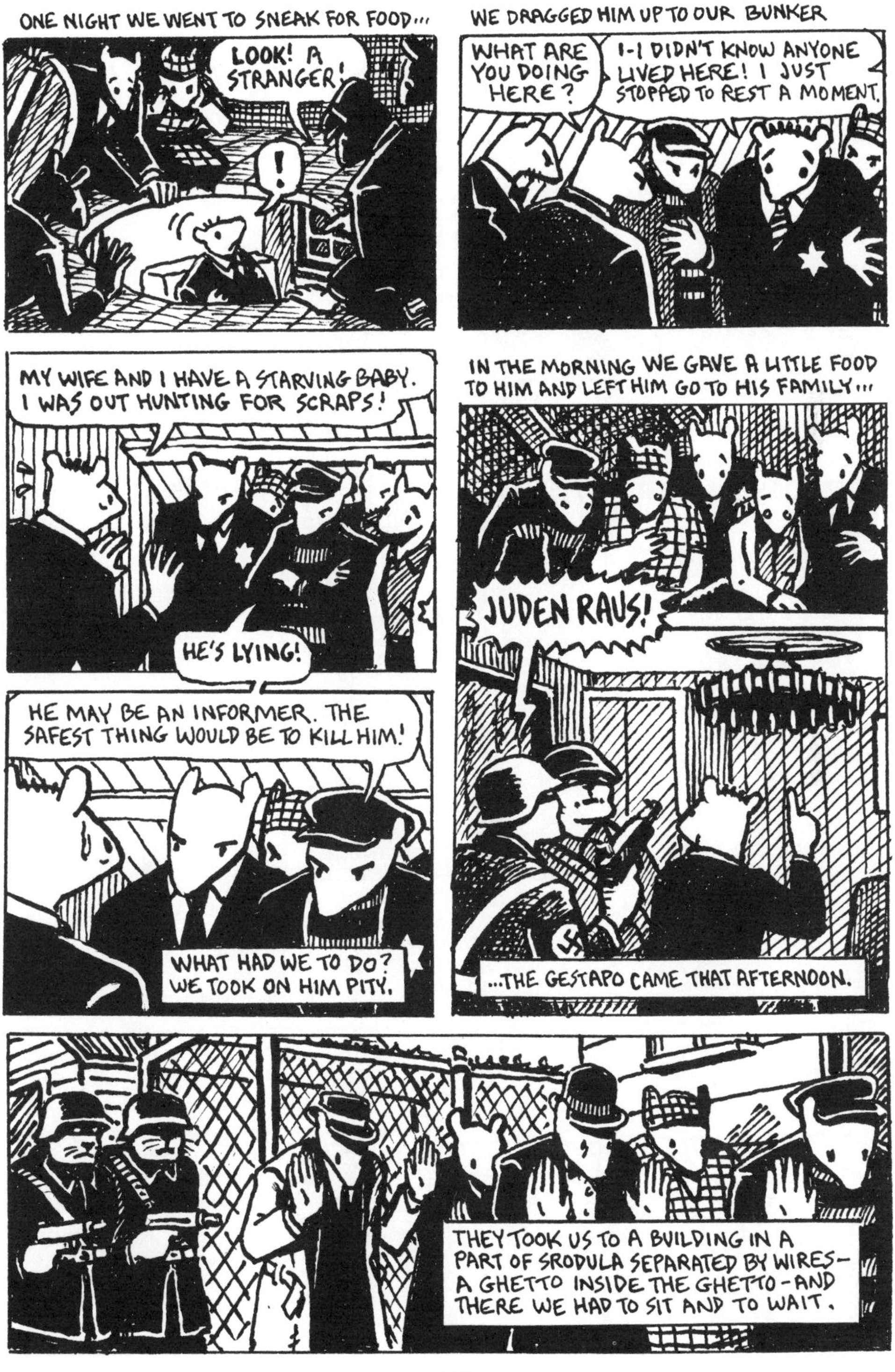
ONE NIGHT WE WENT TO SNEAK FOR FOOD...
LOOK! A STRANGER!
!
WE DRAGGED HIM UP TO OUR BUNKER
WHAT ARE YOU DOING HERE?
I-I DIDN'T KNOW ANYONE LIVED HERE! I JUST STOPPED TO REST A MOMENT.
MY WIFE AND I HAVE A STARVING BABY. I WAS OUT HUNTING FOR SCRAPS!
HE'S LYING!
HE MAY BE AN INFORMER. THE SAFEST THING WOULD BE TO KILL HIM!
WHAT HAD WE TO DO? WE TOOK ON HIM PITY.
IN THE MORNING WE GAVE A LITTLE FOOD TO HIM AND LEFT HIM GO TO HIS FAMILY...
JUDEN RAUS!
...THE GESTAPO CAME THAT AFTERNOON.
THEY TOOK US TO A BUILDING IN A PART OF SRODULA SEPARATED BY WIRES- A GHETTO INSIDE THE GHETTO- AND THERE WE HAD TO SIT AND TO WAIT.

WE WERE MAYBE 200 PEOPLE TOGETHER WAITING... EACH WEDNESDAY WENT VANS TO AUSCHWITZ. WHEN WE WERE CAUGHT, IT WAS THEN MAYBE A THURSDAY.

LOOK, ANJA! THAT'S MY COUSIN, JAKOV SPIEGELMAN, IN THE COURTYARD.

HEY! JAKOV! HELP! JAKOV-HELP US!

VLADEK?! THERE'S NOTHING I CAN DO!

I MADE SIGNS TO SHOW I COULD PAY.

SOME GOLD I HID IN THE CHIMNEY OF OUR BUNKER WHEN THEY TOOK US. BUT A FEW VALUABLES I HAD STILL WITH ME.

OKAY. DON'T WORRY! HASKEL WILL COME HELP YOU!

HASKEL SPIEGELMAN WAS ANOTHER COUSIN.

WOULDN'T THEY HAVE HELPED YOU EVEN IF YOU COULDN'T PAY? I MEAN, YOU WERE FROM THE SAME FAMILY..

HAH! YOU DON'T UNDERSTAND...

AT THAT TIME IT WASN'T ANYMORE FAMILIES. IT WAS EVERYBODY TO TAKE CARE FOR HIMSELF!

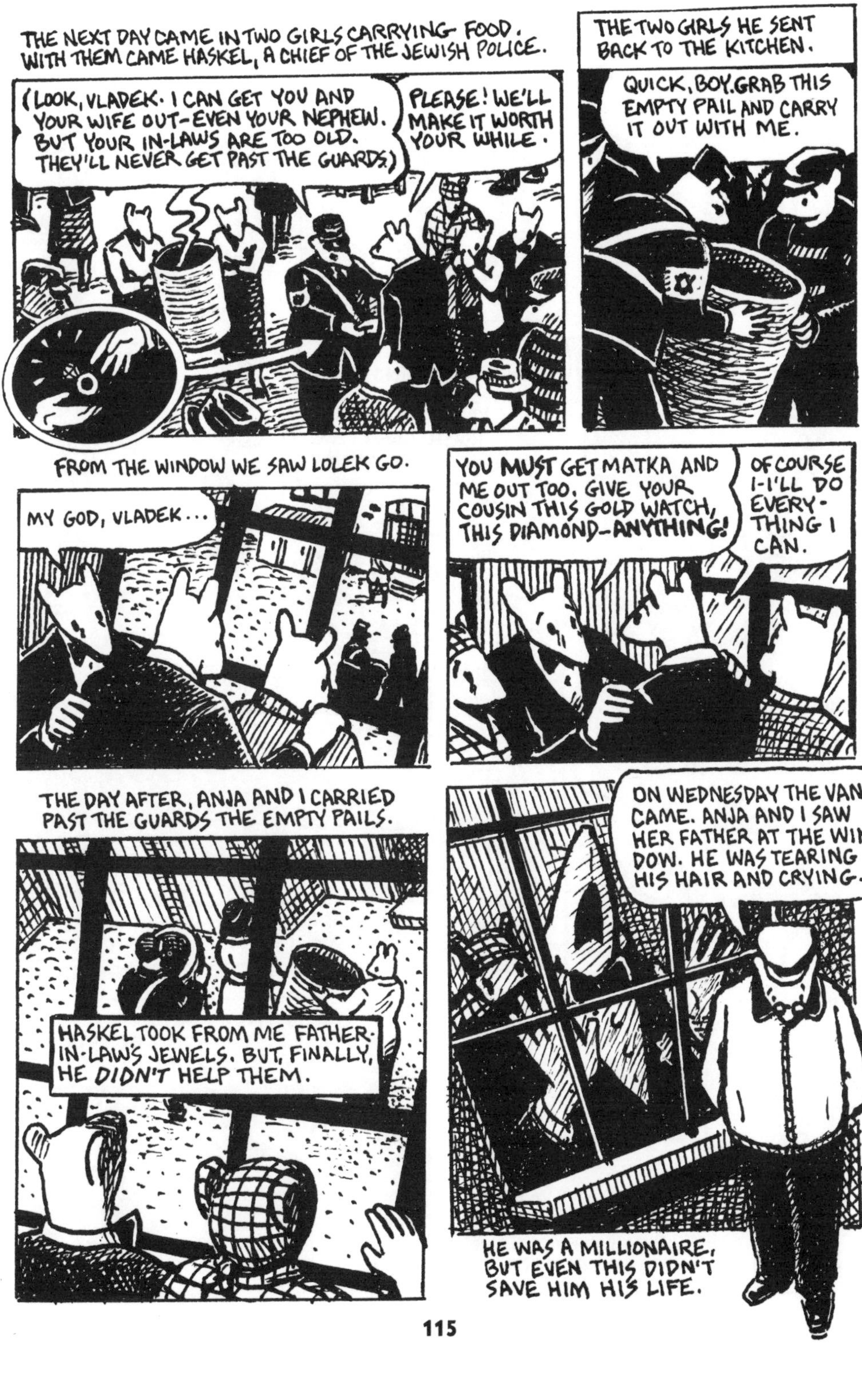
THE NEXT DAY CAME IN TWO GIRLS CARRYING FOOD. WITH THEM CAME HASKEL, A CHIEF OF THE JEWISH POLICE.
(LOOK, VLADEK. I CAN GET YOU AND YOUR WIFE OUT- EVEN YOUR NEPHEW. BUT YOUR IN-LAWS ARE TOO OLD. THEY'LL NEVER GET PAST THE GUARDS.)
PLEASE! WE'LL MAKE IT WORTH YOUR WHILE.
THE TWO GIRLS HE SENT BACK TO THE KITCHEN.
QUICK, BOY. GRAB THIS EMPTY PAIL AND CARRY IT OUT WITH ME.
FROM THE WINDOW WE SAW LOLEK GO.
MY GOD, VLADEK...
YOU MUST GET MATKA AND ME OUT TOO. GIVE YOUR COUSIN THIS GOLD WATCH, THIS DIAMOND- ANYTHING!
OF COURSE I-I'LL DO EVERY-THING I CAN.
THE DAY AFTER, ANJA AND I CARRIED PAST THE GUARDS THE EMPTY PAILS.
HASKEL TOOK FROM ME FATHER-IN-LAW'S JEWELS. BUT, FINALLY, HE DIDN'T HELP THEM.
ON WEDNESDAY THE VANS CAME. ANJA AND I SAW HER FATHER AT THE WIN-DOW. HE WAS TEARING HIS HAIR AND CRYING.
HE WAS A MILLIONAIRE, BUT EVEN THIS DIDN'T SAVE HIM HIS LIFE.

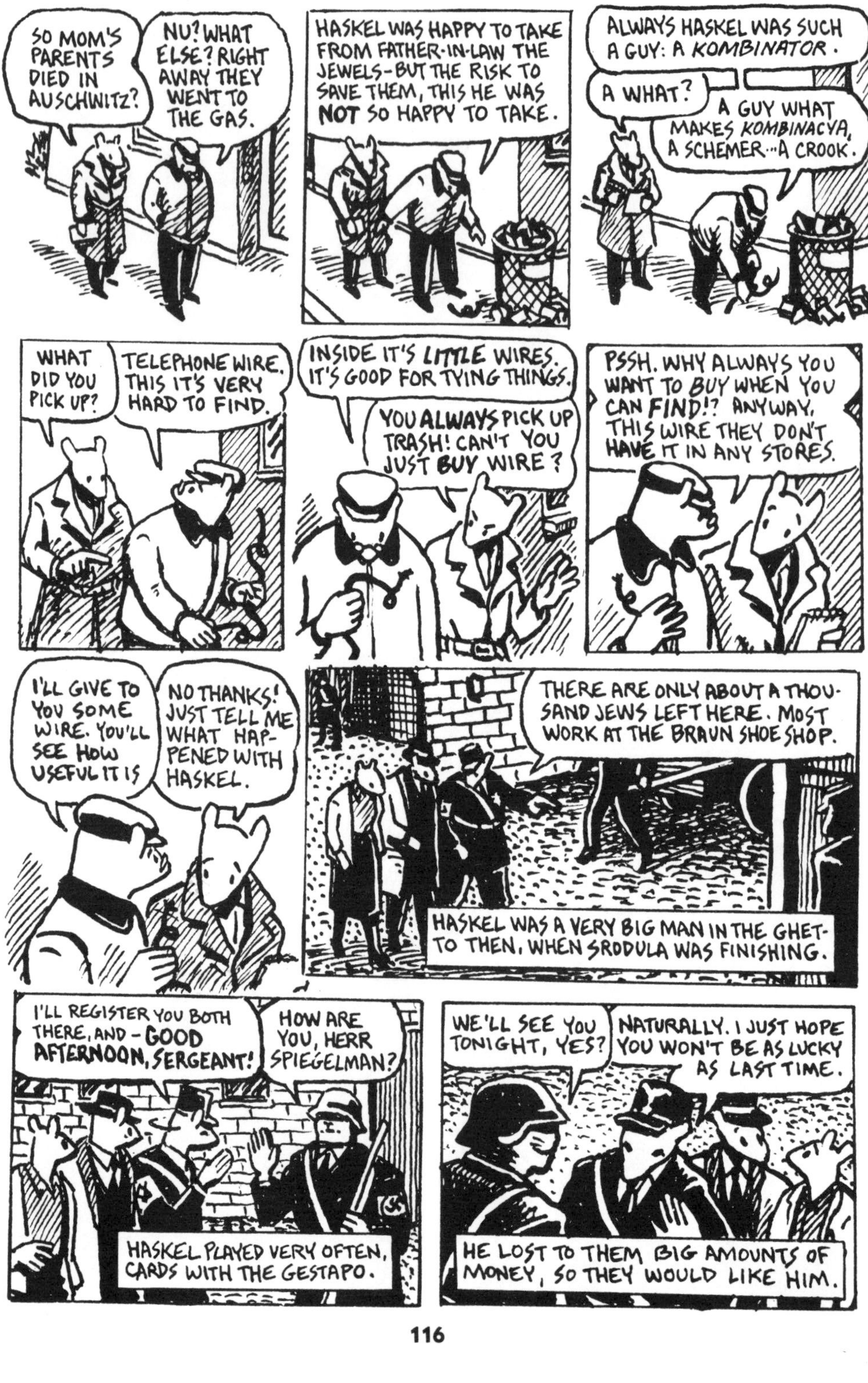

SO MOM'S PARENTS DIED IN AUSCHWITZ?
NU? WHAT ELSE? RIGHT AWAY THEY WENT TO THE GAS.
HASKEL WAS HAPPY TO TAKE FROM FATHER-IN-LAW THE JEWELS-BUT THE RISK TO SAVE THEM, THIS HE WAS NOT SO HAPPY TO TAKE.
ALWAYS HASKEL WAS SUCH A GUY: A KOMBINATOR.
A WHAT?
A GUY WHAT MAKES KOMBINACYA, A SCHEMER...A CROOK.
WHAT DID YOU PICK UP?
TELEPHONE WIRE. THIS IT'S VERY HARD TO FIND.
INSIDE IT'S LITTLE WIRES. IT'S GOOD FOR TYING THINGS.
YOU ALWAYS PICK UP TRASH! CAN'T YOU JUST BUY WIRE?
PSSH. WHY ALWAYS YOU WANT TO BUY WHEN YOU CAN FIND!? ANYWAY, THIS WIRE THEY DON'T HAVE IT IN ANY STORES.
I'LL GIVE TO YOU SOME WIRE. YOU'LL SEE HOW USEFUL IT IS
NO THANKS! JUST TELL ME WHAT HAPPENED WITH HASKEL.
THERE ARE ONLY ABOUT A THOUSAND JEWS LEFT HERE. MOST WORK AT THE BRAUN SHOE SHOP.
HASKEL WAS A VERY BIG MAN IN THE GHETTO THEN, WHEN SRODULA WAS FINISHING.
I'LL REGISTER YOU BOTH THERE, AND - GOOD AFTERNOON, SERGEANT!
HOW ARE YOU, HERR SPIEGELMAN?
HASKEL PLAYED VERY OFTEN, CARDS WITH THE GESTAPO.
WE'LL SEE YOU TONIGHT, YES?
NATURALLY. I JUST HOPE YOU WON'T BE AS LUCKY AS LAST TIME.
HE LOST TO THEM BIG AMOUNTS OF MONEY, SO THEY WOULD LIKE HIM.

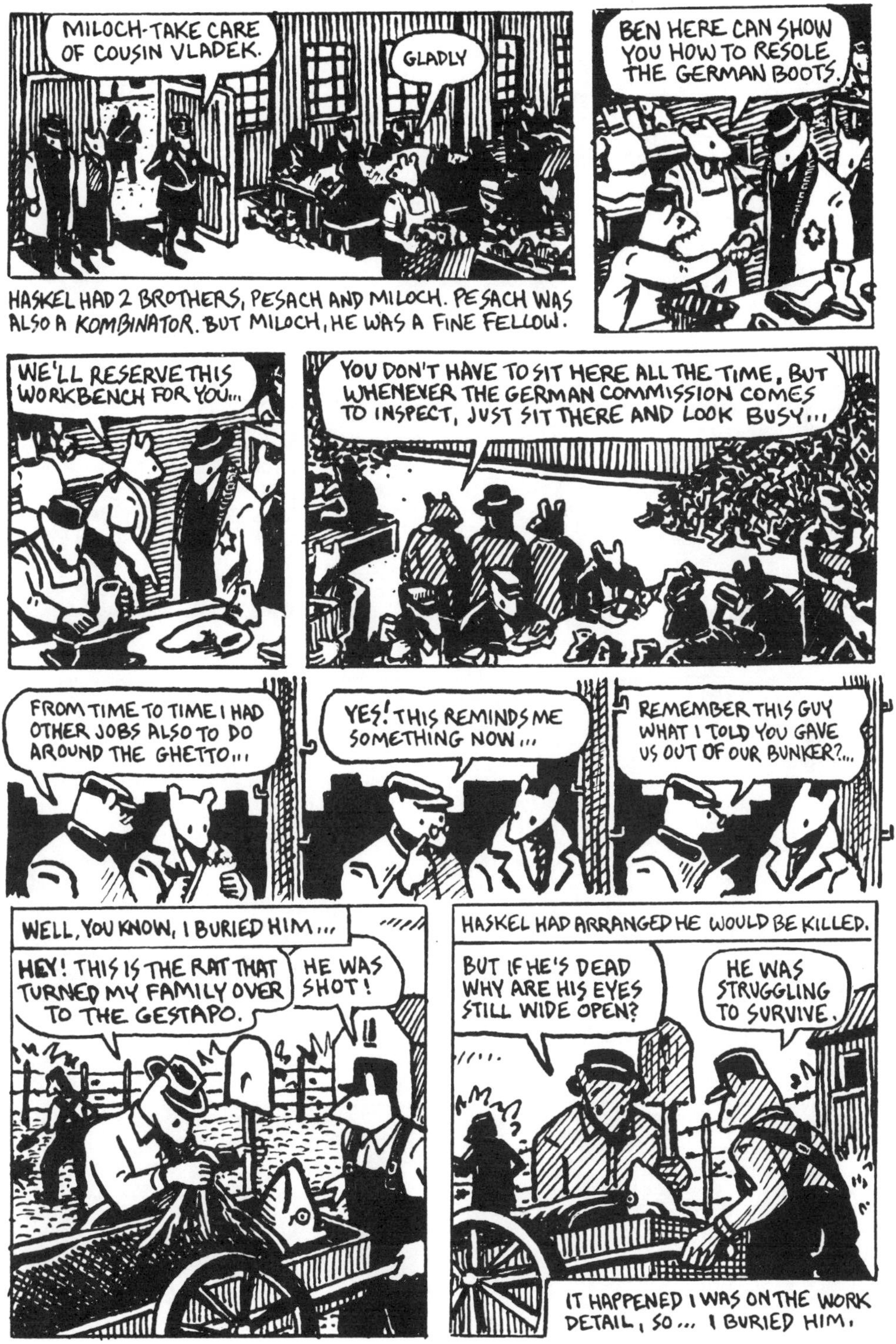
MILOCH-TAKE CARE OF COUSIN VLADEK.
GLADLY
HASKEL HAD 2 BROTHERS, PESACH AND MILOCH. PESACH WAS ALSO A KOMBINATOR. BUT MILOCH, HE WAS A FINE FELLOW.
BEN HERE CAN SHOW YOU HOW TO RESOLE THE GERMAN BOOTS.
WE'LL RESERVE THIS WORKBENCH FOR YOU...
YOU DON'T HAVE TO SIT HERE ALL THE TIME, BUT WHENEVER THE GERMAN COMMISSION COMES TO INSPECT, JUST SIT THERE AND LOOK BUSY...
FROM TIME TO TIME I HAD OTHER JOBS ALSO TO DO AROUND THE GHETTO...
YES! THIS REMINDS ME SOMETHING NOW...
REMEMBER THIS GUY WHAT I TOLD YOU GAVE US OUT OF OUR BUNKER?...
WELL, YOU KNOW, I BURIED HIM...
HEY! THIS IS THE RAT THAT TURNED MY FAMILY OVER TO THE GESTAPO.
HE WAS SHOT!
HASKEL HAD ARRANGED HE WOULD BE KILLED.
BUT IF HE'S DEAD WHY ARE HIS EYES STILL WIDE OPEN?
HE WAS STRUGGLING TO SURVIVE.
IT HAPPENED I WAS ON THE WORK DETAIL, SO... I BURIED HIM.

.... SUCH FRIENDS HASKEL HAD.

BEFORE THE WAR PESACH HAD A RESORT HOTEL IN ZAKOPANE...

IN THOSE DAYS ALSO HE FOUND ALWAYS SCHEMES.

ALL GUESTS HAD TO PAY BIG POLISH TAXES... SO PESACH TOOK BRIBES TO NOT REGISTER THEM. BUT IF AN INSPECTOR CAME, THE GUESTS HAD TO HIDE THEMSELVES AWAY.

ONE TIME HIS WIFE MADE NOT ENOUGH DESSERTS TO GIVE TO EVERYBODY... SO PESACH RAN INTO THE DINING ROOM AND YELLED, "INSPECTORS ARE COMING!"

IT WAS NO INSPECTOR, OF COURSE. BUT 40% OF THE GUESTS RAN FAST FROM THE ROOM. ...PESACH HAD ENOUGH DESSERTS LEFT OVER EVEN FOR THE NEXT DAY!

COME.

ARE YOU READY TO WALK AGAIN?

YES, IT'S TOO DIRTY TO SIT! ...BUT, REALLY, IF I DIDN'T HAVE MY NITROSTAT, IT COULD HAVE BEEN JUST NOW SOMETHING TERRIBLE.

MILOCH SPIEGELMAN—HE SURVIVED THE WAR WITH HIS WIFE AND CHILD AND THEY MOVED TO AUSTRALIA. ABOUT FIVE YEARS AGO HE GOT A BIG HEART ATTACK...

AND LAST YEAR, HE GOT ON THE STREET A SEIZURE—LIKE WHAT I HAD JUST NOW... BUT HE DIDN'T HAVE WITH HIM HIS PILLS. HIS WIFE RAN TO FIND A DRUG STORE.

WHEN SHE CAME BACK MILOCH WAS DEAD!

NU? SO LIFE GOES.

BUT I MUST FINISH QUICK TO TELL YOU THE REST ABOUT SRODULA, BECAUSE WE WILL COME SOON OVER TO THE BANK.

SALE

120

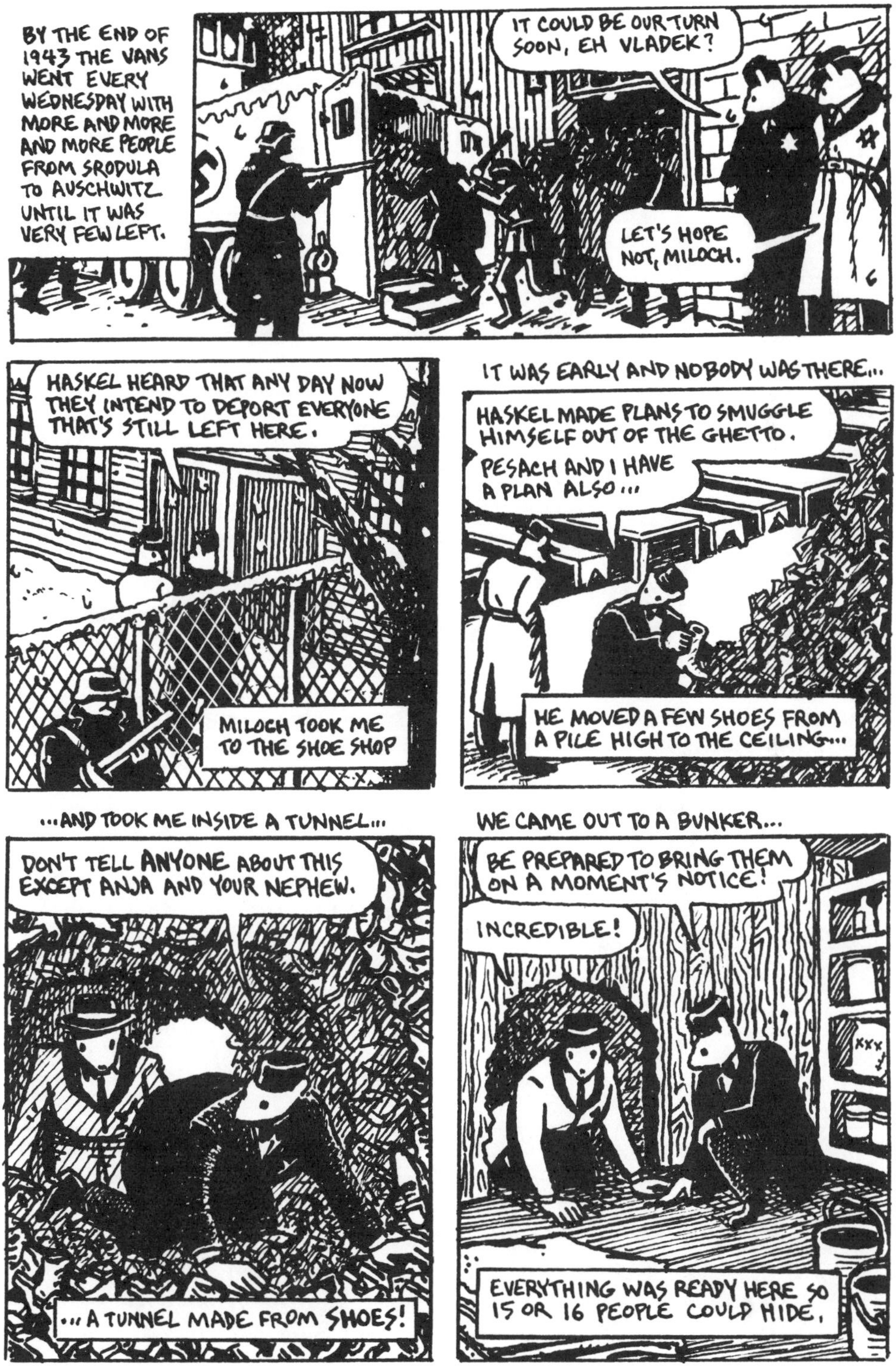
BY THE END OF 1943 THE VANS WENT EVERY WEDNESDAY WITH MORE AND MORE AND MORE PEOPLE FROM SRODULA TO AUSCHWITZ UNTIL IT WAS VERY FEW LEFT.
IT COULD BE OUR TURN SOON, EH VLADEK?
LET'S HOPE NOT, MILOCH.
HASKEL HEARD THAT ANY DAY NOW THEY INTEND TO DEPORT EVERYONE THAT'S STILL LEFT HERE.
MILOCH TOOK ME TO THE SHOE SHOP
IT WAS EARLY AND NOBODY WAS THERE...
HASKEL MADE PLANS TO SMUGGLE HIMSELF OUT OF THE GHETTO.
PESACH AND I HAVE A PLAN ALSO...
HE MOVED A FEW SHOES FROM A PILE HIGH TO THE CEILING...
...AND TOOK ME INSIDE A TUNNEL...
DON'T TELL ANYONE ABOUT THIS EXCEPT ANJA AND YOUR NEPHEW.
...A TUNNEL MADE FROM SHOES!
WE CAME OUT TO A BUNKER...
BE PREPARED TO BRING THEM ON A MOMENT'S NOTICE!
INCREDIBLE!
EVERYTHING WAS READY HERE SO 15 OR 16 PEOPLE COULD HIDE.

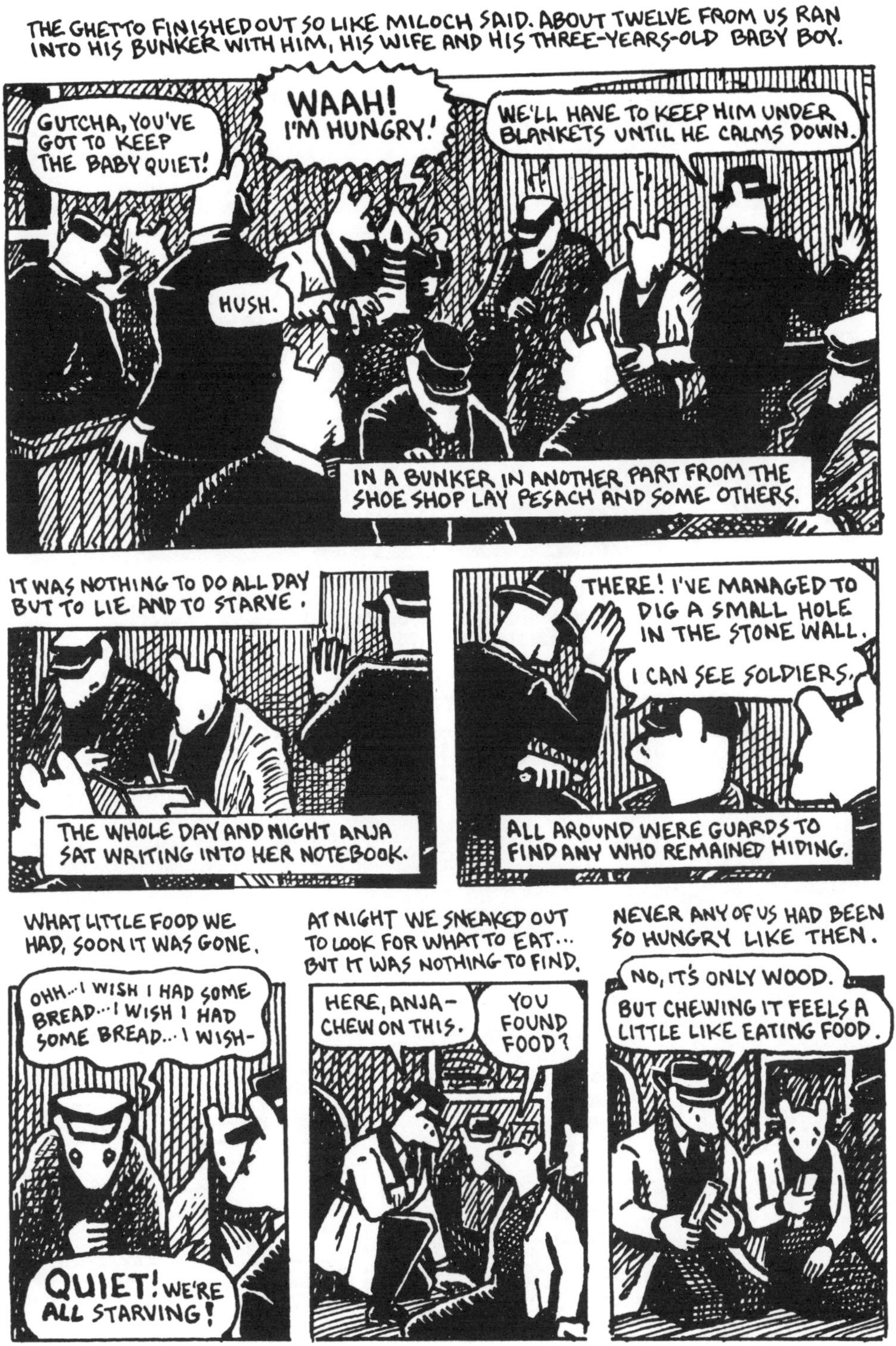
THE GHETTO FINISHED OUT SO LIKE MILOCH SAID. ABOUT TWELVE FROM US RAN INTO HIS BUNKER WITH HIM, HIS WIFE AND HIS THREE-YEARS-OLD BABY BOY.
GUTCHA, YOU'VE GOT TO KEEP THE BABY QUIET!
WAAH! I'M HUNGRY!
WE'LL HAVE TO KEEP HIM UNDER BLANKETS UNTIL HE CALMS DOWN.
HUSH.
IN A BUNKER IN ANOTHER PART FROM THE SHOE SHOP LAY PESACH AND SOME OTHERS.
IT WAS NOTHING TO DO ALL DAY BUT TO LIE AND TO STARVE.
THE WHOLE DAY AND NIGHT ANJA SAT WRITING INTO HER NOTEBOOK.
THERE! I'VE MANAGED TO DIG A SMALL HOLE IN THE STONE WALL.
I CAN SEE SOLDIERS.
ALL AROUND WERE GUARDS TO FIND ANY WHO REMAINED HIDING.
WHAT LITTLE FOOD WE HAD, SOON IT WAS GONE.
OHH... I WISH I HAD SOME BREAD... I WISH I HAD SOME BREAD... I WISH-
QUIET! WE'RE ALL STARVING!
AT NIGHT WE SNEAKED OUT TO LOOK FOR WHAT TO EAT... BUT IT WAS NOTHING TO FIND.
HERE, ANJA- CHEW ON THIS.
YOU FOUND FOOD?
NEVER ANY OF US HAD BEEN SO HUNGRY LIKE THEN.
NO, IT'S ONLY WOOD.
BUT CHEWING IT FEELS A LITTLE LIKE EATING FOOD.

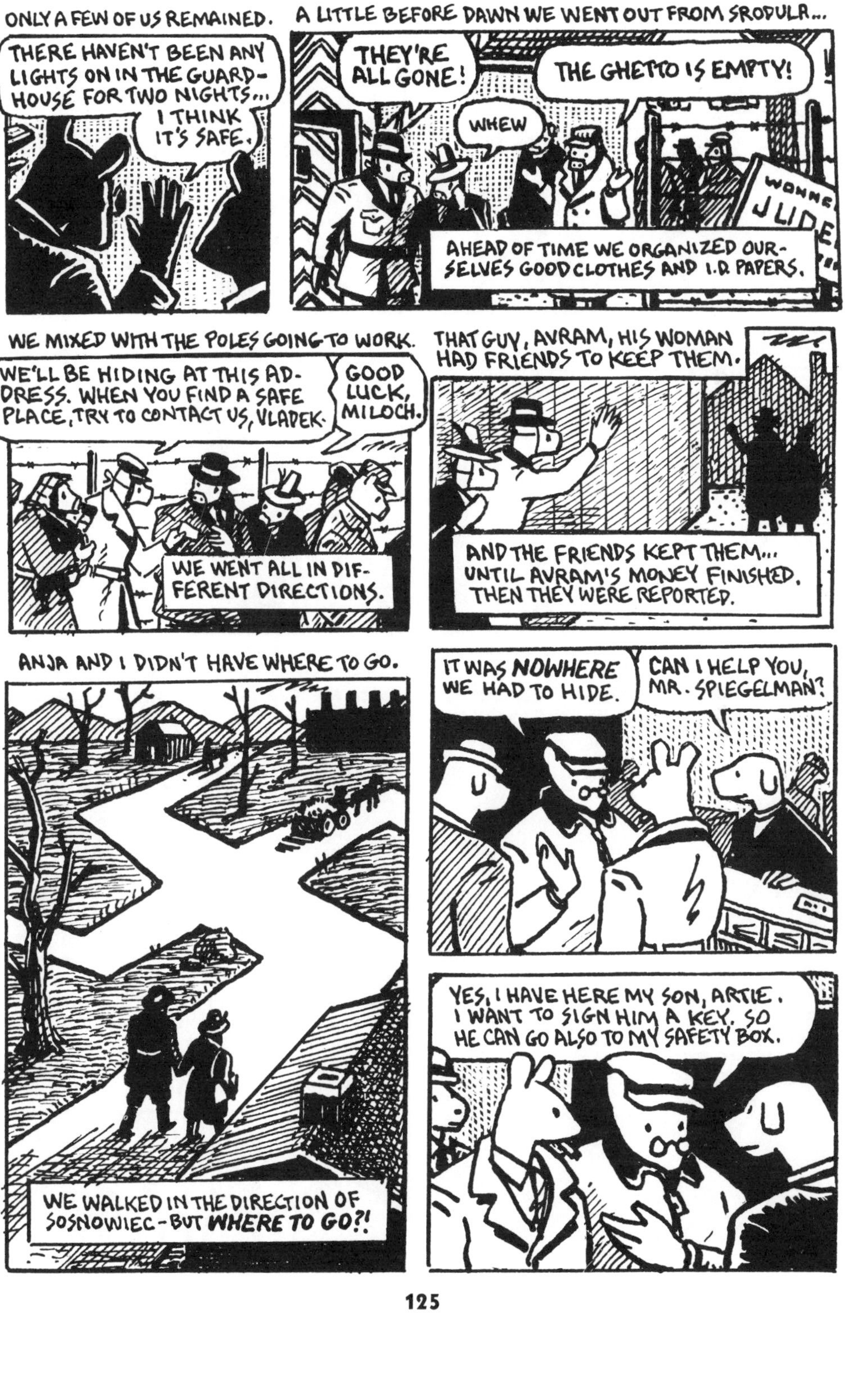
ONLY A FEW OF US REMAINED.
THERE HAVEN'T BEEN ANY LIGHTS ON IN THE GUARD-HOUSE FOR TWO NIGHTS...
I THINK IT'S SAFE.
A LITTLE BEFORE DAWN WE WENT OUT FROM SRODULA...
THEY'RE ALL GONE!
THE GHETTO IS EMPTY!
WHEW
AHEAD OF TIME WE ORGANIZED OURSELVES GOOD CLOTHES AND I.D. PAPERS.
WE MIXED WITH THE POLES GOING TO WORK.
WE'LL BE HIDING AT THIS ADDRESS. WHEN YOU FIND A SAFE PLACE, TRY TO CONTACT US, VLADEK.
GOOD LUCK, MILOCH.
WE WENT ALL IN DIFFERENT DIRECTIONS.
THAT GUY, AVRAM, HIS WOMAN HAD FRIENDS TO KEEP THEM.
AND THE FRIENDS KEPT THEM... UNTIL AVRAM'S MONEY FINISHED. THEN THEY WERE REPORTED.
ANJA AND I DIDN'T HAVE WHERE TO GO.
WE WALKED IN THE DIRECTION OF SOSNOWIEC - BUT **WHERE TO GO?!**
IT WAS **NOWHERE** WE HAD TO HIDE.
CAN I HELP YOU, MR. SPIEGELMAN?
YES, I HAVE HERE MY SON, ARTIE. I WANT TO SIGN HIM A KEY. SO HE CAN GO ALSO TO MY SAFETY BOX.

127

# CHAPTER SIX

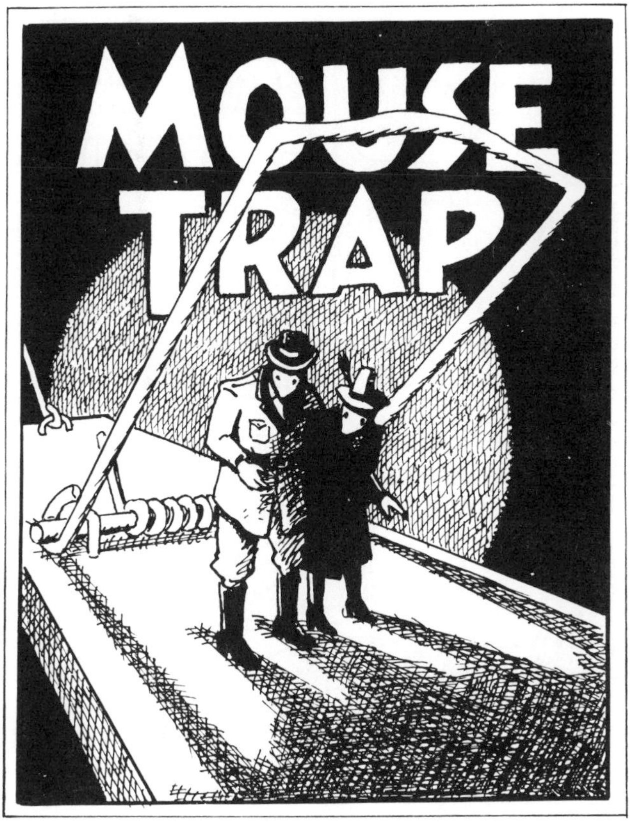
MOUSE
TRAP

Another visit...

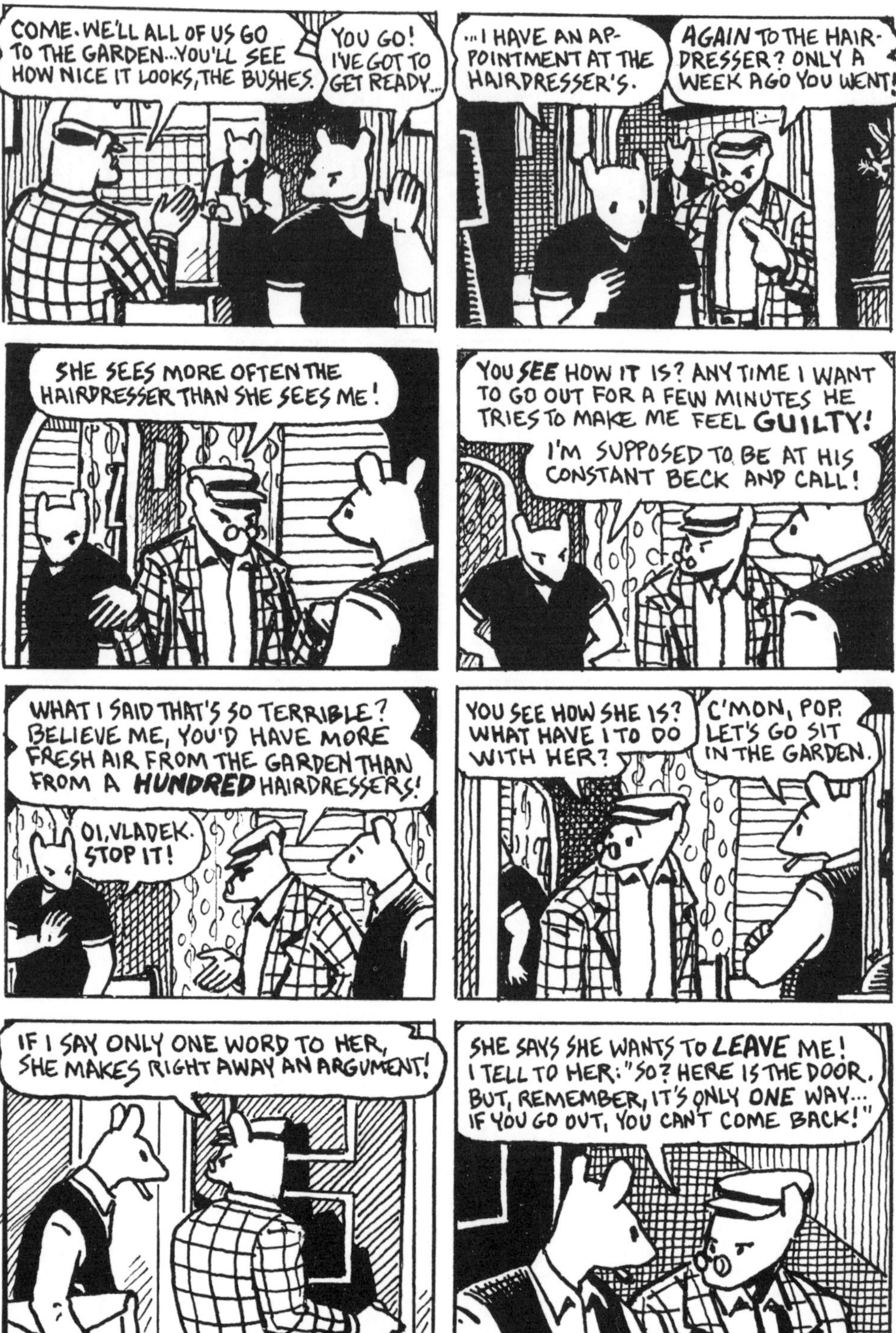
COME. WE'LL ALL OF US GO TO THE GARDEN...YOU'LL SEE HOW NICE IT LOOKS, THE BUSHES.
YOU GO! I'VE GOT TO GET READY...
...I HAVE AN APPOINTMENT AT THE HAIRDRESSER'S.
AGAIN TO THE HAIRDRESSER? ONLY A WEEK AGO YOU WENT!
SHE SEES MORE OFTEN THE HAIRDRESSER THAN SHE SEES ME!
YOU SEE HOW IT IS? ANY TIME I WANT TO GO OUT FOR A FEW MINUTES HE TRIES TO MAKE ME FEEL GUILTY!
I'M SUPPOSED TO BE AT HIS CONSTANT BECK AND CALL!
WHAT I SAID THAT'S SO TERRIBLE? BELIEVE ME, YOU'D HAVE MORE FRESH AIR FROM THE GARDEN THAN FROM A HUNDRED HAIRDRESSERS!
OI, VLADEK. STOP IT!
YOU SEE HOW SHE IS? WHAT HAVE I TO DO WITH HER?
C'MON, POP. LET'S GO SIT IN THE GARDEN.
IF I SAY ONLY ONE WORD TO HER, SHE MAKES RIGHT AWAY AN ARGUMENT!
SHE SAYS SHE WANTS TO LEAVE ME! I TELL TO HER: "SO? HERE IS THE DOOR. BUT, REMEMBER, IT'S ONLY ONE WAY... IF YOU GO OUT, YOU CAN'T COME BACK!"

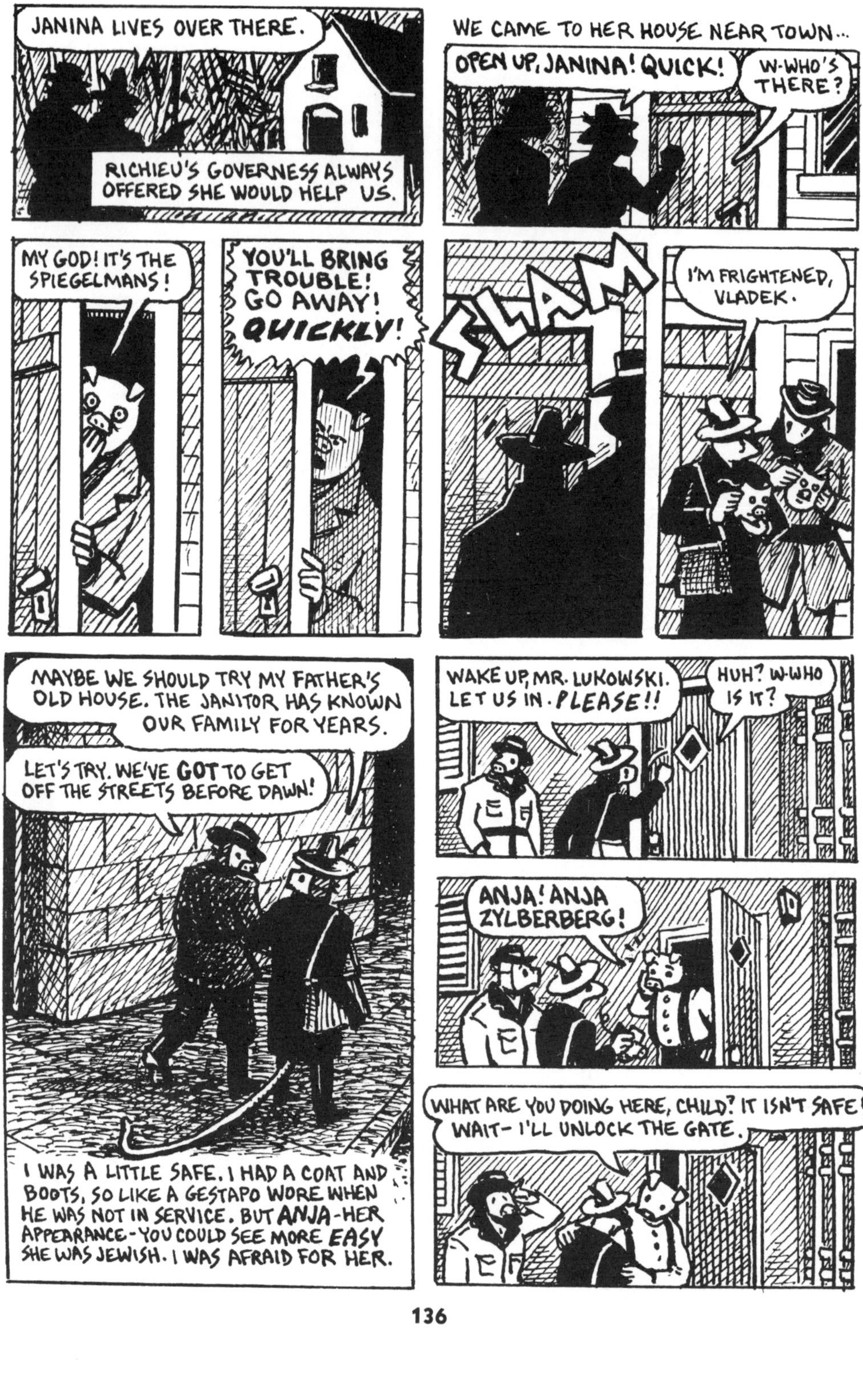
JANINA LIVES OVER THERE.
RICHIEU'S GOVERNESS ALWAYS OFFERED SHE WOULD HELP US.
WE CAME TO HER HOUSE NEAR TOWN...
OPEN UP, JANINA! QUICK!
W-WHO'S THERE?
MY GOD! IT'S THE SPIEGELMANS!
YOU'LL BRING TROUBLE! GO AWAY! QUICKLY!
SLAM
I'M FRIGHTENED, VLADEK.
MAYBE WE SHOULD TRY MY FATHER'S OLD HOUSE. THE JANITOR HAS KNOWN OUR FAMILY FOR YEARS.
LET'S TRY. WE'VE GOT TO GET OFF THE STREETS BEFORE DAWN!
I WAS A LITTLE SAFE. I HAD A COAT AND BOOTS, SO LIKE A GESTAPO WORE WHEN HE WAS NOT IN SERVICE. BUT ANJA-HER APPEARANCE-YOU COULD SEE MORE EASY SHE WAS JEWISH. I WAS AFRAID FOR HER.
WAKE UP, MR. LUKOWSKI. LET US IN. PLEASE!!
HUH? W-WHO IS IT?
ANJA! ANJA ZYLBERBERG!
WHAT ARE YOU DOING HERE, CHILD? IT ISN'T SAFE! WAIT- I'LL UNLOCK THE GATE.

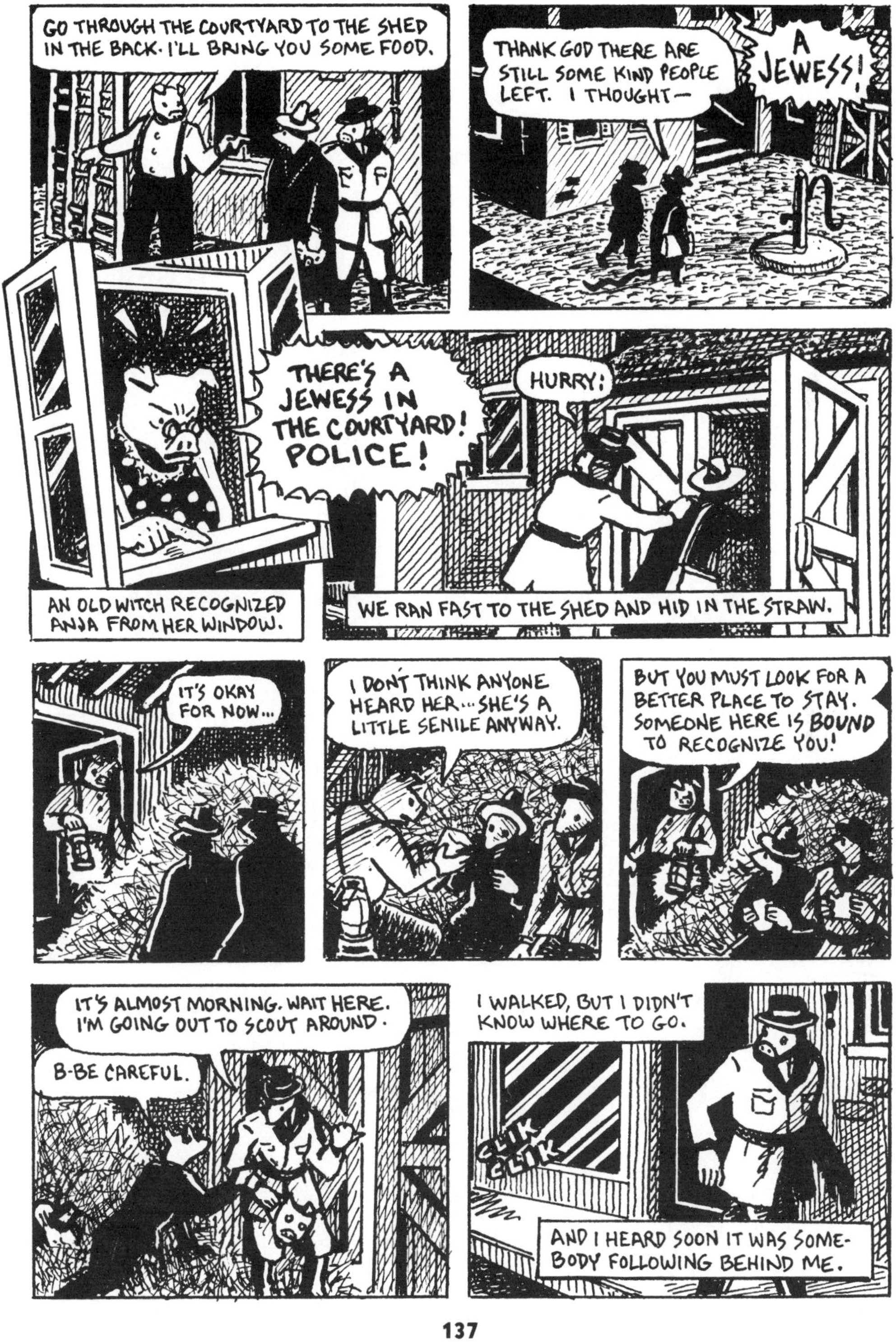

GO THROUGH THE COURTYARD TO THE SHED IN THE BACK. I'LL BRING YOU SOME FOOD.
THANK GOD THERE ARE STILL SOME KIND PEOPLE LEFT. I THOUGHT—
A JEWESS!
THERE'S A JEWESS IN THE COURTYARD! POLICE!
HURRY!
AN OLD WITCH RECOGNIZED ANJA FROM HER WINDOW.
WE RAN FAST TO THE SHED AND HID IN THE STRAW.
IT'S OKAY FOR NOW...
I DON'T THINK ANYONE HEARD HER... SHE'S A LITTLE SENILE ANYWAY.
BUT YOU MUST LOOK FOR A BETTER PLACE TO STAY. SOMEONE HERE IS BOUND TO RECOGNIZE YOU!
IT'S ALMOST MORNING. WAIT HERE. I'M GOING OUT TO SCOUT AROUND.
B-BE CAREFUL.
I WALKED, BUT I DIDN'T KNOW WHERE TO GO.
CLIK CLIK
AND I HEARD SOON IT WAS SOMEBODY FOLLOWING BEHIND ME.

138

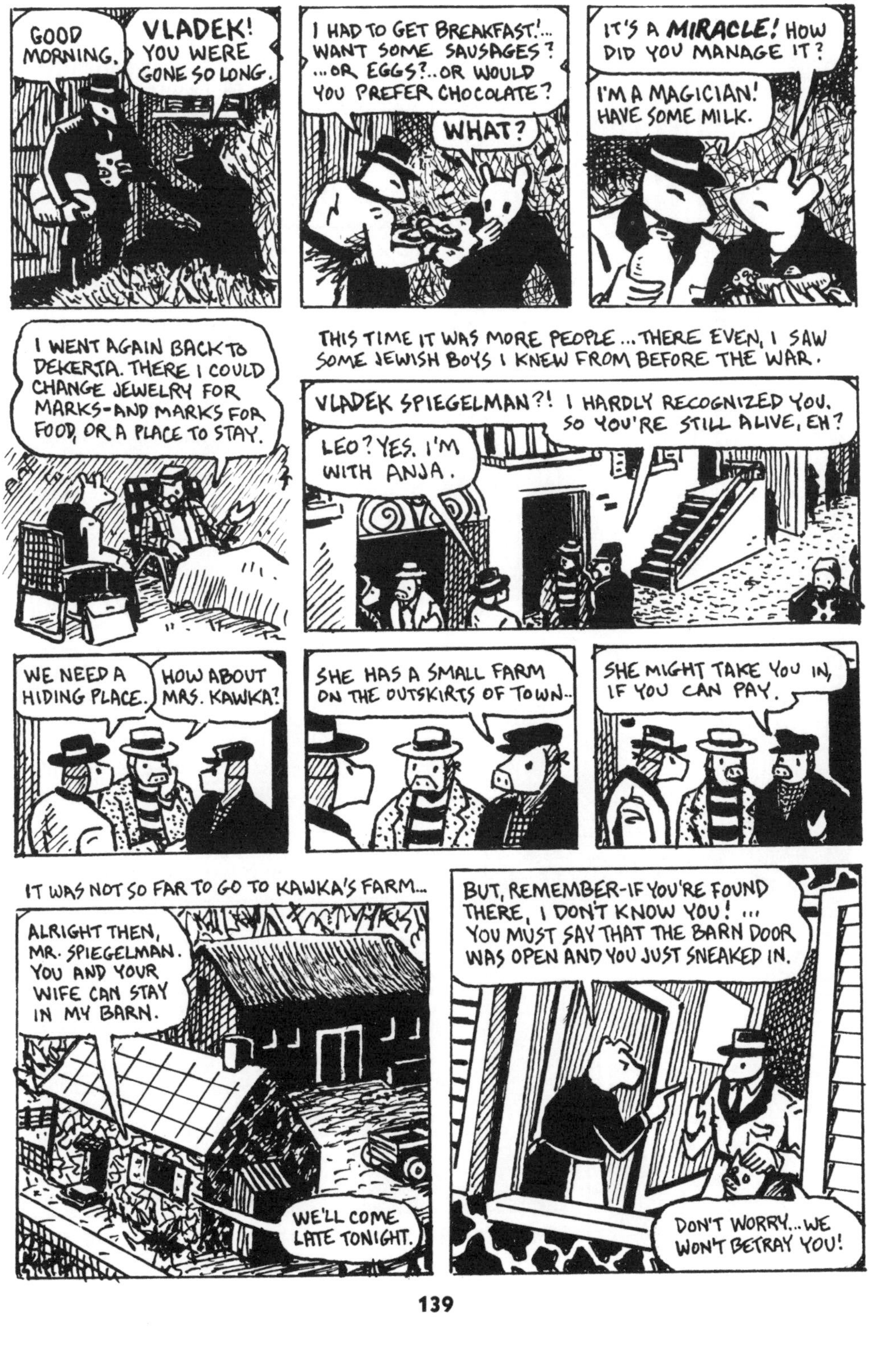

GOOD MORNING.
VLADEK! YOU WERE GONE SO LONG.
I HAD TO GET BREAKFAST!... WANT SOME SAUSAGES? ...OR EGGS?..OR WOULD YOU PREFER CHOCOLATE?
WHAT?
IT'S A **MIRACLE!** HOW DID YOU MANAGE IT?
I'M A MAGICIAN! HAVE SOME MILK.
I WENT AGAIN BACK TO DEKERTA. THERE I COULD CHANGE JEWELRY FOR MARKS-AND MARKS FOR FOOD, OR A PLACE TO STAY.
THIS TIME IT WAS MORE PEOPLE ... THERE EVEN, I SAW SOME JEWISH BOYS I KNEW FROM BEFORE THE WAR.
VLADEK SPIEGELMAN?!
I HARDLY RECOGNIZED YOU. SO YOU'RE STILL ALIVE, EH?
LEO? YES. I'M WITH ANJA.
WE NEED A HIDING PLACE.
HOW ABOUT MRS. KAWKA?
SHE HAS A SMALL FARM ON THE OUTSKIRTS OF TOWN..
SHE MIGHT TAKE YOU IN, IF YOU CAN PAY.
IT WAS NOT SO FAR TO GO TO KAWKA'S FARM...
ALRIGHT THEN, MR. SPIEGELMAN. YOU AND YOUR WIFE CAN STAY IN MY BARN.
WE'LL COME LATE TONIGHT.
BUT, REMEMBER-IF YOU'RE FOUND THERE, I DON'T KNOW YOU! ... YOU MUST SAY THAT THE BARN DOOR WAS OPEN AND YOU JUST SNEAKED IN.
DON'T WORRY... WE WON'T BETRAY YOU!

140

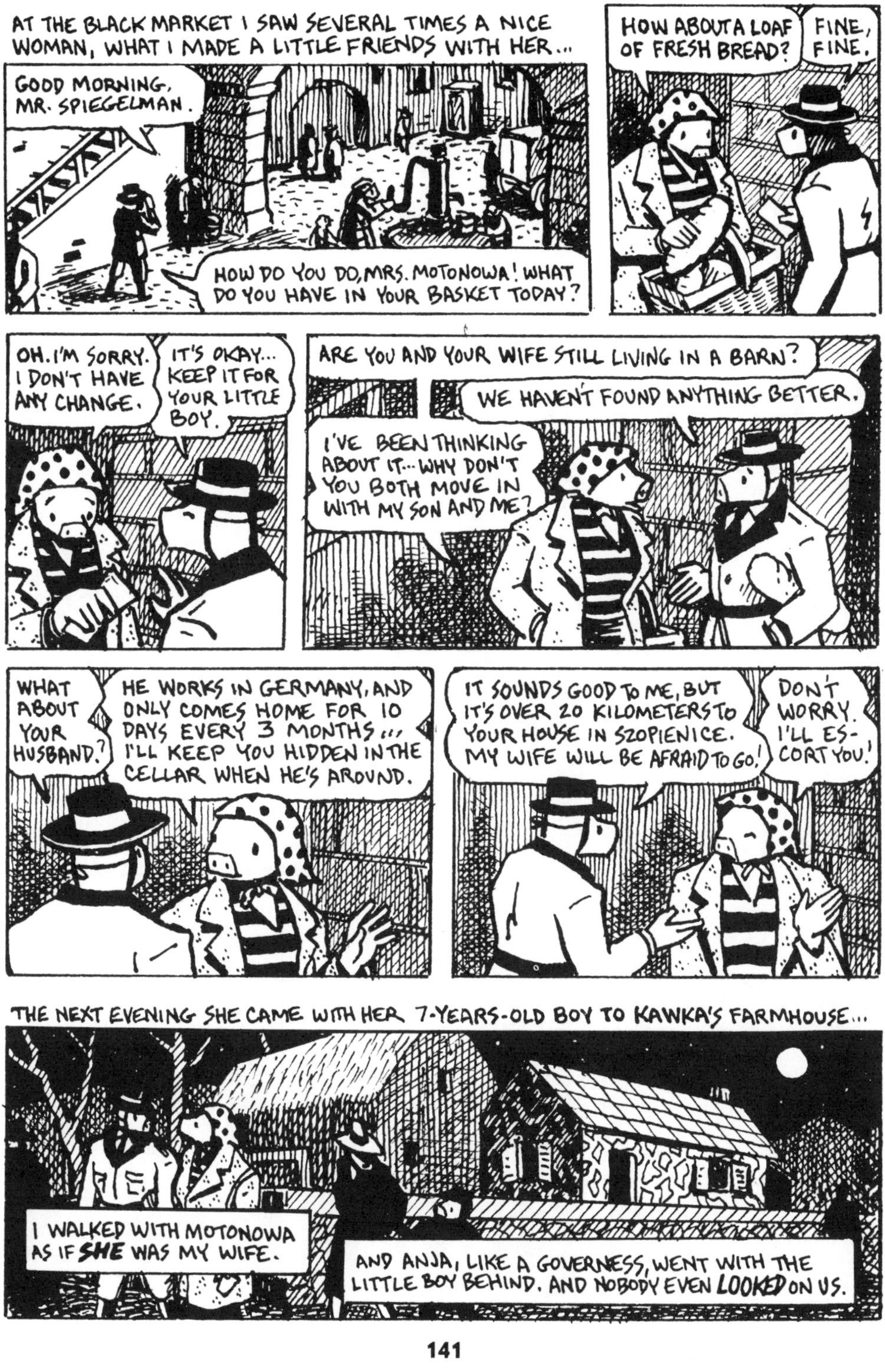
AT THE BLACK MARKET I SAW SEVERAL TIMES A NICE WOMAN, WHAT I MADE A LITTLE FRIENDS WITH HER...
GOOD MORNING, MR. SPIEGELMAN.
HOW DO YOU DO, MRS. MOTONOWA! WHAT DO YOU HAVE IN YOUR BASKET TODAY?
HOW ABOUT A LOAF OF FRESH BREAD?
FINE, FINE.
OH. I'M SORRY. I DON'T HAVE ANY CHANGE.
IT'S OKAY... KEEP IT FOR YOUR LITTLE BOY.
ARE YOU AND YOUR WIFE STILL LIVING IN A BARN?
WE HAVEN'T FOUND ANYTHING BETTER.
I'VE BEEN THINKING ABOUT IT... WHY DON'T YOU BOTH MOVE IN WITH MY SON AND ME?
WHAT ABOUT YOUR HUSBAND?
HE WORKS IN GERMANY, AND ONLY COMES HOME FOR 10 DAYS EVERY 3 MONTHS... I'LL KEEP YOU HIDDEN IN THE CELLAR WHEN HE'S AROUND.
IT SOUNDS GOOD TO ME, BUT IT'S OVER 20 KILOMETERS TO YOUR HOUSE IN SZOPIENICE. MY WIFE WILL BE AFRAID TO GO!
DON'T WORRY. I'LL ESCORT YOU!
THE NEXT EVENING SHE CAME WITH HER 7-YEARS-OLD BOY TO KAWKA'S FARMHOUSE...
I WALKED WITH MOTONOWA AS IF SHE WAS MY WIFE.
AND ANJA, LIKE A GOVERNESS, WENT WITH THE LITTLE BOY BEHIND. AND NOBODY EVEN LOOKED ON US.

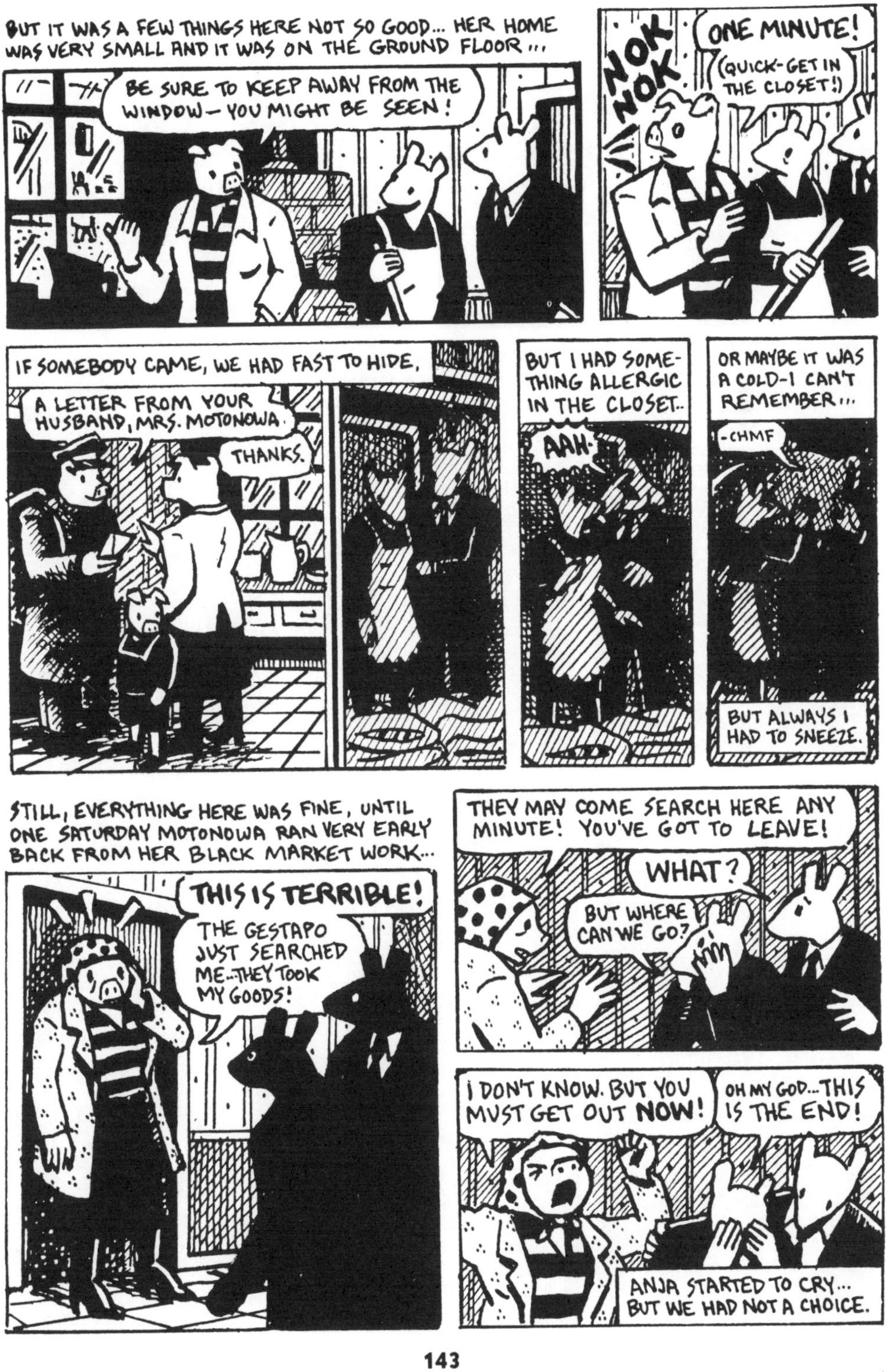
BUT IT WAS A FEW THINGS HERE NOT SO GOOD... HER HOME WAS VERY SMALL AND IT WAS ON THE GROUND FLOOR...
BE SURE TO KEEP AWAY FROM THE WINDOW—YOU MIGHT BE SEEN!
NOK NOK
ONE MINUTE!
(QUICK-GET IN THE CLOSET!)
IF SOMEBODY CAME, WE HAD FAST TO HIDE.
A LETTER FROM YOUR HUSBAND, MRS. MOTONOWA.
THANKS.
BUT I HAD SOMETHING ALLERGIC IN THE CLOSET..
AAH-
OR MAYBE IT WAS A COLD-I CAN'T REMEMBER...
-CHMF
BUT ALWAYS I HAD TO SNEEZE.
STILL, EVERYTHING HERE WAS FINE, UNTIL ONE SATURDAY MOTONOWA RAN VERY EARLY BACK FROM HER BLACK MARKET WORK...
THIS IS TERRIBLE!
THE GESTAPO JUST SEARCHED ME--THEY TOOK MY GOODS!
THEY MAY COME SEARCH HERE ANY MINUTE! YOU'VE GOT TO LEAVE!
WHAT?
BUT WHERE CAN WE GO?
I DON'T KNOW. BUT YOU MUST GET OUT NOW!
OH MY GOD...THIS IS THE END!
ANJA STARTED TO CRY... BUT WE HAD NOT A CHOICE.

144

IT STARTED TO BE LIGHT...

COME. WE WON'T BE NOTICED IF WE MIX WITH PEOPLE OUT ON THE STREET.

I'M SO TIRED AND COLD...

WE CAN REST NOW.

WE CAME FINALLY AGAIN TO THIS PLACE WITH THE COW AND WENT INSIDE.

LATER, KAWKA CAME IN...

W-WHO'S IN HERE?

THE SPIEGELMANS... WE HAD NOWHERE ELSE TO GO.

WELL... I GUESS YOU CAN STAY. BUT, REMEMBER: I DON'T KNOW YOU'RE HERE!

WHY, MRS. SPIEGELMAN, YOU'RE SHIVERING!

YOU CAN COME INTO MY HOUSE FOR AN HOUR OR SO, 'TIL YOU WARM UP.

SHE TOOK ANJA INSIDE AND BROUGHT TO ME SOME FOOD... IN THOSE DAYS I WAS SO STRONG I COULD SIT EVEN IN THE SNOW ALL NIGHT...

THINGS CAN'T BE THIS BAD EVERYWHERE! I'D GIVE ANYTHING TO GET OUT OF POLAND!

YOU KNOW, BEFORE I TOOK YOU IN, I HAD A YOUNG MAN AND HIS SON HERE...

TWO PEOPLE I KNOW SMUGGLED THEM INTO HUNGARY. I HEARD HE AND HIS BOY WERE DOING WELL THERE.

HUNGARY! REALLY?! I'D LIKE TO MEET THOSE SMUGGLERS!

145

SHE TOLD ME THESE TWO ACQUAINTANCES VISITED OFTEN TO HER ON THURSDAY EVENINGS... TODAY WAS MAYBE A MONDAY...

I DON'T GET IT... WASN'T HUNGARY AS DANGEROUS AS POLAND?

NO. FOR A LONGER TIME IT WAS *BETTER* THERE IN HUNGARY FOR THE JEWS... BUT THEN, NEAR THE VERY FINISH OF THE WAR, THEY ALL GOT PUT *ALSO* TO AUSCHWITZ.

I WAS THERE, AND I SAW IT. THOUSANDS—HUNDREDS OF THOUSANDS OF JEWS FROM HUNGARY...

SO MANY, IT WASN'T EVEN ROOM ENOUGH TO BURY THEM ALL IN THE OVENS.

BUT AT THAT TIME, WHEN I WAS THERE WITH KAWKA, WE COULDN'T *KNOW* THEN.

SO... I WENT NEXT DAY TO DEKERTA STREET TO BUY FOOD...

OH GOD! OH GOD! MR. SPIEGELMAN, YOU'RE ALIVE! I'M SO GLAD TO SEE YOU!

MRS. MOTONOWA!

I WANTED TO FIND A NEW CONNECTION TO HIDE US. BUT *REALLY* I DIDN'T THINK TO FIND AGAIN *HER.*

PRAISE MARY, YOU'RE SAFE! I COULDN'T *SLEEP,* I FELT SO GUILTY ABOUT CHASING YOU AND YOUR WIFE OUT.

THE GESTAPO NEVER EVEN CAME TO MY HOUSE. I JUST PANICKED FOR NOTHING.

PLEASE COME BACK AGAIN.

ANJA WAS GLAD OF GOING BACK. AND MOTONOWA ALSO...ALWAYS I PAID HER NICELY.

AND THAT SAME NIGHT WE SAID GOODBYE TO KAWKA AND WENT AGAIN TO SZOPIENICE.

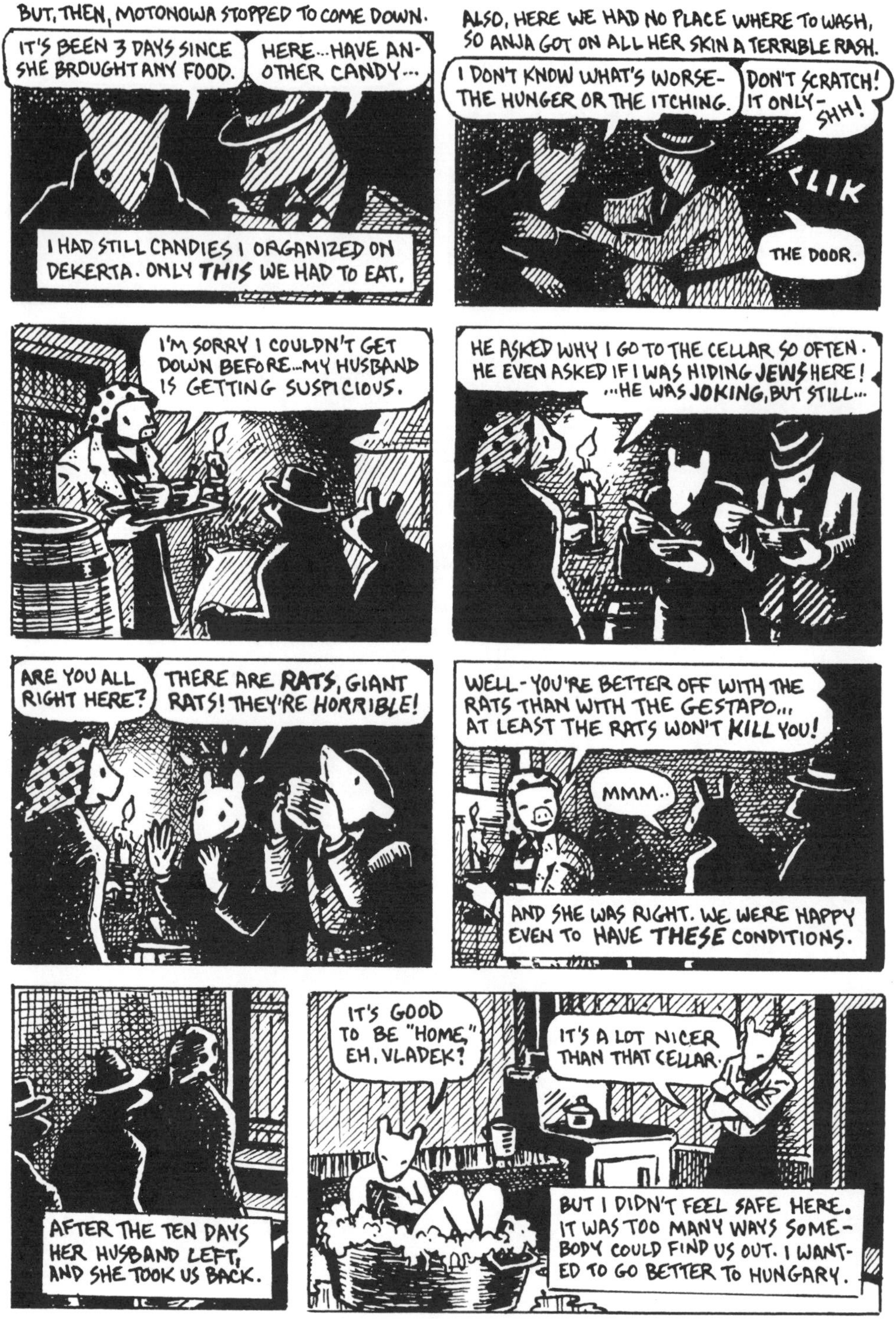
BUT, THEN, MOTONOWA STOPPED TO COME DOWN.
IT'S BEEN 3 DAYS SINCE SHE BROUGHT ANY FOOD.
HERE...HAVE ANOTHER CANDY...
I HAD STILL CANDIES I ORGANIZED ON DEKERTA. ONLY THIS WE HAD TO EAT.
ALSO, HERE WE HAD NO PLACE WHERE TO WASH, SO ANJA GOT ON ALL HER SKIN A TERRIBLE RASH.
I DON'T KNOW WHAT'S WORSE- THE HUNGER OR THE ITCHING.
DON'T SCRATCH! IT ONLY- SHH!
CLIK
THE DOOR.
I'M SORRY I COULDN'T GET DOWN BEFORE...MY HUSBAND IS GETTING SUSPICIOUS.
HE ASKED WHY I GO TO THE CELLAR SO OFTEN. HE EVEN ASKED IF I WAS HIDING JEWS HERE! ...HE WAS JOKING, BUT STILL...
ARE YOU ALL RIGHT HERE?
THERE ARE RATS, GIANT RATS! THEY'RE HORRIBLE!
WELL- YOU'RE BETTER OFF WITH THE RATS THAN WITH THE GESTAPO... AT LEAST THE RATS WON'T KILL YOU!
MMM..
AND SHE WAS RIGHT. WE WERE HAPPY EVEN TO HAVE THESE CONDITIONS.
AFTER THE TEN DAYS HER HUSBAND LEFT, AND SHE TOOK US BACK.
IT'S GOOD TO BE "HOME," EH, VLADEK?
IT'S A LOT NICER THAN THAT CELLAR.
BUT I DIDN'T FEEL SAFE HERE. IT WAS TOO MANY WAYS SOMEBODY COULD FIND US OUT. I WANTED TO GO BETTER TO HUNGARY.

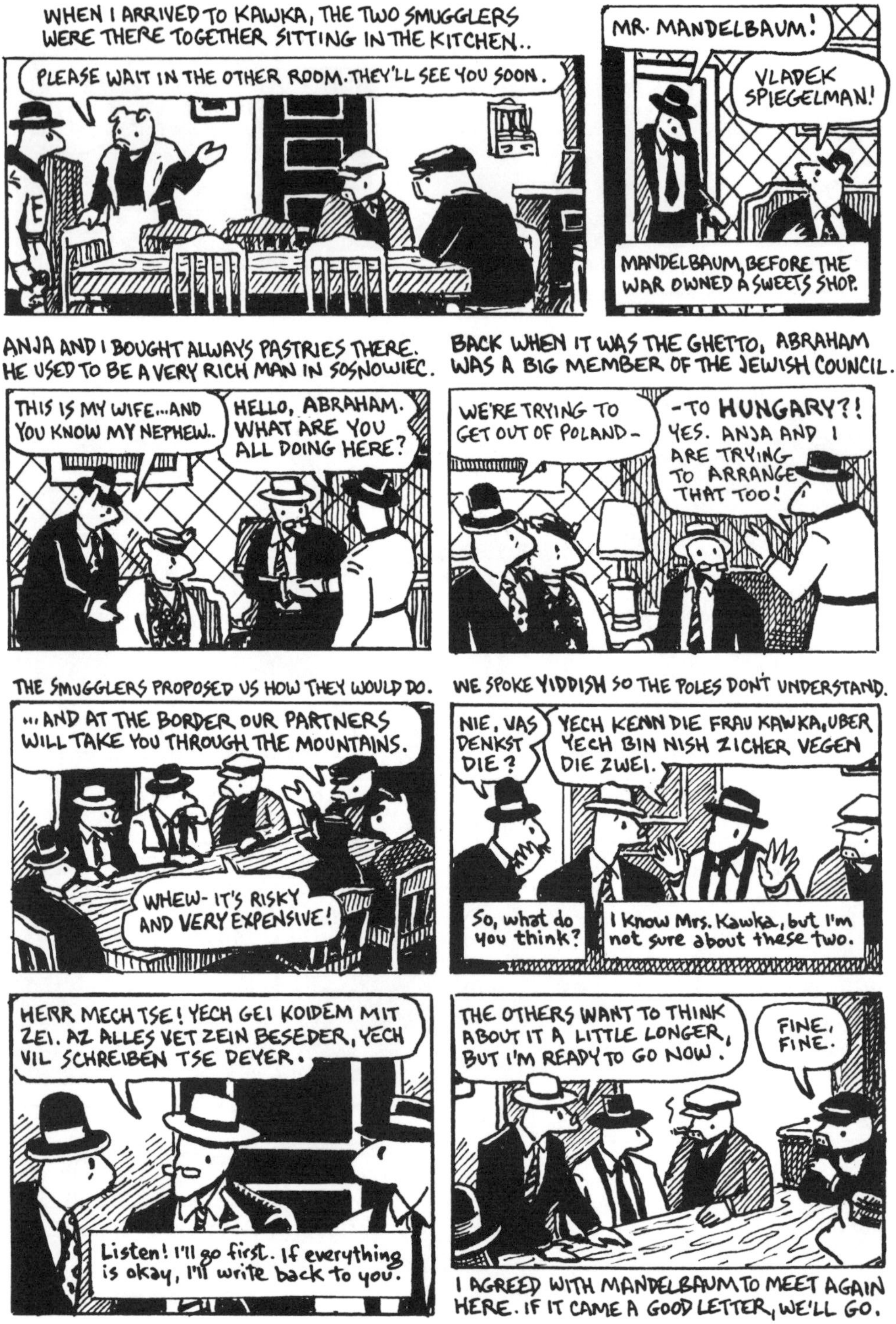
WHEN I ARRIVED TO KAWKA, THE TWO SMUGGLERS WERE THERE TOGETHER SITTING IN THE KITCHEN..
PLEASE WAIT IN THE OTHER ROOM. THEY'LL SEE YOU SOON.
MR. MANDELBAUM!
VLADEK SPIEGELMAN!
MANDELBAUM, BEFORE THE WAR OWNED A SWEETS SHOP.
ANJA AND I BOUGHT ALWAYS PASTRIES THERE. HE USED TO BE A VERY RICH MAN IN SOSNOWIEC.
THIS IS MY WIFE...AND YOU KNOW MY NEPHEW..
HELLO, ABRAHAM. WHAT ARE YOU ALL DOING HERE?
BACK WHEN IT WAS THE GHETTO, ABRAHAM WAS A BIG MEMBER OF THE JEWISH COUNCIL.
WE'RE TRYING TO GET OUT OF POLAND-
-TO HUNGARY?! YES. ANJA AND I ARE TRYING TO ARRANGE THAT TOO!
THE SMUGGLERS PROPOSED US HOW THEY WOULD DO.
...AND AT THE BORDER OUR PARTNERS WILL TAKE YOU THROUGH THE MOUNTAINS.
WHEW- IT'S RISKY AND VERY EXPENSIVE!
WE SPOKE YIDDISH SO THE POLES DON'T UNDERSTAND.
NIE, VAS DENKST DIE?
YECH KENN DIE FRAU KAWKA, UBER YECH BIN NISH ZICHER VEGEN DIE ZWEI.
So, what do you think?
I know Mrs. Kawka, but I'm not sure about these two.
HERR MECH TSE! YECH GEI KOIDEM MIT ZEI. AZ ALLES VET ZEIN BESEDER, YECH VIL SCHREIBEN TSE DEYER.
Listen! I'll go first. If everything is okay, I'll write back to you.
THE OTHERS WANT TO THINK ABOUT IT A LITTLE LONGER, BUT I'M READY TO GO NOW.
FINE. FINE.
I AGREED WITH MANDELBAUM TO MEET AGAIN HERE. IF IT CAME A GOOD LETTER, WE'LL GO.

151

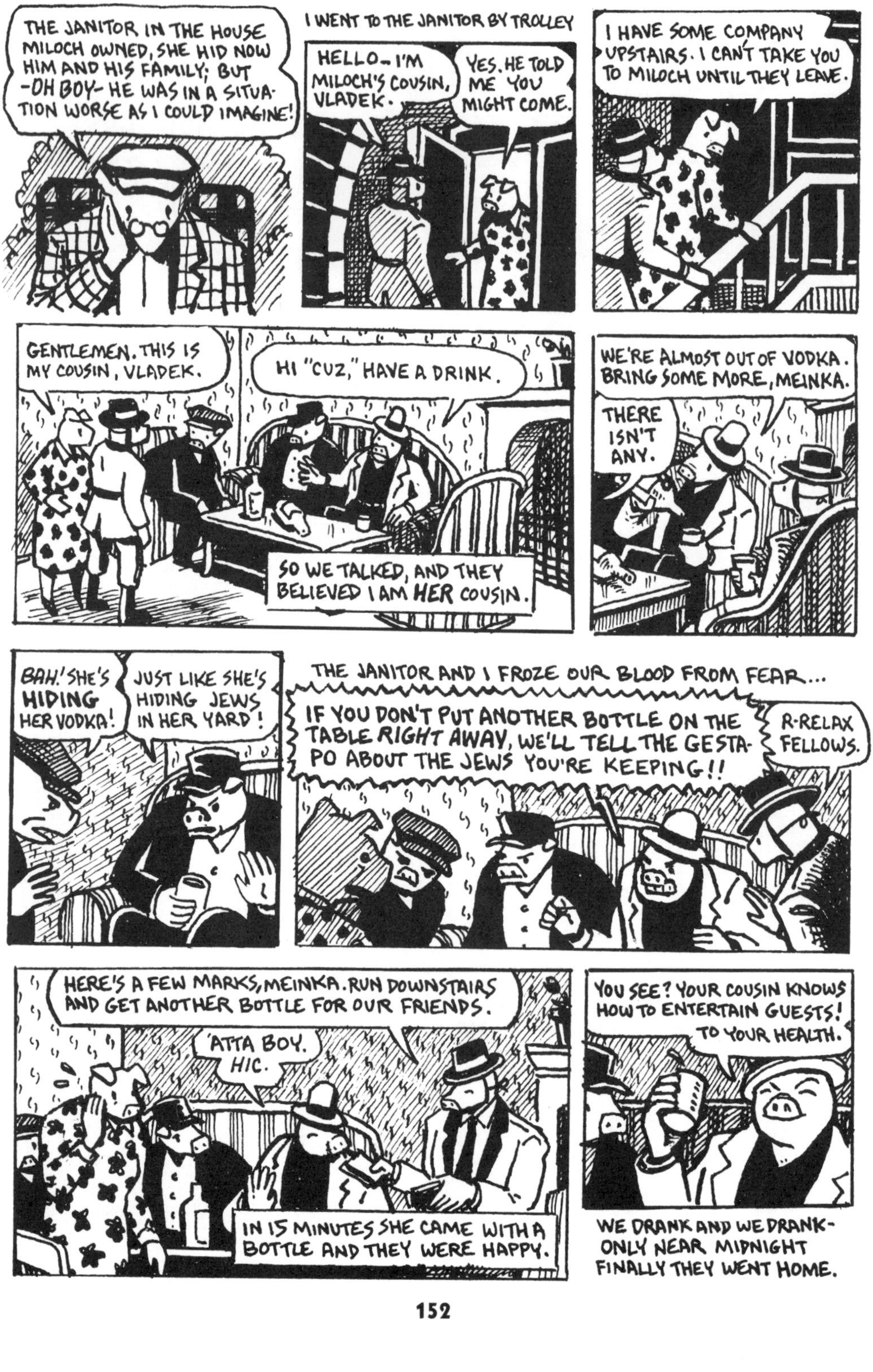
THE JANITOR IN THE HOUSE MILOCH OWNED, SHE HID NOW HIM AND HIS FAMILY; BUT -OH BOY- HE WAS IN A SITUATION WORSE AS I COULD IMAGINE!
I WENT TO THE JANITOR BY TROLLEY
HELLO - I'M MILOCH'S COUSIN, VLADEK.
YES. HE TOLD ME YOU MIGHT COME.
I HAVE SOME COMPANY UPSTAIRS. I CAN'T TAKE YOU TO MILOCH UNTIL THEY LEAVE.
GENTLEMEN. THIS IS MY COUSIN, VLADEK.
HI "CUZ," HAVE A DRINK.
SO WE TALKED, AND THEY BELIEVED I AM HER COUSIN.
WE'RE ALMOST OUT OF VODKA. BRING SOME MORE, MEINKA.
THERE ISN'T ANY.
BAH! SHE'S HIDING HER VODKA!
JUST LIKE SHE'S HIDING JEWS IN HER YARD!
THE JANITOR AND I FROZE OUR BLOOD FROM FEAR...
IF YOU DON'T PUT ANOTHER BOTTLE ON THE TABLE RIGHT AWAY, WE'LL TELL THE GESTAPO ABOUT THE JEWS YOU'RE KEEPING!!
R-RELAX FELLOWS.
HERE'S A FEW MARKS, MEINKA. RUN DOWNSTAIRS AND GET ANOTHER BOTTLE FOR OUR FRIENDS.
'ATTA BOY. HIC.
IN 15 MINUTES SHE CAME WITH A BOTTLE AND THEY WERE HAPPY.
YOU SEE? YOUR COUSIN KNOWS HOW TO ENTERTAIN GUESTS!
TO YOUR HEALTH.
WE DRANK AND WE DRANK - ONLY NEAR MIDNIGHT FINALLY THEY WENT HOME.

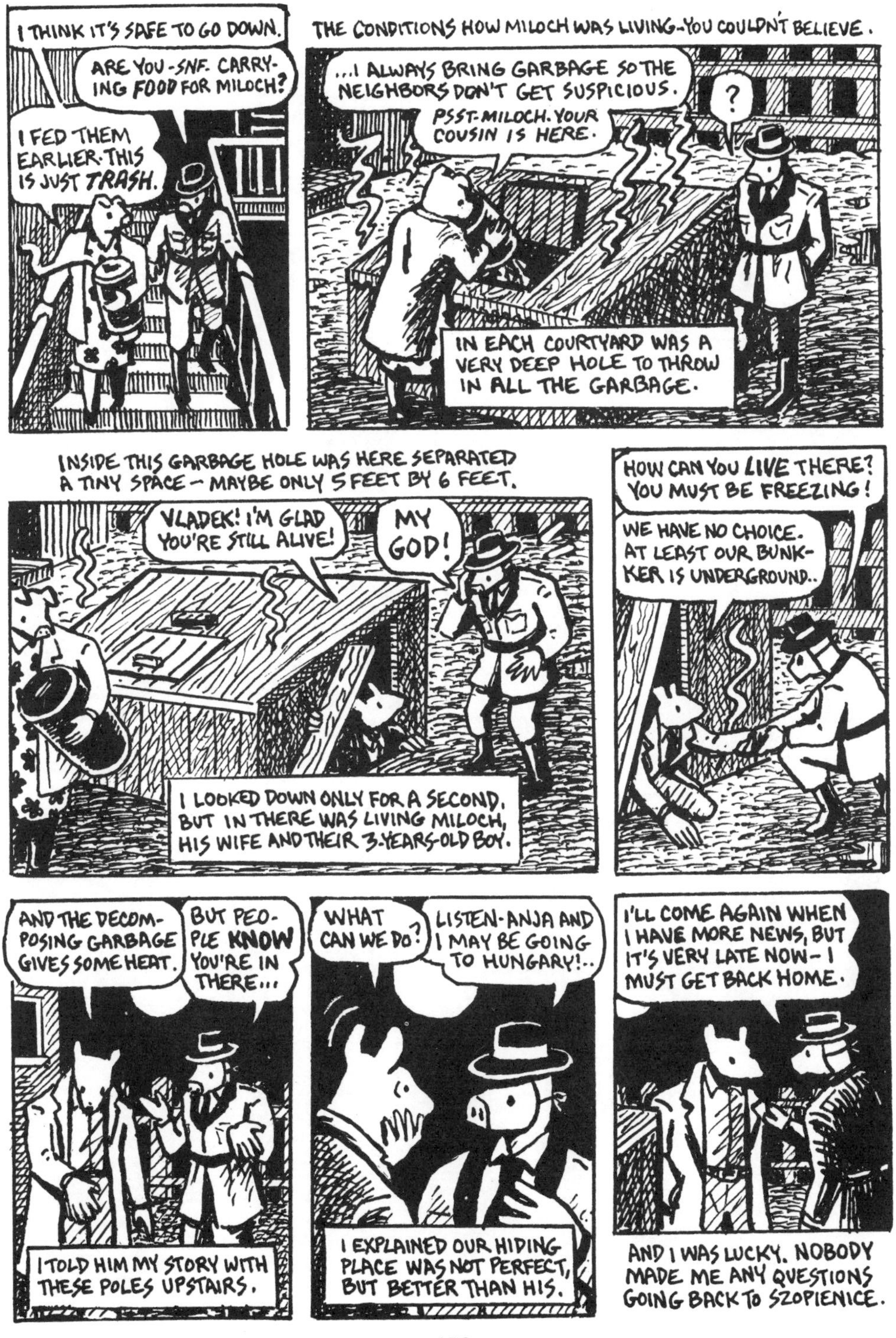

I THINK IT'S SAFE TO GO DOWN.
ARE YOU-SNF. CARRYING FOOD FOR MILOCH?
I FED THEM EARLIER. THIS IS JUST TRASH.
THE CONDITIONS HOW MILOCH WAS LIVING-YOU COULDN'T BELIEVE.
...I ALWAYS BRING GARBAGE SO THE NEIGHBORS DON'T GET SUSPICIOUS.
PSST-MILOCH. YOUR COUSIN IS HERE.
?
IN EACH COURTYARD WAS A VERY DEEP HOLE TO THROW IN ALL THE GARBAGE.
INSIDE THIS GARBAGE HOLE WAS HERE SEPARATED A TINY SPACE – MAYBE ONLY 5 FEET BY 6 FEET.
VLADEK! I'M GLAD YOU'RE STILL ALIVE!
MY GOD!
I LOOKED DOWN ONLY FOR A SECOND, BUT IN THERE WAS LIVING MILOCH, HIS WIFE AND THEIR 3-YEARS-OLD BOY.
HOW CAN YOU LIVE THERE? YOU MUST BE FREEZING!
WE HAVE NO CHOICE. AT LEAST OUR BUNKER IS UNDERGROUND..
AND THE DECOMPOSING GARBAGE GIVES SOME HEAT.
BUT PEOPLE KNOW YOU'RE IN THERE...
I TOLD HIM MY STORY WITH THESE POLES UPSTAIRS.
WHAT CAN WE DO?
LISTEN-ANJA AND I MAY BE GOING TO HUNGARY!..
I EXPLAINED OUR HIDING PLACE WAS NOT PERFECT, BUT BETTER THAN HIS.
I'LL COME AGAIN WHEN I HAVE MORE NEWS, BUT IT'S VERY LATE NOW – I MUST GET BACK HOME.
AND I WAS LUCKY. NOBODY MADE ME ANY QUESTIONS GOING BACK TO SZOPIENICE.

A FEW DAYS AFTER, I CAME AGAIN TO THE SMUGGLERS. AND MANDELBAUM WAS ALSO THERE.

LOOK, VLADEK— MY NEPHEW IS SAFE! THEY BROUGHT ME A LETTER FROM HIM.

IT WAS IN YIDDISH AND IT WAS SIGNED REALLY BY ABRAHAM. SO WE AGREED RIGHT AWAY TO GO AHEAD.

BUT ANJA JUST DIDN'T WANT WE WOULD GO...

PLEASE, VLADEK, CALL IT OFF!

BUT IT'S ALL AR-RANGED. I'VE EVEN GIVEN THEM HALF THEIR MONEY!

NO! NO! NO! IT'S SOME KIND OF TRICK!

BE REASONABLE. I SAW ABRAHAM'S LETTER WITH MY OWN EYES!

WH-WHAT DID IT SAY?

"DEAR AUNT AND UNCLE, EVERYTHING IS WON-DERFUL HERE. I AR-RIVED SAFELY. I'M FREE AND HAPPY. DON'T LOSE A MINUTE. JOIN ME AS SOON AS YOU CAN. YOUR LOVING NEPHEW, ABRAHAM."

I-I DON'T KNOW...

WE LEAVE THE DAY AFTER TOMORROW FROM THE KA-TOWICE TRAIN STATION.

AND FINALLY I CONVINCED HER.

SO, I WENT ONE MORE TIME OVER TO MILOCH IN HIS GAR-BAGE BUNKER AND DIRECTED HIM HOW HE MUST GO TO SZOPIENICE AND HIDE...

AND, YOU KNOW, MILOCH AND HIS WIFE AND BOY, THEY ALL SURVIVED THEMSELVES THE WHOLE WAR... SITTING THERE ... WITH MOTONOWA...

BUT, FOR ANJA AND I, IT WAS FOR US WAITING ANOTHER DESTINY...

WE CAME WITH NO PROBLEM BY TROLLEY CAR TO OUR MEET-ING POINT WITH THE MANDEL-BAUMS AND THE SMUGGLERS.

EVERYTHING IS ARRANGED. HERE ARE YOUR TICKETS.

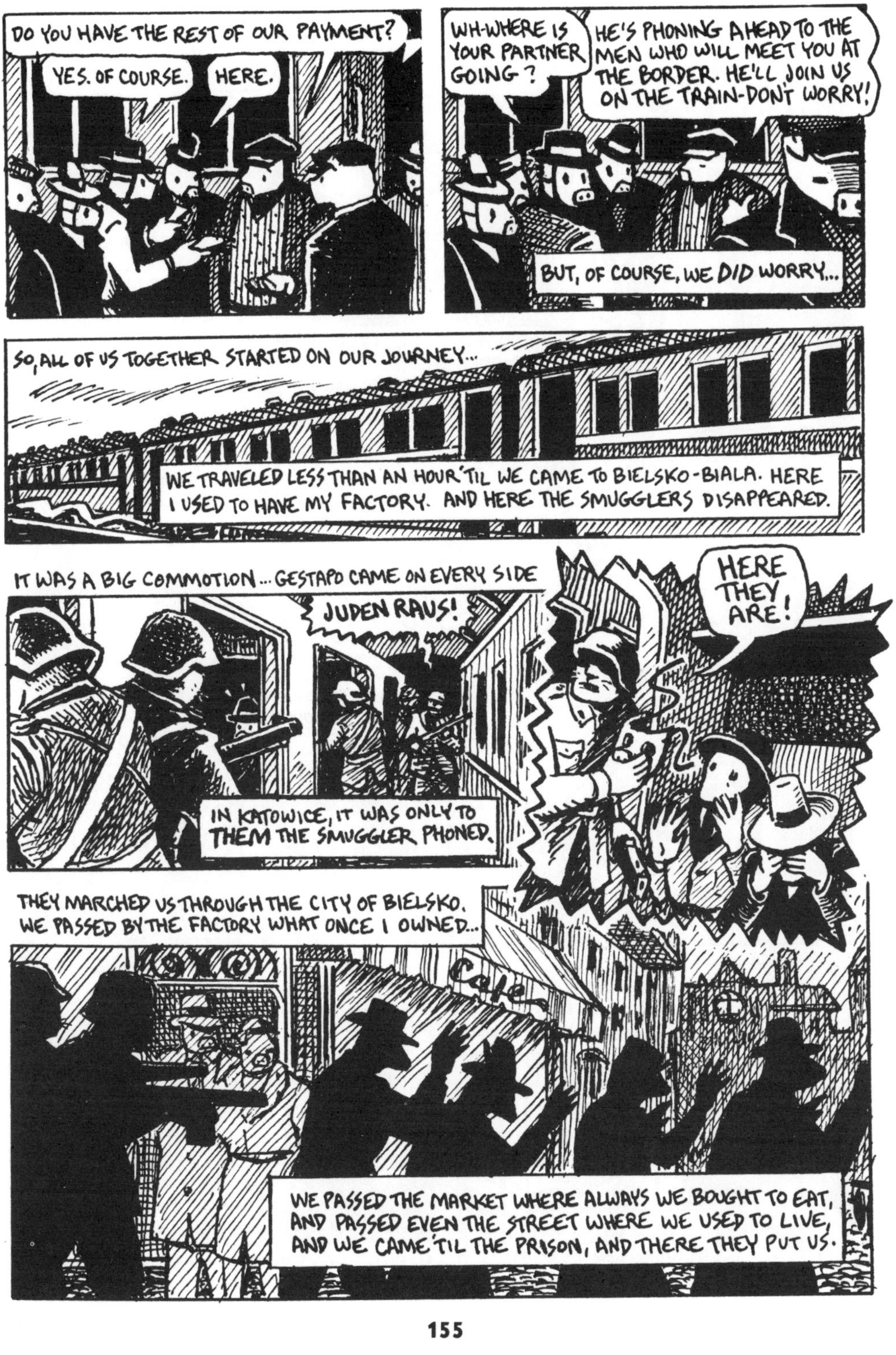
DO YOU HAVE THE REST OF OUR PAYMENT?
YES. OF COURSE.
HERE.
WH-WHERE IS YOUR PARTNER GOING?
HE'S PHONING AHEAD TO THE MEN WHO WILL MEET YOU AT THE BORDER. HE'LL JOIN US ON THE TRAIN-DON'T WORRY!
BUT, OF COURSE, WE DID WORRY...
SO, ALL OF US TOGETHER STARTED ON OUR JOURNEY...
WE TRAVELED LESS THAN AN HOUR 'TIL WE CAME TO BIELSKO-BIALA. HERE I USED TO HAVE MY FACTORY. AND HERE THE SMUGGLERS DISAPPEARED.
IT WAS A BIG COMMOTION... GESTAPO CAME ON EVERY SIDE
JUDEN RAUS!
HERE THEY ARE!
IN KATOWICE, IT WAS ONLY TO THEM THE SMUGGLER PHONED.
THEY MARCHED US THROUGH THE CITY OF BIELSKO. WE PASSED BY THE FACTORY WHAT ONCE I OWNED...
Cafe
WE PASSED THE MARKET WHERE ALWAYS WE BOUGHT TO EAT, AND PASSED EVEN THE STREET WHERE WE USED TO LIVE, AND WE CAME 'TIL THE PRISON, AND THERE THEY PUT US.

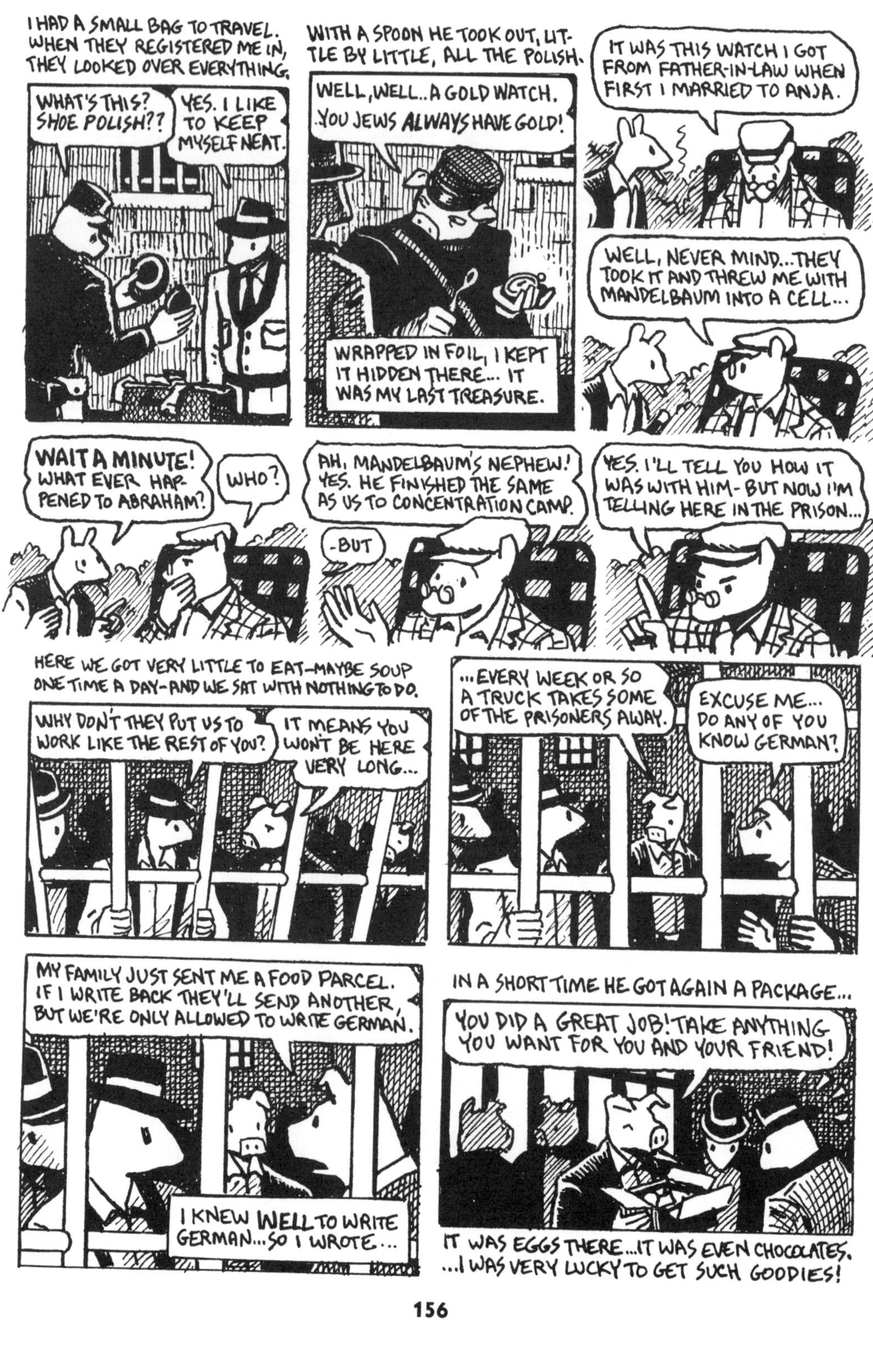
I HAD A SMALL BAG TO TRAVEL. WHEN THEY REGISTERED ME IN, THEY LOOKED OVER EVERYTHING.
WHAT'S THIS? SHOE POLISH??
YES. I LIKE TO KEEP MYSELF NEAT.
WITH A SPOON HE TOOK OUT, LITTLE BY LITTLE, ALL THE POLISH.
WELL, WELL.. A GOLD WATCH. YOU JEWS ALWAYS HAVE GOLD!
WRAPPED IN FOIL, I KEPT IT HIDDEN THERE... IT WAS MY LAST TREASURE.
IT WAS THIS WATCH I GOT FROM FATHER-IN-LAW WHEN FIRST I MARRIED TO ANJA.
WELL, NEVER MIND...THEY TOOK IT AND THREW ME WITH MANDELBAUM INTO A CELL...
WAIT A MINUTE! WHAT EVER HAPPENED TO ABRAHAM?
WHO?
AH, MANDELBAUM'S NEPHEW! YES. HE FINISHED THE SAME AS US TO CONCENTRATION CAMP.
-BUT
YES. I'LL TELL YOU HOW IT WAS WITH HIM- BUT NOW I'M TELLING HERE IN THE PRISON...
HERE WE GOT VERY LITTLE TO EAT-MAYBE SOUP ONE TIME A DAY-AND WE SAT WITH NOTHING TO DO.
WHY DON'T THEY PUT US TO WORK LIKE THE REST OF YOU?
IT MEANS YOU WON'T BE HERE VERY LONG...
...EVERY WEEK OR SO A TRUCK TAKES SOME OF THE PRISONERS AWAY.
EXCUSE ME... DO ANY OF YOU KNOW GERMAN?
MY FAMILY JUST SENT ME A FOOD PARCEL. IF I WRITE BACK THEY'LL SEND ANOTHER, BUT WE'RE ONLY ALLOWED TO WRITE GERMAN.
I KNEW WELL TO WRITE GERMAN...SO I WROTE...
IN A SHORT TIME HE GOT AGAIN A PACKAGE...
YOU DID A GREAT JOB! TAKE ANYTHING YOU WANT FOR YOU AND YOUR FRIEND!
IT WAS EGGS THERE...IT WAS EVEN CHOCOLATES. ...I WAS VERY LUCKY TO GET SUCH GOODIES!

"Spiegelman portrays the Nazis as cats, the Jews as mice, the Poles as pigs and the Americans as dogs. They are all terrifyingly human. This is comic strip art which has nothing to do with Tom and Jerry. Anyone moved by Briggs's *When the Wind Blows* … will appreciate Spiegelman's genius for dealing with a subject many would say cannot be dealt with at all"
– *The Times*

"You need be neither a Jew nor a death-camp ghoul to be moved. Anyone who has ever tried to understand the mystery of their parents, and how the 20th century has treated them, will find in *Maus* a key that turns the lock"
– Ian Jack in the *Observer*

"This intensely personal account of a family's survival, of hair-breadth escapes and incarceration, deals artfully with experiences and emotions that many might fervently wish to forget. Of how, when life is stripped to subsistence level, trust and betrayal take on unprecedented dimensions… In the tradition of Aesop and Orwell, it serves to shock and impart powerful resonance to what, after all, is a well documented subject. And the artwork is so accomplished, forceful and moving, without resorting to sentimentality, that it *works*" – *Time Out*

"*Maus* memorialises Spiegelman's father's experience of the Holocaust – it follows his story, frame by frame, from youth and marriage in pre-war Poland to imprisonment in Auschwitz …The 'survivor's tale' that results is stark and unembellished … One of the clichés about the Holocaust is that you can't imagine it – like nuclear war, its horror outfaces the artistic imagination. Spiegelman disproves that theory"
– *Independent*

### ALSO PUBLISHED

*Maus: A Survivor's Tale*

Part II: And Here My Troubles Began

(From Mauschwitz to the Catskills and Beyond)